Native North American Theology Through A Christian Lens

Contrasts and Comparisons

Rev. John W. Friesen, Ph.D., D.Min, D.R.S.

Cover Design by David J Friesen

Produced by:

John W. Friesen, Ph.D, D.Min., D.R.S.,
Professor, Werklund School of Education
University of Calgary
2500 University Drive, NW.
Calgary, AB, Canada, T2N 1N4

drsfriesen.com

Dedicated to
Caleb Joshua David Droppert,
our thirteenth grandchild

What I am suggesting here is that if you want to bridge the two spiritual cultures, *the key is to discover who you are and commit yourself to that*. With that as a goal, then the ceremonial experiences become a direct contributing factor.

You will find that the ceremonial experiences will favor and enhance that. It's not just words. The more you discover yourself, the more capable you become in tuning into someone else.

(Joseph E. Couture in *Couture and Cowan*, 2013, p. 293) [italics mine]

CONTENTS

FOREWORD

Seldom does an author coalesce so many disparate yet worthy elements into a coherent mosaic of a book. The Rev. Dr. John Friesen has fulfilled this incredible challenge in this, his latest book. Certainly. The author has produced the mature work of a mature scholar on labyrinthine cultural and religious content. He has synthesized what others have not – Judaic, Christian, and First Nations religious cosmologies, values, terminologies, and symbol systems. In fact, Professor Friesen has fulfilled what he once dreamt. Chief John Snow of the Morley Reserve west of Calgary appeared in a dream that pointed to a proper way of life for a minister to First Nations people. In the dream, Chief Snow instructed Friesen in these words: "You must speak from the heart. People need to hear what you know, and you must share it with them." In short, sincere and spontaneous honesty had to become the ministerial path of the Reverend Friesen. Subsequently, Friesen delivers a mindful and heartfelt account of the sacred subject matter presented in this book. As the dream directed, the Reverend Friesen obeyed Chief Snow's counsel.

The First Nations belief that the Great Spirit or Great Mystery created the natural and spiritual world as an indivisible whole constitutes a leitmotif in this text. For a sacred specialist from a First Nation, to see an eagle flying above a religious congregation may also be to see the eagle simultaneously relaying an optimistic spiritual message from the Great Creator or Great Medicine to humankind. A circle joins the mystical energies of nature and spirit, yet an openness to the myriad mysteries of the Great Medicine remains in First Nations spirituality for the seeker.

By what authority can and does the Rev. Dr. John Friesen speak about First Nations spiritual paths? Among the authorizations he sets forth that may establish his worthiness to address First Nations spirituality, notably from an intercultural perspective, are five eagle feathers bestowed upon him and his wife Dr. Virginia Friesen, several of which honored them at indigenous ceremonies. A Plains Cree elder who had four piercings from participating in four Sundance ceremonies gifted John Friesen with an eagle feather, a feather seen as sacred among North American Plains People.

Several singular themes surface though Professor Friesen's account of Native People of North America from a Christian perspective. The author does not see through a glass darkly; rather, he sees through a glass brightly. Analogically, his insightful lens corrects the perplexing intellectual myopia, presbyopia, and other visual impairments that many suffer pertaining to North American Aboriginal religions and ways of life and Christian denominations and its ways of life. By contrasting and comparing the Christian religion with Aboriginal religion, creation by contrast becomes a novel and inventive Rosetta Stone for interpreting both Native and Christian paths. To consider theology in terms of rumination becomes discerningly honest.

Professor Friesen introduces religious terms in a style that is accessible and comprehendible to readers with general and specialized interests in the text's content. Whether the reader has ministerial credentials or not, Friesen delivers a penetrating hermeneutic on divinity, soteriology, deontology, sacramentalism, ecclesiology, eschatology, missiology, and reconciliation. By carefully and accurately simplifying these complex terms and concepts, he demonstrates that, despite slight improvements in comprehension from the non-Native citizenry, the belief systems and practices of First Nations people continue to be misinterpreted and misunderstood. The content Friesen elucidates that pertains to the ongoing confusion about North American Aboriginal people becomes a justification in itself for the value of the text.

Actually, Friesen illuminates numerous cultural and religious concepts, events, and phenomena. A short list of his generous offerings that apply to First Nations people follows: the significant contrasts between Christianity and Native spirituality, the symbolization of the Divinity-Blackfoot braiding of the hair, the Tuskegee account of creation and the flood stories of the Cowichan and Pima, the malleable and resurgent Trickster, the vision quest and good medicine, the medicine wheel and medicine bundles, the multifunctional significance of the number four, the naming of *The Great Spirit* (or *The Great Mystery*, *The Great Medicine*, and *The Great Creator*), the interconnectedness and the circle-of-life, the spiritual practice of pipe-smoking and sweat lodges, the elder traditions and their sayings, the sacredness of places and plants, the give-a-way dance and the spiritual sharing among elders and medicine people like Black Elk, confrontation with Imperialist Christianity, and the openness to a spiritual dialog to listen to one another like the Seneca Chief Red Jacket. In addition, Friesen covers missiology, which deals with missionary efforts designed to benefit the welfare of others. The term *missiology* should not be confused with the term *misology* or the fear or hatred of argument or reasoning. Missiology has a history, for better or for worse, of pursuing and even reveling in argument and reasoning, and Friesen covers its highs and lows over time with fervor and light.

As a final commentary to this culturally and spiritually beneficial text, Professor Friesen reconciles a number of differences between European North American Christianity and Native North American spirituality by transcending the dialectic of Christian versus Aboriginal cultural and religious blessings and curses. With respect to divergent worldviews, values, and languages, he reconciles paradigmatic differences that make a difference. If his book is intended to decrease anxieties about the differences between Christianity and First Nations spirituality, Friesen fulfills his purpose. He challenges existing phobias about the incompatibility of Christianity and Native spirituality. In challenging the fears as being predominantly unwarranted, Friesen transmutes many base views of frightening differences between Christianity and Native religion into befriending similarities, much as the learned First Nations spiritual personages of Chief John Snow and Elder Joseph Couture did before him. To close, the Rev. Dr. Friesen shows in this text that he veritably earned his gifted eagle feathers.

Richard Fiordo, Ph.D.,
Professor of Communication,
University of North Dakota

PREFACE

Readers who bypass reading the preface of a book tend to miss out on discovering the reason why it was written. This study is the result of many years of personal inquiry coupled with a passion to understand the spiritual beliefs of North America's First Peoples. It also represents a personal attempt to work out a synthesis between having been raised and formally trained in the Christian faith, and the result of many years of researching, experiencing, and learning about North American Great Plains First Peoples theology. While the much of this book's contents originates from secondary sources, from time to time I also inject information from personal experiences that afforded me valuable insights. I would also like to think that the many years spent in Aboriginal communities have influenced me perhaps to understand and even adopt some of their ways of thinking.

One of the things I learned while in the presence of respected Indigenous leaders has been to appreciate nature's ways. I can also say with deep heart-felt thanks that in every Indigenous community I have visited over the past several decades, from the Canadian Northwest through Montana, Idaho and the Dakotas, to Arizona, Kansas, and Texas, there have been kind individuals who graciously spent time with me and freely offered valued information.

A case in point happened when my wife, Virginia, and I visited the Fort Belknap Indian Reservation in Montana a decade or two ago. While conversing with a gentleman from the Fort Belknap Office of Education, I inquired as to the existence of a tribal history for the community. I was informed that one was indeed available, but only in manuscript form. It had not yet been published in book form. However, my host informed me, he would be happy to photocopy all 400 pages of it for me if I cared to wait!

For the next two hours my new friend and I stood before a photocopy machine that occasionally refused to cooperate with our requests of it, while the two of us shared and exchanged information. When the task was done, I offered payment, but my host graciously refused my offer. He indicated that his people were happy to share information about their culture and history to anyone interested in it. On my return home, I gratefully sent a gift of several books to my new colleague, in the meanwhile counting my blessings at having been able to obtain this informative resource. This experience was typical of many other visits I undertook to Native communities in both Canada and the United States over the years Two other examples are these: the manager of the Apache Information Center in Oklahoma provided me with rare sources pertaining to tribal historical information and invited me to make free use of their archives. The folks at the Comanche headquarters gave me a license tag that is currently mounted on the front bumper of my car and proudly reads, "The Comanche Nation: Lords of the Plains."

Closer to home, I would be remiss if I did not mention by name many local Aboriginal individuals who from time to time offered their wisdom and lent their support as I continued my journey to understand more about Aboriginal ways.

ACKNOWLEDGEMENTS

As any author knows, a work of this nature could not be completed without the kind assistance of colleagues and friends. This book is no exception, and I must thank the following individuals, among others, who have been especially helpful in this regard. Sadly, a number of these kind people are now deceased, but their generous acts in the form of sharing Indigenous knowledge, lingers on. The list includes:

- *Assiniboine*: Rev. Bernice Saulteaux.
- *Blackfoot* (Kainai): Wanda Black Rider, Mike Head, Dr. Maurice Manyfingers, Pete Standing Alone, and Roy Weaselfat.
- *Blackfoot* (Piikani): Denise Yellowhorn and Kathy Yellowhorn.
- *Blackfoot* (Siksika): Dr. Vivian Ayoungman, Dr. Andrew Bear Robe, Stewart Own Chief, Donna Weaselchild, Verna Weaselchild, and Russell Wright.
- *Cree* (Plains): Lloyd Buffalo, Charlene Burns, Walter Lightening, and Jerry Saddleback.
- *Cree* (Woodland): George Calliou, Joe Cardinal, Dr. Joseph Couture, Floyd and Marlene Steinhauer, and William Wuttunee.
- *Ojibway* (Anishinabae): Rev. Cheryl Jourdain.
- *Sioux* (Lakota): Dr. Phil Lane and Dr. Beatrice Medicine.
- *Stoney* (Nakoda Sioux): Lucy Daniels, Wilfred Fox, Cherith Mark, Rod and Reatha Mark; Fred and Beatrice Powder, Reba Powderface, Clara Rollinmud, Doris Rollinmud, Roland Rollinmud, Rev. Dr. John Snow and Mrs. Alva Snow, Wally and Francis Snow, Ivan and Trudy Wesley, and Lazarus and Lily Wesley.
- *Tsuu T'ina*: Marie Crowchild, Fred Eagletail, and Hal Eagletail.

Finally, as always, I want to thank my wife, Dr. Virginia Lyons Friesen (who usually co-authors books with me), for her amazingly consistent support in travel and research, editing, taking photographs, and participating in other kinds of backup. While we usually write books together, I did this one on my own so she could have some time to engage in her favorite hobby of making quilts. No doubt about it, we will be warm next winter!

J.W. F.
Werklund School of Education
University of Calgary

INTRODUCTION

This book has been a major undertaking involving life long experiences and a half a century of academic research. Essentially, my very pleasant personal experiences in a variety of Indigenous communities in western Canada provided me with the motivation to undertake this task, and because of my link to academe, this resultant treatise also has a strong literary foundation.

To begin with, I have always been intrigued by the study of theology, and while doing so, I have constantly been amazed at the number of "truths" about Divinity and God and heaven that theologians sometimes manage to decipher from a single, somewhat obscure passage of scripture. Determined to discover the secret of this form of expertise in hermeneutical interpretation, over the years between 1957 and 2006 I enrolled in and completed a course in contemporary theology six times with six different institutions—Bethany Bible College in Hepburn, SK; Concord College in Winnipeg, MB; The Kansas School of Religion at the University of Kansas; Evangelical Theological Seminary in Naperville, IL; Lutheran Theological Seminary in Saskatoon, SK; and, Trinity Theological Seminary in Newburg, IN. In addition, I completed many related courses at the seven postsecondary institutions from which I graduated over the years. Needless to say, I am still not thoroughly enlightened about what it is that theologians do. All I can do is offer what I consider to be an admixture of personal musing, reading, observing, listening, and reflection.

My enamor with Aboriginal theology also has a lengthy history; beginning with the moment I began to read. In third grade I discovered a book entitled, *Autobiography of an Indian Woman*, which I devoured with considerable interest. Written sometime during the first third of the 20th century, I have not since been able to locate the book, but I do remember being hooked on its contents, and determined to learn more about these interesting people. Although born in Saskatchewan, my family moved to Trail, BC, shortly after my arrival, stayed a dozen years, and then migrated back to the land of my birth—and theirs! During the intervening years our family took annual trips to Saskatchewan from British Columbia, and usually passed through Aboriginal territory on our way through southern Alberta. I looked wistfully through the windows of our ancient automobile wondering if I would ever have opportunity to learn more about my new "literary friends." This opportunity came sooner than I dreamed possible.

In 1948 a physician advised my father to leave his job with the Canadian Mining and Smelter Company in Trail and move to the Saskatchewan prairies for his health. In response Dad purchased a quarter section of land (160 acres/64.7 hectares) in Saskatchewan for $25.00 and a 1929 Model "A" Ford car and our family suddenly became farmers. While not yet teenagers, my older brother, David, and I, without previous experience of any kind, quickly learned how to harness a horse, drive a steel-wheeled tractor, gather eggs in straw-stacks, swill hogs, and milk cows. The two of us were quite surprised to learn that the one-room school we were to attend was two and one-half miles away, a distance we would traverse on foot. The good news (for me) was that half of the 42 students, in grades one to eight, were Métis or nonStatus Indian children! This was exciting news because it gave me opportunity to attend school with Indigenous children and perhaps learn more about their culture and history. I should mention that Aboriginal children, who were registered by the federal government as Status Indians, were enrolled at that time in a residential school some seventeen miles away and operated by the Roman Catholic Church. The one-room country school my brother and I attended offered only eight years of elementary school, therefore, I later pursed a high school diploma by enrolling with the Saskatchewan Government Correspondence School.

Years later, in 1967, after completing thirteen years of post-secondary education, I was offered an academic position at the University of Calgary, which had opened a year earlier as an independent campus. Having completed a doctorate in philosophy of education, for the next ten years I taught four sections of the course with 40-50 students in each class. However, I was pleasantly surprised to learn that four Aboriginal reserves (reservations) were located within a one-hour drive of the city, and I decided to avail myself of the opportunity to learn more about their cultural lifestyle as soon as I could.

A colleague, Dr. Louise C. Lyon, with a similar perspective on educational relevance, also arrived at the University of Calgary in 1967, and approached me about working with her to develop a course on Native education. Her thinking was that our institution was not properly serving the large population of Indigenous peoples in the Calgary area. Our faculty did not offer a single course that included Native content. We took the matter up with our department chair and he reluctantly agreed that we could offer such a course, but insisted that it would have to run on Saturdays so as not to use up needed university classroom space. He also informed us that we would not be paid for this service, but students would be given credit for taking the course. We did this for four years, starting with ten students in the first course. As enrollment continued to grow, the course eventually became part of regular university offerings.

In 1972, another dream of mine was realized when the University of Calgary decided to offer courses in teacher education on nearby Indian reserves, if instructors were willing to commute to these communities. I signed up, and from 1977 to 2010, I taught courses in Blackfoot (Siksika) Chipewyan, Woodland Cree, Plains Cree, and Stoney (Nakoda Sioux) communities. For three years I was also privileged to work with the Calgary Police Service by delivering courses for Calgary police officers in Indigenous studies on the Tsuu T'ina (Sarcee) Reserve. In each context within which I worked, I was able to become friends with local elders who were always very kind in explaining local customs and beliefs. I recall that when teaching at Old Sun College on the Blackfoot Reserve I had the opportunity every week to share a lunch table with the late Russell Wright, who very willingly shared his insights with me.

As the next three decades went by I had many unique opportunities to expand my knowledge about Indigenous cultures in North America. Over the years, my wife, Virginia, and I made many research trips through Plains Indian country from Calgary to Texas, including at least fifteen visits to the American southwest pueblo country. We share a common interest in Aboriginal studies, and over the last decade have co-taught a variety of courses on the topic. We have also presented papers at many universities and colleges across the continent, and co-authored more than a dozen books.

In 1986, my friend of many years, the late Rev. Dr. John Snow, Chief of the Wesley Band on the Stoney Indian Reserve, asked me if I would help out at least monthly as minister for the local United Church. At that time the congregation was without a minister and with little prospect of finding one. I leaped at the opportunity since I was between pulpits at the time, and found that the opportunity to serve soon expanded to a weekly responsibility. This did not particularly interfere with my plans since I had always wanted to maintain an academic position to pay my living expenses while serving as a part-time pastor to any church that could not afford a full-time minister. I originally began my ministry at a little country church in Kansas in 1960, and was ordained in 1965 by what is now the United

Methodist Church in the United States. In addition, five of the seven postsecondary institutions from which I had graduated were affiliated with various religious denominations, so I felt that I had gained a bit of a global perspective on Christian theology.

When I began my ministry at the Morley United Church in the Stoney First Nations community, I soon realized that the theological and denominational training I received was not particularly appropriate to serving an Indigenous congregation. However, I was quite willing to adjust my thinking to local conditions and needs. The Morley congregation was very receptive to my presence among them, but unlike my experiences in non-Native churches, no one ever confronted me on any issue. I soon learned that if my parishioners did not agree with my ideas, or were displeased with what I was doing, they would simply stop attending church—at least for a while. Personal confrontation is not a strong Stoney Nakoda suit. Far be it from a Stoney person to embarrass anyone on a personal matter. I quickly learned to appreciate this perspective.

When we began serving Morley United Church my wife, Virginia, soon found herself fulfilling a multiplicity of unpaid roles. She faithfully played piano, led the choir, taught Sunday School, served as social convener, and became co-janitor and co-trustee with myself. As the years went by several times we helped the church locate a minister to serve the church, but only a few of these individuals stayed very long on the job. At that point we would return to help out. At present we are serving our sixth term since 1986 with the longest stint lasting fifteen years.

The Stoney people are a Plains First Nation, close friends of the Plains Cree, and very much appreciative of the workings of the Creator in nature. Although we were commissioned to serve in a leadership capacity at Morley United Church, we learned as much from members of the congregation about spirituality as they learned about biblical theology from us—maybe more! For example, consider the following event.

One beautiful Sunday morning, as the congregation was leaving the church, an elder, the late Fred Powder, glanced toward the heavens watching an eagle circling the sky above the congregation. "This is a sign from God," he said. "The Creator is smiling on us. Good things will happen." This remark is typical of Stoney people who exercise a keen sensitivity toward the natural world and view all its workings as integral to their traditional spirituality. Every encounter with natural processes, including those initiated by any of God's creatures, has the potential to influence one's spiritual journey. We learned from the Stoneys that the Creator works in a myriad of ways and those engaged in spiritual questing must be open to all of them.

Observing the eagle gliding above us led me to wonder how the first European visitors to North America could have missed the opportunity to experience this remarkable spiritual orientation. The European objective in coming to North America was not to learn about local cultural practices, but to claim new territory and exploit local resources. North Americans have learned since then, but Christian theologians who acknowledge the complexity of Indigenous spirituality still tend to apply Eurocentric paradigms to Indigenous systems. This approach does not necessarily work even though we share with Indigenous people the belief that, "The earth is the Lord's, and everything in it" (Psalm 24:1a).

Admittedly, it takes a bit of courage these days for a non-Native individual to write about so mystical a subject as Aboriginal spirituality, but I believe I have valid credentials for doing so. My wife and I have five eagle feathers in our home, some of which have been awarded to us in special ceremonies. Eagle feathers are considered very sacred by Plains Indigenous peoples, indicative of a very highly regarded award. A Plains Cree elder, who had been pierced four times in four separate Sundance ceremonies, personally gave one of the eagle feathers to me in a public ceremony. A Sundance is the most sacred spiritual observance among North American Plains people. The purpose of the feather I received is to authorize me to teach about Native spirituality. To do so, I must first remove my ring and my watch and any other jewelry, engage in a sweet-grass cleansing ceremony, and then commence to share my perceptions. This same elder also informed me that the title to a book that I recently had published was questionable. The book in question is entitled, *You Can't Get There From Here: The Mystique of North American Plains Indian Culture & Philosophy* (Friesen, 1995).

"Your title is wrong," my mentor insisted, "because you are proving that it *can* be done. You are beginning to understand Aboriginal spirituality; you *are* getting there!" I was somewhat taken aback by his observation, and felt greatly honored by his support.

My second experience of authorization to take up this challenge was equally dramatic. I considered Chief John Snow a dear friend who taught me many things, and I felt deeply honored to conduct his funeral in 2006. Shortly after Chief John Snow's untimely death, he visited me in a dream that so greatly affected me that I immediately woke up my wife to share its message with her. This was the dream.

It seems that I was a guest at a band council meeting (which had also happened in real life), and was seated immediately to the left of Chief John Snow at the council table. Lazarus Wesley, another close friend and elder, was seated on my left side. I was asked to share my thoughts with those who had gathered, although I had not expected to do so. I hesitated, mentioning to Chief Snow that I had not prepared to speak and had no notes with me.

"You do not need notes," Chief Snow informed me. "You must speak from your heart. People need to hear what you know, and you must share it with them."

This dream and the presence of Chief Snow was so real that I awakened with a start, woke Virginia, and proceeded to tell her about the dream. Today that dream is as vivid to me as it was several years ago when it occurred. And although I *do* teach about various aspects of Indigenous spirituality (as in this book), I am always aware that when I do, that I am venturing onto hallowed, privileged ground—somewhat like Moses at the burning bush, described in the Old Testament (Exodus 3:1-2). Therefore, I (metaphorically, at least), remove my shoes.

I sometimes wonder why Christians who claim to believe in the Bible and have no difficulty endorsing the efficacy of Divine truths contained in dreams and visions recorded there, refuse to acknowledge this means of receiving revelation in more recent times. The Indigenous peoples of North America still value this form of Divine communication, and so do I.

I do want to clarify that this book is mainly intended for non-Aboriginal people, so as a result, the chapter outline follows a distinct Eurocentric discussion model. This approach may make it easier for those not familiar with the complexity that underlies Indigenous belief systems. I must also emphasize the danger of giving in to what has been called a pan-Indian approach in undertaking this task (Battiste 2000, pp. 35-36). Social scientists have identified some fifteen distinct cultural areas that were fully functional at the time of European contact, and noted that *some* of the First Peoples in *some* of these areas held *some* fairly major beliefs in common—but not necessarily all of them (Cajete, 2000; Colorado, 1988; Henderson, 2000; and Nabigon, 2006). It would therefore be a bit presumptuous to make too many general observations about Indigenous spirituality as if to imply that any conclusions made represent all of the cultural areas. In fact, most of my observations were derived from working in communities that represent the Aboriginal people of the Great Plains and being heavily influenced specifically by my experiences in Stoney Nakoda country.

Despite these cautions about generalizing observations and conclusions about North American Native cultures, it is helpful to note that the late Professor Åke Hultkrantz (1987, p. 20ff.) of the Institute of Stockholm, spent many years visiting and researching various North American Aboriginal religious systems, and noted some remarkable similarities among the beliefs of the Indigenous cultures he studied. Hultkrantz discovered four prominent spiritual beliefs that he insisted could be applied to traditional Aboriginal lifestyles across the continent. These were: (a) a similar worldview; (b) a shared notion of cosmic harmony; (c) an emphasis on direct experience with powers and visions; and, (d) a common view of the cycle of life and death.

The notion of worldview may be defined as the way members of a culture perceive the workings of the universe. Traditionally, each Native North American nation had a repertoire of stories or legends in store that explained the tribe's relationship to the universe, and most of these involving interactions between human beings and other living creatures. Even today it is believed that a close affinity exists between the two parties. This perception adds a special dimension to the study of Native theology.

A Note on Vocabulary

There appears to be a wide variety of terms in pertaining to the identification of the original peoples of North America in the literature, and these vary depending on context and preference in usage. Terms currently "on the market" include Aboriginals, AmerIndians, Indigenous people, First Nations, First Peoples, Native North Americans, Natives, and North American Indians. The term "Indian," initially incorrectly employed by Christopher Columbus, is slowly fading into disuse, and has virtually been banned in Canadian literature. Recently a colleague suggested that the labels "Pre-Canadians" or "Pre-Americans" would be more apt! There are writers, Aboriginal and non-Aboriginal who prefer a particular usage to the exclusion of all the others. This is not my preference. I should also mention that in this discussion various terms to describe the Aboriginal/Indigenous peoples will be capitalized as a means of emphasizing the legitimacy of their status as nations, in the same way that identities of other nationalities are capitalized—for example, Australians, Brazilians, Canadians, Danish, and so on.

In 2011, the Canadian government decided to replace the word "Indian" with "Aboriginal," in official documentation, but the government of the United States of America still uses the term "Indian." Despite arguments to the contrary, in this book the above terms will be used interchangeably, partly to relieve monotony in delivery, and partly because it is sometimes difficult to know which usage might be suitable in a particular context. The term "Indian" as well as the word "tribe" will occasionally appear when employed in a historical context or when reference is to policy or practices involving the United States of America.

Using "correct" terminology is always a challenge. In fact, at times in seems as though the political correctness movement has seriously stymied attempts at meaningful communication. As historian, J. R. Miller (2004, p. 62) has appropriately observed: "Political correctness confines or even closes off completely the scope of investigation, ensuring that whatever 'truth' emerges will be partial at best."

On another note, readers will frequently encounter use of

such terms as fundamentalist, evangelical, conservative Christians, and liberal-minded Christians in this book. These terms are used to differentiate the following theological camps in Christianity. Fundamentalists refers to those Christians who adhere to biblical inerrancy, the virgin birth of Jesus Christ, the satisfaction of the theory of the atonement, the bodily resurrection of Jesus Christ, and the facticity of the miracles of Jesus. Fundamentalists seldom work with other denominations, including fellow fundamentalist denominations, because they are so concerned with getting their doctrines right. They also oppose the teaching of evolution in any form (Placher, 1983, p. 297).

Evangelicals have sometimes been called "fundamentalists with PhD's." This group does have an historical connection with fundamentalists, but is less concerned with maintaining the fundamentals of faith than they are with reaching out to other denominations, relating to government, preserving separation of church and state, promoting Christian education, engaging in evangelism through use of the media, and obtaining the guarantee of freedom for home and foreign missions (Smith, 1992, pp. 58-59). Though evangelicals try to submit to the teachings of the Bible as the sole and final authority, they realize that their interpretations of the Bible are influenced by prior convictions of truthfulness (Klein, Bloomberg, and Hubbard, 1993, p. 110). Both fundamentalists and evangelicals may be classified as conservative Christians, albeit with fundamentalists standing quite far to the right of evangelicals.

The roots of liberal Christianity in North America can possibly be traced to the writings of Walter Rauschenbusch (1861-1918), sometimes known as the founder of the social gospel movement. Rauschenbusch claimed that conservative Christians pay too much attention to the concept of salvation and not enough to the call for social change implied in the symbol of the kingdom of God. Rauschenbusch seems to have followed the writings of German theologian

Albrecht Ritschl (1822-1889) who found Karl Marx's analysis of social issues useful (Placher, 1983, p. 287). Since then liberal-minded Christians have tended to avoid discussions of biblical doctrine, concentrating instead on social issues such as equality, justice, and fair play.

It will become obvious to readers that sometimes passages and references in this book appear to be repeated in various discussions, and indeed they are. This is because in several chapters similar aspects of Christian beliefs and/or Aboriginal thought and practice *must* be cited in order to make comparisons. Hopefully these items will not detract too much from the body of the text or the overall message of the book.

It should be noted that unless otherwise indicated, all biblical quotations are from the New International Version of 2011. A 1953 version of the King James Version is also cited.

CHAPTER ONE

Background To Theological Rumination

They had what the world has lost. They have it now. What the world has lost, the world must have again, lest it die (John Collier, American Indian Commissioner, 1933-1945 in Bordewich, 1996, p. 71).

John Collier believed that traditional Indigenous cultures were morally and aesthetically superior to the modern industrialized ethos of individualism and competition. As Indian Commissioner for the American government from 1933-1945, Collier worked tirelessly to help his fellow Americans understand that traditional Indian beliefs and ceremonies were a national resource that must be preserved at any price. He was convinced that the future of Western civilization depended on helping America's First Peoples maintain and strengthen their cultural foundations. After all, basic American values were an admixture of diverse backgrounds, and none of them could be considered purely European. Why not blend traditional Indian values into the mix?

It is an oft-stated piece of misinformation that Europeans per se arrived in North America and took over local cultures. In fact, the first to arrive were people from a variety of backgrounds. These included Basque whalers, west-coast English fishermen, Dutch traders, and French missionaries. It took some time for local Aboriginal people to decipher differences among these groups, even though they shared a similar background in terms of the economic structures, political systems, and religious beliefs they imported from home (Miller, 2000, pp. 15-16). Nonetheless, as soon as the first visitors arrived, things got off to a rocky start, religiously speaking.

Churchill (1998, p. 97) suggests that the campaign to undermine and destroy Indigenous cultures over the past five centuries is unparalleled in history, both in terms of its sheer magnitude, and in its duration. This trend continued in both Canada and the United States right through to, as well as after, the American Declaration of Independence in 1776, and Canadian Confederation in 1867. For example, the size of the invasion in terms of numbers alone was significant. During the nineteenth and twentieth centuries, millions of Europeans continued to pour into these two countries (Buckley, 1993, p. 3).

The new arrivals to North America represented a variety of interests—economic, nationalist, political, and religious, and it was those with the latter concern who most often reacted negatively to the differences they identified between their theological convictions and those held by local residents. These newcomers were insufficiently prepared to accept the presupposition that Native North Americans were worshipping the same God that they were worshipping. Seton and Seton (1966, p. 8) documented this assertion by an unidentified Indigenous chief:

> ...we Indians are worshipping the same God that you are—only in a different way. When the Great Spirit, God, made the world, He gave the Indians one way to worship and He gave the Whiteman another way, because we are different people and our lives are different.... We like to see you worship Him in your own way, because we know you understand that way.

Religiously-inclined immigrants were not alone in both misunderstanding and condemning local Indigenous customs. In fact, even though early missionaries and anthropologists disagreed on metaphysical fundamentals, both groups could be accused of ethnocentrism by the way they mislabeled Indigenous beliefs and practices without objectively examining them. Today it is believed that anthropologists are committed to studying, describing, and analyzing cultural patterns without engaging in judgment about them, but this has certainly not always been the case. Consider, for example, the theories advanced by early anthropologists such as Lewis H. Morgan who in 1877 conjectured that societal progress was intricately linked to technology. This led him to conceive the idea that North American tribal societies were significantly inferior to those of "more advanced" societies like those in England, France, or Spain. Morgan cited seven "proofs" that the Aryan kinship family form of civilization enjoyed "intrinsic superiority," namely finer developed forms of subsistence, government, speech, family structures, religion, and architecture, as well as the origin of privately owned property. In Morgan's words:

> The latest investigations respecting the early condition of the human race are tending to the conclusion that mankind commenced their career at the bottom of the scale and worked their way up from savagery to civilization through the slow accumulation of experimental knowledge (Morgan, 1963, p. 3).

A half-century after Morgan's assessment of North American Indigenous cultures, anthropological perspectives had not changed very much. Consider the following assessment of North American Indigenous spirituality by respected American anthropologist, Edward B. Tyler (1965, p. 19).

It has been shown how what we call inanimate objects—rivers, stones, trees, weapons, and so forth—are treated as intelligent beings, talked to, propitiated, punished for the harm they do.... Our comprehension of the lower stages of mental culture depends much on the thoroughness with which we can appreciate this primitive, childlike conception, and in this our best guide may be the memory of our own childish days.

Promoters of organized religion who first visited North America promulgated the same assessments of local cultures as their academic counterparts did. The highly motivated missionaries who arrived in the New World were certainly not wicked people, of course, but merely individuals who strove to fulfill the mandate of furthering their interpretation of the Christian Gospel by any means, namely: "Go into all the world and preach the gospel to all creation. Whoever believes and is baptized will be saved, but whoever does not believe will be condemned" (Mark 16:15-16). Unfortunately, what was perceived as the urgency of this mission did not usually translate to the patience required to deliver effectively on the challenge. Most missionaries simply preached and taught the Gospel without first becoming familiar with what local Indigenous people already believed and practiced. When they *did* discover what they considered to be an inferior culture, they set about altering the social ideology of local Indigenous people (Bonvillain, 1986, p. 29).

The Reverend John McDougall became a Methodist missionary to the Stoney Nakoda Sioux First Nation located just west of Calgary, Alberta shortly after his ordination in 1872. Although he worked with these folk for several decades, he remained convinced that British civilization was in many respects superior to Native ways. His slogan, "Christianize, educate, and civilize" implied that the third goal of this triad was to inject the elements of British democracy into Stoney society. He felt that the Stoney people not only needed to learn about British social organization, they also *wanted* to learn about them. As McDougall put it:

Sometimes the Chief would ask me to tell about white men and how they resolved matters. I would respond with a short address on government and municipal organization, or at another time speak of civilization and some of its wonders, or give a talk on education…(McDougall, 1895, p. 75).

A contemporary of McDougall, The Reverend Dr. Carman, was more poignant in his assessment of West Coast British Columbia's First Nations societies.

No man, till (sic) has seen it, can form any idea of the moral, spiritual and intellectual death of the pagan Indians. Oh, what darkness! Oh what blindness! Oh what ignorance! What utter torpor and vacuity of mind! One would say it must take generations of time and toil to lift them anywhere near the level of Christian civilization (Chalmers, 1995, p. 19).

Sir John A. Macdonald, Prime Minister of Canada in 1885, concurred with this assessment and made this observation: "[Indians] are simply living on the benevolence and charity of the Canadian Parliament… beggars should not be choosers" (Wright, 1992, p. 313).

One of the objectives of incoming missionaries in wanting to amend the "undesirable ways" of local tribes was to focus on their children. Hence, a series of day schools and later residential or boarding schools were developed to provide European forms of civilization to Aboriginal children. Residential schools were basically begun because officials thought they would speed up the process of assimilation (Dickason and Newbigging, 2010, p. 229). School officials were also faced with the challenge of educating Indian children when their nomadic parents did not remain in one locality for very long periods of time. The goal of Indigenous education therefore became one of confinement for many Indian children. The adopted policy, developed with government cooperation, was this:

> If it were possible to gather in all Indian children and retain them for a certain period, there would be produced a generation of English-speaking Indians, accustomed to ways of civilized life, which might then be the dominant body among themselves, capable of holding its own with its white neighbors, and thus would be brought about a rapidly decreasing expenditure until the same should forever cease, and the Indian problem would have been solved (Canada, 1895, p. xxiii).

It is important to keep in mind a number of facts pertaining to the residential school phenomenon. In Canada, for example, only about one-third of Indigenous children attended residential schools, although accounts of personal experiences were for the most part quite unpleasant. Most Native children attended day schools that were equally committed to belittling Indian culture. Reports of these experiences are generally shocking, although some former students claim actually to have enjoyed the experience (Friesen and Friesen, 2008, p. 99; Grant, 2004, p. 95). On the positive side, if there is one, residential schools *did* produce capable band managers, advocates for social justice, and Native political leaders equipped with skills necessary to effectively negotiate with, and sometimes oppose, government actions (Warry, 2007, p. 61).

Positive Appraisals

Lest the impression be left that every incoming European immigrant who encountered Native North American culture formed a negative or judgmental impression of their beliefs and practices, let the record show that this was indeed not the case. At times immigrants of various backgrounds including explorers, early anthropologists, and missionaries were positively impressed with Indigenous ways. The following chronologically formulated excerpts are illustrative of these impressions.

Sometimes described as an early anthropologist with religious leanings, John MacLean observed in 1896 that a faithful study of Indian beliefs and customs would compel would-be learners to acknowledge that "… under the blanket and coat of skin there beats a human heart…. there is beauty, sweetness and wisdom in their traditions and courage, liberty, and devotion in their lives" (MacLean, 1896, p. iii). A few years later, however, anthropologist George Bird Grinnell expressed his surprise that Aboriginal observations about nature were brilliant enough to astonish civilized people. Grinnell published a book about North American Aboriginal peoples and described them with what might be called reluctant admiration:

> The Indian has the mind of a child in the body of an adult…. His mind does not work like the mind of a white man…. By this I mean that it is a mind in many respects unused and absolutely untrained as regards all matters which have to do with civilized life. The Indian is a close observer, and in respect to things with which he is familiar—which are within the range of his common experience—he draws conclusions that are entirely just so accurate in fact as to astonish the white man, who is here on unknown ground (Grinnell, 1900, pp. 7-8).

Grinnell did concede that in the areas of life with which they were familiar, the brilliance and performance of Indigenous people often did astonish their early European visitors.

A generation later, a Jesuit priest, Father Aaron M. Beede, who worked with the Lakota Sioux Nation for twenty-five years, observed that the people of his flock were a true church of God. He described the Sioux as "… true worshippers of the one true God, and their religion is one of truth and kindness. They do not need a missionary, but they do need a lawyer to defend them in the Courts" (Seton and Seton, 1966, p. 38). Later Father Beede abandoned his role as missionary and studied for the bar so he could more effectively serve the people in a legal capacity. He was unfortunately defrocked for his views and documented in his writings that local non-Native Indian agents despised him for taking up a legal role.

Father Beede's positive assessment of Indian ways was paralleled by the perceptions of anthropologist, Robert Lowie, who contended that the concept of cultural universals applied equally to Indigenous cultures. Lowie insisted that Native Americans grappled with the same challenges of everyday living as their brotherly counterparts in countries around the world, and they employed the same psychological processes of association, observation, and inference that people in other cultures did. In Lowie's words: "When a Hopi Indian in Arizona raises corn where a white tiller fails…. He is solving his everyday problems, not only competently, but with elegance" (Lowie, 1952, p. xvi).

A Belgium Jesuit priest, Father Pierre-Jean de Smet (1801-1873) spent many years in the northwestern American plains, working with several different Aboriginal tribes, always trying to negotiate peace among warring tribes (Ewers, 1989, p. 165ff.). De Smet had a great deal of respect for Aboriginal ways, and was often called on to negotiate disputes among the Blackfeet, Crow, Flathead, and Sioux nations. De Smet saw his ministry as a mixed mission, carefully mingling Christian beliefs with local cultural practices. On one occasion he prepared a Christian chant and translated it into the Blackfoot language for the Piikani tribe (formerly Peigan tribe), thereby building a bridge between the two not diametrically opposed religious systems. The chant contained this message: "God Almighty; Peigans are all his children; He is going to help us on earth; if you are good, he will save your soul" (Ewers, 1989, p. 189). Through de Smet's influence, several First Peoples in northwestern North America came to believe that Christianity was a more powerful war medicine than any they had previously encountered or possessed.

A foremost authority on linguistics, ethnology, and history of religion, a German Roman Catholic priest, Father Wilhelm Schmidt (1868-1954) argued vigorously that the religious system of the First Peoples of North America was monotheistic, and similar in nature to that introduced by early European missionaries (Schmidt, 1965). Schmidt denounced anthropological assertions that the First Peoples of North America were animistic or polytheistic in belief. He argued that even a cursory glance at Indigenous religious systems would validate this assumption. In Schmidt's words:

> A quite typical attribute of the primitive Supreme Being is that he is altogether good; all good that men enjoy comes from him. Among the North Central Californians he wishes men to live in a sort of paradise, with the least possible effort and the greatest possible pleasure…. As regards morality, the primitive Supreme being is without exception unalterably righteous…. (Schmidt, 1965, p. 27).

Schmidt went on to explain that non-Aboriginal students of Indigenous spiritual systems were often too impatient to notice that variations with European explications of Divinity were not sufficient reason to argue that they were other than monotheistic. In Schmidt's words:

Among other races, the fact of their monotheistic belief has been obscured. This is partly due to crosses with later forms, partly to differentiation, partly to other causes, all of which can be discovered by exact historical analysis (Schmidt, 1965, p. 23).

As the decades rolled into the middle of the 20th century, negative images of the First Peoples slowly began to disappear. Gradually, even phrases more indicative of social concern such as "solving the Indian problem" were exchanged for more positive nomenclature (Josephy, 1989, p. 31f; Schurz, 1978, p. 13ff.). Native writers began to emerge, and armed with European-derived literary skills, capably pointed out specific instances where the belief systems of their people had been misunderstood and misinterpreted. Several of these writers were quite polemic in their writings, clearly disturbed by past descriptions published by non-Aboriginal writers. Several Indigenous writers adopted a more understanding stance, suggesting that a cooperative effort to set the record straight would be a more productive approach. Métis writer, Maria Campbell had this to say:

> I believe that one day, very soon, people will set aside their differences and come together as one. Maybe not because we love one another, but because we need each other to survive. Then together we will fight our common enemies. Change will come because we won't give up (Campbell, 1973, pp. 1956-1957).

A Stoney Nakoda chief of some 26 years, the late John Snow was equally positive:

> How do we, as the Great Spirit's people, build a path into the next hundred years? And the answer comes loud and clear to me. "The Great Spirit has been our guide in the past, He is our guide today, and He will

be our guide into the future"…. As I stand on the top of the hill that overlooks the beautiful Bow River Valley, with the sacred shining mountains in the background as a refuge, I am reminded of our proud heritage… the wise elders, and the buffalo that roamed as monarch of the plains, the eagle that guarded the skies. They all speak of the brotherhood and oneness of the universe (2005, p. 220).

William Wuttunee, the first Aboriginal (Cree) lawyer to practice law in Western Canada was even more optimistic when he observed that someday the tables would turn. He projected that sometime in the future Native people, having reached a form of equality in Canada, would reach out past the edges of their own campaign to set things right and strive to assist others. In his words: "The day will come when Indian will not be concerned with struggling for their basic civil rights only, but for the basic rights of all individuals" (Wuttunee, 1971, pp. 138-139). There are times when that day seems a long way off, but we appear to have made some headway since writer Heather Robertson made this observation four decades ago: "So utterly fallacious, misleading and mischievous is the information given out by white people about Indians, that it is impossible for Canadians not to be racist in their attitudes" (Robertson, 1970, p. 6). Even today, North America's First Peoples are still in pursuit a positive image in the media, as well as pursuing the same standard of living that the rest of North Americans enjoy. North Americans need to finally dispel the image of Aboriginal people still portrayed in old western movies, dime novels, and nickelodeons, as warriors in eagle feather adorned war bonnets raising their rifles above their heads as they swoop down on a wagonload of stouthearted pioneers (Andrist, 1993, p. 2; Wilson, 1986, p. 353). This image, like all of those that describe the continent's Indigenous People in negative light, were created by incoming Europeans and their descendants, not by Aboriginals themselves (Francis, 1992, p. 8).

ment in Vietnam, civil rights unrest propelled by unhappy minority

The turbulent decade of the 1960s forced attention to a number of social sectors including Aboriginal rights, America's involvement in Vietnam, civil rights unrest propelled by unhappy minority groups (one of them known as the "Black Power" movement"), the rise of multiculturalism, and the emergence of hippie culture. The latter group decried the perpetual quest for materialism and fled to previously unoccupied areas of the wilds in an effort to revive the simplistic lifestyle of frontier North America.

Another related development has been a renewed academic interest in the status of Native Americans. For example, somewhat perturbed by uninformed descriptions of Indigenous cultures, American historian Alvin Josephy, Jr. (1968, p. 4) attributed the superficial, distorted, or negative stereotypes he encountered in the literature to lack of familiarity with Indigenous ways. He contended that anyone spending more than a little time with the first residents of North America would certainly come to appreciate their beliefs and practices. An academic colleague, Bruce Trigger (1969, p. 5) concurred, suggesting that most early descriptions of Native ways were primarily penned for purposes of propaganda, and only secondarily as works of history. Many North Americans who read the early works and then did some research on their own, were surprised to discover that Aboriginal People had long since earned the right to vote and participate in their nation's economy on the same basis as other citizens.

The two decades that followed the 1960s witnessed the production of many literary works that acknowledged the contributions of First Peoples in dimensions other than ethnological or historical. Specific attention was turned to Native religion and spirituality, some of it unfortunately muddied with New Age concerns. Books that exemplified these various themes include these titles:

Spirits of the Sacred Mountains: Creation Stories of the

American Indian, by William E. Coffer (1978);

The Pipe and Christ: A Christian-Sioux Dialogue, by William Stolzman (1998);

Sacred Ground: Reflections on Lakota Spirituality and the Gospel, by Ron Zeilinger (1986);

Mother Earth Spirituality: Native American Paths to Healing Ourselves and Our World, by Ed McGaa, Eagle Man (1995);

The Spiritual Legacy of the American Indian, by Joseph Epes Brown (1992);

Renewing the World: Plains Indian Religion and Morality, by Howard L. Harrod (1992);

Amerindian Rebirth: Reincarnation Belief Among North American Indians and Inuit, edited by Antonia Mills and Richard Slobodin (1994);

Look to the Mountain: An Ecology of Indigenous Education, by Gregory Cajete (1994);

The Way of the Pipe: Aboriginal Spirituality and Symbolic Healing in Canadian Prisons, by James Waldram (1997);

Native American Religious Identity, edited by Jace Weaver (1998);

Spirit and Reason: The Vine Deloria, Jr., Reader, by Vine Deloria, Jr., edited by Barbara Deloria, Kristen

Foehner, and Sam Scinta (1999);

Aboriginal Spirituality and Biblical Theology: Closer Than You Think, by John W. Friesen (2000a); and,

Kaandossiwin: How We Come to Know, by Kathleen E. Absolon (Minogiizhigokwe) (2011).

As concerns about spiritual revitalization continue to be an area of concern in North American Native communities, other sectors of their lifestyles are also being addressed. These include a wide range of spiritual, pedagogical, and political concerns such as Aboriginal self-government, land claims, urban adjustment, economic development, and the pursuit of quality health, education, and welfare services. As is typical of Aboriginal thinking, all of these concerns have a spiritual foundation, particularly those that are connected to the land (Valaskakis, 2005, p. 92). Unless all parties involved in resolving these issues are aware of this very fundamental premise, it is doubtful that meaningful dialogue and/or negotiations can occur.

CHAPTER TWO

Creating A Theological System By Contrasting Theological Concepts

In order to get the discussion started, it is first necessary to identify the purpose of this chapter. Eurocentric theology is usually perceived as the study of Creator God *and* the relationship between God and the universe. Of course, that is a purely Christian definition because it assumes that God exists, He is male, and He relates to His creation, the primary object of which are humans. As subsequent theological discussions get underway a series of derived doctrines and matters of Divinity are usually delineated, thereby providing sustenance for "official" theological debates and general confusion for people-in-the-pews. Minor variances in theological interpretation also provide an ample rationale by which to encourage denominational splits, often on quite picayune points. Usually the list of topics discussed in theological works includes some of the concepts discussed here, although this list is by no means exhaustive. Workable definitions of these concepts are more or less standard in Christian theological studies, although theologians differ in the *choice* of concepts they expand on. In delineating these here, brief contrasts with Native North American conceptualizations will be identified, and presented in alphabetical order. Most of these concepts will be elaborated on in subsequent discussions.

Atonement

Atonement is a term that implies reconciliation has taken place between discordant parties. In the Christian tradition this has specific reference to the work of Christ on the cross, whom by His sacrificial death redeemed alienated humankind and brought about reconciliation between humankind and God (Fitzwater, 1953, p. 426). The Old Testament Israelites celebrated a Day of Atonement as a *predictive* ritual, symbolizing an act of national humiliation (Leviticus 23:26-32).

Generally speaking, atonement is not a highlighted term in Indigenous peoples theology, since emphasis on guilt is virtually nonexistent. Community induced shame replaces individual guilt, and individuals are encouraged by various means to try to live out their manifest destiny by making appropriate restitution for wrongs done, and by trying to improve themselves morally and spiritually in alignment with their Divine calling. The nature of an individual's purpose in life can be determined and confirmed in a variety of ways, and community support is always available.

Covenant

Covenant is a term that implies the existence of a binding and solemn agreement between two parties, and in theology, the covenant is between God and humankind. Biblical history outlines a series of covenants, the first being that between Noah the ark builder and God, with the latter promising that there would never be another universal flood upon the earth.

I will remember my covenant between me and you and all living creatures of every kind. Never again will the waters become a flood to destroy all life. Whenever the rainbow appears in the clouds, I will see it and remember the everlasting covenant between God and all living creatures of every kind on earth (Genesis 9:15-16).

From the making of the first great biblical covenant, the shape of the future was revealed, because God at that time made His purposes known through His promises (Richards and Martin, 1981, p. 28).

A second Old Testament covenant was made between God and Abraham. The covenant was that Abraham would increase to father a numerous people, he would be materially enriched, his name would be known throughout the land, and he would not only be blessed but *be* a blessing to others. All of this was conditioned on Abraham leaving the land of Ur and migrating to a new land that God would show him (Genesis 12:1).

A third covenant took place at Mount Sinai between God and the nation of Israel. This was the occasion in which Moses received the Ten Commandments from God and delivered them to the nation of Israel. The nation of Israel, in turn, promised to keep them. In Exodus 34: 27 the event is recorded in this way: "Then the Lord said to Moses, "Write down these words, for in accordance with these words I have made a covenant with you and with Israel."

A fourth Old Testament covenant made between King David and the Lord God was similar to the one made between God and Abraham. "The Lord declares to you that the Lord himself will establish a house for you: When your days are over and you rest with your ancestors, I will raise up your offspring to succeed you, your own flesh and blood, and I will establish his kingdom" (2 Samuel 7:11c-12).

The New Testament makes reference to Old Testament agreements, but proposes a new covenant of a different nature with the nation of Israel.

> This is the covenant I will establish with the people of Israel after that time, declares the Lord. I will put my laws in their minds and write them on their hearts. I will be their God, and they will be my people. For I will forgive their wickedness and will remember their sins no more" (Hebrews 8:10, 12).

The new covenant is based on the believer's acceptance of the sacrifice made by Jesus Christ on behalf of God's people. In the new covenant, Jesus is made the guarantee of a better covenant (Hebrews 7:22). In essence, He becomes the high priest, a role that was typified in the Old Testament by the high priest who annually made sacrifices on behalf of the people. In the New Testament, Jesus Himself *is* the sacrifice, as 1 Corinthians 11:25 notes: "This cup is the new covenant in my blood; do this, whenever you drink it, in remembrance of me." A covenant is a solemn promise confirmed by an oath or sign. When Christ spoke of the cup commemorating a new covenant He was pointing to the promises of salvation arranged by God on the basis of Christ's death (Boice, 1986, p. 603).

Contemporary theological discussions about covenants tend to reference a movement called covenant theology, a perspective that originated around the turn of the 20th century, as an outgrowth of Calvinistic theology. From this perspective the idea of the self-sufficient, ontological Trinity is the final reference point in all prediction (Douglas, 1991, p. 240). Three key concepts emerging from covenant theology are the covenant of works, humankind as the covenant breaker, and the initiation of the covenant of grace. Originally, humankind through the first man, Adam, was mandated to carry out God's expectations with regard to expectations that Adam would perform good works. Adam, as the representative of those who came after him, broke the covenant; thus God initiated a new covenant of grace that offers redemption through faith in the work of God's Son, Jesus Christ. God's wrath for covenant breakers is restrained through faith in Christ.

The First People of North America are quite familiar with the notion of contracting agreements in the form of governmental treaties. When European settlers arrived in North America they faced the challenge of what to do with regard to the people already resident here. They could work out agreements with the locals, enslave them, or try to banish them from the country. While newcomers initially accepted the principle that the Indigenous peoples were just owners of the land, they decided to negotiate treaties with them. Treaty making was seen as a feasible method for gaining a foothold on the continent without alarming the locals (Deloria and Lytle, 1983, p. 3). Many of the first treaties were negotiated in good faith even though later their terms were not always fulfilled (Fumoleau, 1973, pp. 4-5; Morris, 1991, p. 285). The legal definition of treaty making was elaborated as "a compact or agreement between two or more independent nations" (Cumming and Mickenberg, 1971, p. 53; Venne, 2002, p. 44). However, the terms of many treaties were later broken for various reasons, and negotiations to make restitution for violations are much in vogue today.

A number of Plains Aboriginal communities, notably Blackfoot (Blackfeet) believe they have an unwritten covenant with the Creator that they insist has never been broken. The braiding of the hair commemorates the Divinity-Blackfoot contract. Other Indigenous people hold a similar belief, and identify their covenant with the Creator in the choice of the name of their tribe, meaning "the people." This covenant implies that Creator God is pleased with His people, but He also has expectations that they will live according to His revealed moral and spiritual codes. A wide variety of rituals and ceremonies contain within them aspects of God's expectations, and they are regularly commemorated with both sacramental and mandated meaning.

Creation

Creation is addressed by writers of all world religions, many times in the form of stories called legends or fables. Christians tend to accept on faith that God freely created the world out of nothing, just as the first chapter of the Book of Genesis records. There is, however, an ongoing debate as to whether or not the Genesis account is to be taken literally or perceived as a myth. Creation from nothing implies a productive act where there is no material cause and no subject matter to work with, so that the entire being of created things comes from their created cause. As Garrigou-Lagrange (1950, p. 125) explained; "Before creation, nothing of the created thing existed, not even its matter, however unformed you may suppose it. The production of the created being has indeed an efficient cause and an exemplary cause (the Divine idea), but no material cause." In more simple language it means that Christians accept the fact of creation by God entirely on faith.

Creation stories abound in Native North American communities, some of them closely resembling the Old Testament Genesis account. Flood stories also appear quite frequently, much to the surprise of those who cling tenaciously to the notion that the biblical account is singular in existence. Interestingly, but not unexpectedly, the Tuskegee legend of the origin of the earth shows the predominance of animals in the earth's creation (Clark, 1989, p. 284). As is common among AmerIndian oral literature, the sacred number four occurs frequently in this legend.

Summarized, the discourse of the legend goes like this: before the earth came into being there was nothing—no people, animals, or fish in sight. Water was everywhere. Birds were flying around aimlessly, looking for some place to land. They decided to have a council to contact the Creator about their dilemma. They also wanted to determine if it would be best to have all water or all land. Some of the creatures preferred to have only water, while others pointed out that land was necessary to grow food. Eagle was appointed chief, and he decided that it would be good to have some land. Subsequently, he sent out Dove, who flew around for four days and returned with a report that there was no land to be found anywhere.

Crawfish, who was swimming nearby, volunteered to hunt for land. He disappeared under water for four days and then rose to the surface with some dirt in his claws. He made a ball of the dirt and gave it to Eagle who flew away with the dirt. Eagle remained out of sight for four days, then returned with the observation that land could be created from the limited amount of dirt that Crawfish had located. Everyone was very excited by the news and quickly followed Eagle to where he had envisaged the formation of land. Then a miracle occurred; as the mud was flung out into the water, land seemed to grow in size and the waters abated. Soon there was an abundance of land on which to grow food. The creatures of the earth and air were very happy.

The Tuskegee people say that long, long ago their tribe was chosen by the Great Spirit to be the first people to live upon the new earth.

Ecclesiology

Ecclesiology is generally referred to as the study of religious structure or organization, and in a Christian context includes reference to a variety of related offices such as bishops, church boards, deacons, deaconesses, elders, ministers, overseers, priests, and so on (1 Timothy 3:1-12). Thiessen (1959, pp. 404-405) noted that the first form of religious organization occurred under the leadership of Moses who received advice on the matter from his father-in-law Jethro.

Jethro observed that Moses alone regularly served as judge for the nation with no one to assist him. Thus Jethro offered Moses some advice.

> When his father-in-law saw all that Moses was doing for the people, he said, "What is this you are doing for the people? Why do you alone sit as judge, while all these people stand around you from morning till evening?" (Exodus 18:14)

Thus began the first form of institutional administration in Judeo-Christian church history. From that point on a variety of formats have sprung up ranging from hardheaded independent congregational rule to church presbyteries to Episcopal systems. Mickey (1980, p. 139) outlines the traditional Christian version of the church's role this way: "Scriptural Christianity affirms that the Church of Jesus Christ is the community of all true believers under His Sovereign Lordship.... it is holy because it belongs to God and is set apart for His purposes in the world."

When the first Europeans migrated to North America, they greatly underestimated the complex nature of local cultures, probably because local systems were constructed and functioned somewhat differently from European religious models. Spiritual offices of various kinds existed, and could be differentiated from other forms of leadership. All were either attained by hereditary succession or apprenticeship, or simply by community recognition of special gifts over time. Chapter ten offers a fuller description of Native American ecclesiology pertaining to the role of elders.

Eschatology

Eschatology is the study of last things, that is, it is the study of what happens to individuals after death. Eschatology has always been a topic of great interest to curious Christians, particularly those who tend toward a more evangelical bent (Strong, 1956). Generally speaking, there are three major positions on this subject: (a) those who believe that death ends all; (b) those who believe in "soul sleep," meaning that nothing happens to the dead until Christ returns to earth, at which time they are resurrected; and, finally, (c) there are those who believe that immediately after death one's soul goes either to heaven to be with Jesus and with one's loved ones who have gone before, or to the "lake of fire" along with "the cowardly, the unbelieving, the vile, the murderers, the sexually immoral, those who practice magic arts, the idolaters, and all liars..." (Revelation 21:8a). This will not be a pleasant state because of "the fiery lake of burning sulfur," which is "the second death" (Revelation 21:8b).

A second topic of interest to eschatologists is what will happen when the world finally comes to an end with the Second Coming of Jesus Christ. Once again, there are three basic positions on the subject: amillennialism, premillennialism, and postmillennialism. The word *millennium* is Latin for one thousand years. Essentially the differences among these perspectives have to do with the belief in a one thousand year reign referred to in the Book of Revelation (20:4b): "They had not worshipped the beast or its image and had not received its mark on their foreheads or their hands. They came to life and reigned with Christ a thousand years." Amillennialists do not accept the notion that Christ will reign upon the earth when He returns in His Second Coming. He will simply resurrect the dead and take them to heaven with Him.

Premillennialists hold that the Second Coming of Christ will occur *before* the establishment of the millennium. Postmillennialists propose that Christ's Second Coming will occur *after* His one thousand year reign on earth. What is interesting is that these kinds of speculations have occurred virtually since the day Christ ascended into heaven. They appear to be posited with total disregard for the biblical warning: "For you know very well that the day of the Lord will come like a thief in the night" (1 Thessalonians 5:2; 2 Peter 3:10). As Christ Himself stated, "But about that day or hour no one knows, not even the angels in heaven, nor the Son, but only the Father. Be on guard! Be alert! You do not know when that time will come" (Mark 13:32-33). Despite these cautions, speculating about the end times continues among Christians.

Traditionally, North American Native peoples could be considered minimally eschatological, since their way of life emphasized the mandate of fulfilling present obligations, with the adjoining belief that the future would look after itself. A definite belief in the hereafter existed, but its state and function remained relatively vague. Similarly, the future survival of the soul was not a particular concern to Aboriginal people (Lowie, 1965, p. 180). Conceptualizations of heaven did exist, but were rarely elaborated (Hultkrantz, 1953, p. 37; MacLean, 1896, pp. 100, 446). The motto for living might be summarized like this: "Live right, and the future will look after itself." Charles Alexander Eastman (Ohiyesa) of the Santee Sioux Nation put it this way: "In the life of the Indian there was only one inevitable duty—the duty of prayer, the daily recognition of the Unseen and Eternal. His daily devotions were more necessary to him than daily food" (Friesen, 1998, p. 21). Chapter eleven offers a fuller account of Native North American eschatology.

Ethics

Ethics is always a topic of intrigue for moral philosophers and theologians, probably because it has to do with what constitutes appropriate behavior. Simply defined:

> Ethics is the science that deals with conduct, in so far
> as this is considered right or wrong, good or bad. A
> single term for conduct so considered is "moral con-

duct," or the "moral life." Another way of stating the same is to say that Ethics aims to give a systematic account of our judgments about conduct, in so far as these estimate it from the standpoint of right or wrong, good or bad (Dewey and Tufts, 1908, p. 1).

Christians tend to use the Bible as a guide to moral behavior, while some theologians attempt to find Scriptural support for every particularized enactment. Passages to justify behaviors that do not fall strictly within the parameters of Scripture are condemned or justified on the basis of Scriptural verses that offer *general* principles for moral living. Here is one example. The apostle Paul wrote to the Corinthian Church: "So whether you eat or drink or whatever you do, do it all for the glory of God" (1 Corinthians 10:31). Paul further clarified this principle in his second letter to the Corinthian church: "And he died for all, that those who live should no longer live for themselves but for him who died for them and was raised again" (2 Corinthians 5:15). Christians are therefore called upon to serve God because of the tremendous sacrifice He made for them through His Son, Jesus Christ (Boice, 1986, p. 320). Individuals who do not accept the authority of the Scriptures usually prefer to derive codes of ethics from reason, employing such concepts as intuition, teleology, or empiricism. Perhaps to confuse the matter a bit, Scottish philosopher David Hume put it this way: "Reason is, and ought only to be, the slave of passions" (Dewey and Tufts, 1908, p. 232).

Before European contact, the Indigenous People of North America had in place a very well delineated code of ethics pertaining to virtually all aspects of life, and although there were differences among the various tribes that occupied the continent, a significant number of ethical principles could be considered universal. These included belief in connectedness of all living phenomena; respect for, and obeisance to the workings of the earth; being, not doing; family concerns are primary; obligation to share resources; respect for individuality; and government by consensus (Boldt, 1992, p. 118; Friesen, 1995, p. 33ff.). Informal means of social control like ridicule or teasing, the enactment of certain rituals and ceremonies, and the impartation of moral legends by elders served as reminders of moral obligations.

Evangelism

Evangelism is a term that implies reaching out to others with "the truth" as one sees it. Christians usually base their mandate to convert unbelievers on the Great Commission; "... Go into all the world and preach the gospel to *all* creation. Whoever believes and is baptized will be saved, but whoever does not believe will be condemned" (Mark 16:15-16, italics mine).

Evangelical Christians have sometimes been criticized for the zeal they demonstrate from time to time in their attempts to "win souls." Nowhere in North American history have such campaigns been more intense than those concerning the conversion of the First Peoples. Evangelicals have often quoted St. Paul to justify their efforts: "... I have become all things to all people so *that by all possible means I might save some*" (1 Corinthians 9:22b, italics mine). In writing to the Philippian church Paul reiterates the importance of preaching the Gospel to the unconverted. He acknowledges that some do so on the basis of selfish ambition, envy and rivalry, and in his mind: "But what does it matter? The important thing is that in every way, whether from false motives or true, Christ is preached. And because of this I rejoice" (Philippians 1:18). Today more liberal-minded Christians have virtually backed way from trying to implement the Great Commission, choosing instead to "love and accept everybody without trying to change them in any way." Apparently they leave that to the Spirit of God.

The evangelization of individuals and tribes other than their own was not a valued goal among the traditional Indigenous peoples of North America. At times, individuals from neighboring tribes were captured or received as "payment" for someone whose life had been taken by that neighboring tribe, but evangelism per se was not practiced. Sioux Chief Red Fox explained it this way:

> Brother, the Great Spirit has made all of us, but He has made a great difference between His White and Red children… why may we not conclude that He has given us a different religion according to our understanding? The Great Spirit does right. He knows what is best for His children. We are satisfied (Friesen, 1998, p. 21).

Faith

Faith is "confidence in what we hope for and assurance about what we do not see." So states the writer of the Book of Hebrews (11:1). Everyone lives by faith to some extent, although this is not commonly noted. When farmers plant crops, they have faith that plants will come up so that seeds may be harvested; when students graduate from university, they assume that their diplomas will provide them enhanced economic opportunities. In fact, the very act of sitting down on a chair involves faith—faith that the chair will not break under the weight of the occupant! Faith in the Divine is, of course, quite another thing. Those who have faith in God or in the Creator, or even in the "Good Guy Upstairs," tend to believe that they have an added resource on which to rely when the going gets tough. Barring belief in this kind of faith object, nonbelievers have only their own resources to rely on. It can safely be said that historically few cultures placed as great an emphasis on faith in the Divine as Native Americans of North America. Faith in a Higher Power or Great Mystery pervaded every facet of their cultures. Although unknown to them, their daily motto is aptly summarized in Proverbs

3:5-6: "Trust in the Lord with all your heart and lean not on your own understanding; in all your ways acknowledge him and he will make your paths straight."

Fall of Humankind—Original Sin

Fall of humankind—original sin: "For as in Adam all die, so in Christ all will be made alive" (1 Corinthians 15:22). In traditional Christianity the explanation for the sinful condition of humankind is as follows: "The original state of man was that childlike innocence or morally indifferent naturalism which had in itself the possibility of ideal development, but in such a way that its realization could be reached only by struggle with its natural opposite" (Strong, 1956, p. 519). Adam, the first man apparently ruined things for everyone by violating God's order in the Garden of Eden. By that act, his descendants inherited original sin; in other words, by Adam's action, everyone failed to live up to God's moral standard.

The basic presupposition of traditional Aboriginal theology is that "God is good; God is great; let us thank Him..." Creator God has provided amply for His children who are expected to do their best in living out their unique individual assignments. This includes sharing with others. A particular event known as the fall of man cannot be documented. However, an individual "fall" can occur if that person deliberately chooses to ignore his or her calling. Such an event parallels the actions of the individual in the parable of the talents or gold bags who, when he was assigned a bag of gold, went and buried it in the ground. His colleagues, however, who received five and two bags of gold respectively, both doubled the amount they were given (Matthew 25:14-25).

Grace

Grace is often described as unmerited favor (Piper, 1995, pp.

11-12). For sinful human creatures, the only way to get back into God's favor is through a way He Himself prepared through the work of Jesus Christ. As Garrigou-Lagrange (1959, p. 293) clarified:

> Man in his fallen state, can without grace, by God's concurrence in the natural order, know certain natural truths, though this concurrence of God is gratuitous in this sense, that it is accorded to men in varying degrees. Yet, even within the natural order, fallen man cannot without supernatural grace attain all truths, in particular not the more difficult truths.

Garrigou-Lagrange was quite clearly making reference to *spiritual* truths, which the natural man cannot know without being reconciled with God, and reconciliation is possible through faith in Christ alone. In the words of St. Paul, "The person without the Spirit does not accept the things that come from the Spirit of God but considers them foolishness, and cannot understand them because they are discerned only through the Spirit" (1 Corinthians 2: 14).

If grace may be defined as the practice of granting or endorsing some degree of flexibility, adaptability, or widening of the parameters of individual belief and behavior, with the consistent availability of forgiveness for failure, there was an ample supply in the traditional North American Indigenous belief system. It was believed that the Creator appreciated individual differences both in gift and practice. However, individuals did not perceive themselves as consistently being able to meet God's standard. Hence, it was necessary daily to renew one's covenantal commitment to the Creator. On a parallel note, many Old or New Testament saints acted quite differently from one another, and the Creator appears to have blessed them whenever they sought to maintain an open relationship with Him.

Incarnation

Incarnation refers to God taking human form in Christ so that Christ can properly represent fallen humankind on the day when God's final judgment will take place (Boice, 1986, p. 556). Many Christian theologians argue that the incarnation of Jesus Christ was a *necessary* happening for sinful humankind. It was necessary so that someone who was truly representative of humankind, namely Jesus Christ the Son of God, as well as equal with God, could represent humankind (John 14:20; Philippians 2:6).

Many North American First People traditionally assumed a "middle" kind of Deity, commonly called by various names such as the trickster. The Mi'kmaq and Maliseet peoples believed in the incarnated Glooscap, who possessed Divine powers, aided the Creator in creation, and was always available to assist the people when they needed him (Miller, 1995, p. 108). The Aboriginal belief in incarnation, which coincided nicely with Christian theology, made it an easier task for incoming missionaries when they presented the Christian Gospel, and may explain why many local Aboriginal communities so readily accepted it.

Justification

Justification and regeneration are theological terms that are often used interchangeably by those not formally connected to the field of theology. Being justified in the eyes of God refers to believers who have accepted Christ as Savior and therefore are theologically acceptable to God when He perceives them through the veil of Christ's sacrificial work on the cross. Romans 3:24 makes this abundantly clear: "all are justified freely by his grace through the redemption that came by Christ Jesus." Ephesians 2:8-10 echoes this thought: "For it is by grace you have been saved, through faith—and this is not from yourselves, it is the gift of God—not by works, so that no one can boast." (For further explanation on justification, see the section on *Regeneration* in this chapter.)

Miracles

Miracles are a frequent subject in both the Old and New Testaments. Miracles are perceived as happenings that can only occur with Divine origination or intervention. Today many liberal Christian leaders are skeptical that miracles happen, ever occurred, or are needed to bolster individual faith. As an anonymous skeptic put it, "Miracles are the swaddling clothes of the infant church, not the garments of the full grown." Ironically, many world religions have accounts of miraculous happenings in regard to the growth and development of their faith, and Native Americans are no exception. They have always and still do believe very strongly in Divine miracles. For them, and for many Bible believing Christians, belief in the possibility of miracles is very closely linked to personal faith.

Natural Law

Natural law constitutes a strong plank in Neo-Scholastic philosophy, and dates back at least to the writings of Thomas Aquinas (1225-1274). Aquinas conjectured that certain dispositions or natural inclinations are a fundamental component of human nature. These dispositions include preservation of life, propagation of the species, and an inclination to search for truth (Stumpf, 1993, p. 190). Although Aquinas believed strongly that laws should primarily be designed on the basis of reason, he also believed that a particular segment of the human disposition was made up of natural laws, that is, the propensity and desire to fulfill the three inclinations outlined above. Beyond that, humankind generally desires to formulate rules for living on the basis of reason.

Anthropologists tend to portray tribal societies as having

great respect for the natural order of things. The First Peoples believe that the Creator carefully designed the natural environment for *all* of His creation, and expected that the various creatures, including humankind, would behave in alignment with the laws He set in place for them. This means that natural laws, like the seasons, and other rhythms and cycles of nature should be respected. By contrast, modern society feigns belief in naturalism, but in actuality prefers to rely on human reason and/or democratically (representative, that is), arrived at decision-making.

Nature of Humankind

Nature of humankind (human nature) is an often discussed topic phrased in these queries; Is humankind basically evil, good, or neutral at birth? Are very young children passive, active (self-starters), or interactive with their immediate environment? (Bayles, 1966, p. 14ff.). Traditionally, conservative Christian writers have portrayed human beings as depraved at birth, citing a Scriptural passage like Psalm 51:5, "Surely I was sinful at birth, sinful from the time my mother conceived me." Children were perceived as having a natural inclination toward evil.

Conversely, modern educators, beginning with Jean Jacques Rousseau (1712-1778) have tried to promote the notion that human nature is basically good. Rousseau stated that…

> everything is good as it comes from the hands of the
> Maker of the world, but degenerates once it gets into
> the hands of man…. We are born with the capacity to
> learn…. The pretense is made that when children are
> left free they are likely to acquire wrong postures and
> to get misshapen limbs from their movements. This is
> one of the rationalizations of false wisdom, and is not
> borne out by experience. Let the mothers nurse their

children and a general reform of morals will follow
as a matter of course (Rousseau, 1962, pp. 11, 21, 16).

Rousseau preferred that early in life children would become active in
their search for truth, and parents and educators should be alert to
encourage this inclination.

There are, of course, students of human nature who would
argue that people are basically good, but subject to the whims of the
society in which they are raised. The society of their upbringing will
determine the nature of good or evil and also determine whether or
not children they give life to, are good or evil in inclination. Further,
the definitions of these inclinations will also be determined by that
society. John Dewey (1957, pp. 91, 101) spoke of the "plasticity of
impulse" and the "alterability of human nature," implying that moral flexibility is a built-in human trait. The question that emerges is
whether change is definable by individuals themselves, or by society,
or by both. The same question applies to the matter of moral goodness, evil, or neutrality.

If the tri-category of perceiving human nature as good, evil,
or neutral was adhered to in delineating traditional Aboriginal theology, it could probably best be categorized as neutral, that is, no
specific delineations were ascribed to it at birth. Each individual
was expected to find his or her unique place in the band, tribe, or
clan, and hence, in the universe, but always had available the option
to pursue either good or evil. The Creator would probably be most
pleased when individuals discovered the role designed for them and
lived to fulfill it in honor to God, to one's community, and to one's
brothers and sisters. This is entirely in keeping with James 1:27: "Religion that God our Father accepts as pure and faultless is this: to
look after orphans and widows in their distress and to keep oneself
from being polluted by the world."

Parables

Parables are biblical stories that were told to inform hearers whether or not a particular form of behavior was appropriate. Before the written word, all preliterate societies treasured a host of stories, legends, or myths that were related for a variety of purposes. Native Americans of the Plains, for example, had a store of legends that were intended for the purposes of entertainment, cultural instruction, moral guidance, and spiritual impartation. Biblical parables and moral legends of the Plains First Peoples are very similar in nature, and when told, leave it entirely up to the hearer to decipher and personalize the intended meaning (Friesen and Friesen, 2009, p. 135).

A popular Plains First Peoples legend that defines appropriate moral behavior is the story about wasted talent. The story line goes like this.

It came about that an Indian warrior once decided to play a trick on nature's ways. He chose to target the eagle for his experiment. He climbed into an eagle's nest and stole an egg out of the nest. Then, when no creature was looking, he put the eagle egg into a prairie chicken's nest that already had several eggs in it. The warrior reasoned that the mother would never know that he had added an egg to her workload. He was correct.

The mother prairie chicken faithfully sat on her eggs and soon they hatched. As the chicks grew and developed, she noticed that one of them was a bit larger than the others, but it never occurred to her that one of her chicks was really a baby eagle.

When the eagle chick grew up observers noted that he was unusually large, but he acted just like a prairie chicken. He ate prairie chicken food, walked like a prairie chicken, made sounds like a prairie chicken, and flew like a prairie chicken. Since prairie chickens do not fly very high, he always flew close to the ground.

One day the now grown young eagle saw another eagle flying high in the sky, soaring over the mountaintops. He was clearly impressed with what he saw. "Who is that bird?" he asked his friends. "He flies so high; I wish I could fly like that!"

"That is the king of the birds," his friends said. "You just saw the king of the birds flying high in the sky. Don't worry about it though. You will never be able to fly like that. You are a prairie chicken."

The young eagle never tried to fly high like that. He always remained close to the ground, never realizing the gift that the Creator had given him (Friesen, 2000b, p. 47).

Prayer

Prayer is the activity of worshipping, thanking, interceding, and/or making requests of the Divine Being called Creator God. Prayer is a universal activity among all world religions although adherents of some of the various faiths are probably quite certain that God will hear only those individuals who hold to their particular religious/spiritual persuasion. I am sure that these belief systems comprise a significant number.

Jesus made it quite clear that prayer is not to be taken lightly. "Therefore I tell you, whatever you ask for in prayer, believe that you have received it, and it will be yours. And when you stand praying, if you hold anything against anyone, forgive them, so that your Father in heaven may forgive you your sins" (Mark 11:24-25). The New Testament writer, James, concurred when he remarked, "The prayer of a righteous person is powerful and effective" (James 5:16b).

Chief Tecumseh of the Shawnee Nation reminded his people of the obligation to engage in prayer:

> When you arise in the morning, give thanks for the light, give thanks for the morning, for your life and strength. Give thanks for your food and the joy of living. If you see no reason for giving thanks, rest assured, the fault lies within yourself (Friesen, 1998, p. 14).

Prophecy

Prophecy in a classic Christian context is defined as foretelling or predicting future events through the medium of Divine guidance. Both Old and New Testaments contain accounts of individuals possessing the gift of prophecy, but Christianity is not alone in recognizing this role. Ramm (1958, p. 253) argued that proof of fulfilled prophecies has been central in Christian apologetics for centuries, and secularists have long been enamored with the predictions of French astrologer, Michel de Nostradamus (1503-1566). Kaltreider (1998) who is partially of Aboriginal descent has published a series of fulfilled Native American prophecies based on the visions of Sioux elder, Chasing Deer. No doubt today's philosophers are critically analyzing all of these perspectives with a penchant for skepticism.

Redemption, Repentance, Reconciliation

Redemption, repentance and reconciliation are terms that suggest that a recommended change in attitude and behavior has been or is in the making. Redemption was once defined as a legal act dating probably from the fourth century BC. If an enemy captured a Roman citizen, it was the duty of his family to pay a ransom to the enemy and have the prisoner returned (redeemed) to them (Elul, 1976, p. 66).

Today the term redemption is used in Christian theology to describe the situation of humankind in the fall of Adam and Eve. Humankind needs to be redeemed in order to return to the family of God. God has paid the ransom in the form of Christ's sacrificial death on the cross. The apostle Paul informed the Philippian jailor of this opportunity when he announced, "...believe in the Lord Jesus, and you will be saved—you and your household" (Acts 16:31).

Repentance has to do with a sincere and thorough change of mind toward *wanting* to be forgiven for past errors. Christians believe that when an individual repents of his or her sinful ways, it involves a radical change in personality. To repent is to turn away from a sinful way of life and become reconciled to God (Purkiser, 1960, pp. 180-181). As the Scripture states, "Therefore, if anyone is in Christ, the new creation has come: The old has gone, the new is here! (2 Corinthians 5:17).

Traditional North American Indigenous theology posits a slightly different scenario than that outlined above, and tends to adhere to a more developmental process in delineating these terms. The traditional practice in Native North American culture was that children would be taught to search for their Divine calling as soon as they were able to conceive of it. This could be done in various ways, and spiritual elders guided most related processes. Those who heard and listened to the voice of the Creator would then engage themselves in a progressive learning curve, always trying to move closer to the ideal that the Creator had set for them as individuals. Repentance per se, was not a valued term in the sense that severe breaks were made with the Creator's plan. Thus any misstep was replaced with the sincere desire to do better.

Even today, individual freedom of choice is highly valued in Aboriginal societies. If individuals *do* choose to follow a path of evil or "bad medicine" which, by the way, is experientially real (Waldram, 1997, p. 180), it will be necessary to repent of any evildoing should they decide to pursue God's calling for them. After all, God is merciful and He is "not wanting anyone to perish" (2 Peter 3:9).

Regeneration

Regeneration means quite literally to be born again or born anew. It should be evidenced by a complete mind change, evidenced by a change in the direction of living. Jesus Christ Himself made this quite clear to his learned friend, Nicodemus, when the latter sought to understand Jesus' teaching. This is Jesus' response to Nicodemus in John 3:3: "Jesus replied, "Very truly I tell you, no one can see the kingdom of God unless they are born again." Jesus further explained that to be regenerated means to believe in and accept Jesus Himself as one's personal Savior. "For God so loved the world that he gave his one and only Son, that whoever believes in him shall not perish but have eternal life" (John 3:16). The Apostle Peter was even more specific when he addressed a skeptical group of inquiring Jewish rulers, elders, and teachers of the law: "Salvation is found in no one else, for there is no other name under heaven given to mankind by which we must be saved" (Acts 4:12). In the mind of evangelical Christians, people are either believers through faith in the work of Christ or they are not believers; there is no middle road.

The North American Native view of salvation (with some liberal license) is as follows. Creator God is perceived as a loving Being who provides graciously for all of His creation in conjunction with the resources of Mother Earth. He also has expectations of His creatures, humans and animals alike; He expects them to live in accordance with the natural laws He has laid out for the various species. Men and women are specifically expected to care for Mother Earth and her various creatures, and remain daily in spiritual communion with the Creator. Children are taught right from wrong in a myriad of ways and in an ascending fashion, so it is not expected that they will someday experience a specific salvation experience. The traditional Native American perspective falls right in line with the injunction of Proverbs 22:6; "Start children off on the way they should go, and when they are old they will not turn from it." (For further explanation on regeneration, see the section on *Justification* in this chapter.)

Resurrection

Resurrection is probably one of the hardest truth for non-believers to accept, and in this context refers to Christ having been raised from the dead on the third day after His death. For Christians, the resurrection was a necessary happening so that God's redemptive plan could be completed. God decreed this; "the wages of sin is death" (Romans 6:23), but death had to be overcome so that hope for eternal life could be secured. Jesus defeated death. As Paul argued:

> ...how can some of you say that there is no resurrection of the dead? If there is no resurrection of the dead, then not even Christ has been raised. And if Christ has not been raised, our preaching is useless, and so is your faith....you are still in your sins (1 Corinthians 15:12b-14, 17b).

Christ's resurrection is also important in the fact that it now becomes possible for others to be resurrected since Christ became the "firstfruits of those who have fallen asleep" (1 Corinthians 15:20). This means that since one person has been raised, there is now the potentiality for a universal awakening of the dead (Küng, 1976, p. 357). Indeed, when the Second Coming of Christ occurs, "the dead in Christ will rise first" (1 Thessalonians 4:16c).

Native North Americans traditionally concerned themselves with following the Creator's path in the here and now. Operating on fairly general conceptualizations about the hereafter, related terms were not always distinctly elaborated. The concept of resurrection *was* part of the vocabulary of some Plains tribes who surmised that the intermediary deity they conceptualized (for example, called Glooscap among the Mi'kmaq and Maliseet) had the ability to die and be resurrected.

Revelation

Revelation occurs when an element of the essence of Divinity is made available to humankind, that is, certain individuals obtain special information about the workings of God, sometimes in relation to specific events or situations. According to the biblical tradition, this information may be obtained through dreams, visions, trances, appearance of angels, prophetic utterances, or through direct conversation. For example, God spoke directly to Noah, informing him that he was to become the builder of a huge ark (Genesis 6:14); an angel of God spoke directly to Hagar, wife of Abram, telling her that she would give birth to a special son and she should name him Ishmael (Genesis 16:7, 11); King David was reprimanded by the prophet, Nathan, for arranging Uriah's death so David could marry his widow (2 Samuel 12:1-12); an angel appeared to Joseph in a dream, urging him to marry Mary, who became the mother of Christ (Matthew 1:20); and the Apostle Peter was the recipient of a vision or trance during which he was informed that people are all equal in God's eyes (Acts 10:9-15).

There has long been reluctance on the part of adherents to specific belief systems, like Christianity; to acknowledge the validity of supernaturally derived information claimed by other religionists. This reluctance has made it difficult for people of different backgrounds to appreciate each other's beliefs, and on many occasions has led to unfortunate misunderstandings and conflict, and even war.

Aboriginal peoples of North America believed (and believe) very strongly in Divine revelation that may be accessed through a variety of avenues including dreams and visions, vision quests, and other specified ceremonies.

Sacraments, Rituals, Ordinances

Sacraments, rituals, ordinances are physical enactments that lend authenticity to one's spiritual search and assist in appreciation of basic transcendental beliefs. Generally speaking, religions are made up of three specifics: (a) beliefs and practices that inspire fear, awe, or reverence; (b) a prescribed lost of expected behaviors; and, (c) a long-term promise of eventual respite (hope). Sacraments, rituals, and ordinances are part and parcel of the first criterion, Sacraments being the most powerful of the three concepts. Taking part in a Sacrament implies Divine participation in the enactment; rituals are set forms or procedures of public observance; and ordinances are customs or practices established by social usage or by ecclesiastical authority. While all religious persuasions adhere to these phenomena in one fashion or another, spiritual leaders in each religious persuasion will likely determine their exact definition.

Cultures relying on the oral tradition, like North American

First Peoples, utilized a wide variety of enactments by which to perpetuate valued beliefs. Many of their ceremonies, rituals, and other spiritual practices were very complex in nature, and their meaning was almost completely indecipherable to outsiders. It is only recently, and with the permission of spiritual elders, that some Native writers have felt the liberty to describe these. Two major purposes for enacting rituals and ceremonies have been (a) to perceive them as teaching tools (that is, learning by doing), and, (b) to remind people of their spiritual privileges and obligations.

Salvation

Salvation is a term that implies a need for redemption or deliverance. The Christian interpretation is clear-cut. Through the fall of man, initiated by Adam and his wife, Eve, all humankind became sinful and alienated from God. The Old Testament recipe for salvation was through the enactment of quite complicated rituals, while the New Testament pathway to being reunited with God is through faith in Jesus Christ, God's Son. This implies belief in and acceptance of Christ's sacrifice on the cross and His subsequent death and resurrection. A wider interpretation allows for the applicability of this concept to other faiths, namely that leaders of each belief system have spelled out the route by which Divine favor can be achieved.

In traditional North American Aboriginal theology, salvation was viewed as a perpetual progressive process. It began at conception, and at birth each child was perceived as a gift of God, theologically innocent, and therefore in right relationship with God. As the child grew up he or she would be guided to the search for Divine approval. Anyone who discovered "the path" set out for them by the Creator would be "saved" by following that path. Salvation was not perceived as a distinct action to be undertaken at any specific time in life. Children were taught this Divine arrangement from the time of their birth and carefully guided in ways that would help them remain on the path.

Sanctification

Sanctification means literally, "being setting apart." Although there are varying interpretations of this term, the general Christian context suggests that believers are expected to avoid behavior patterns that dishonor God. Several more fundamentalist, charismatic-inclined denominations interpret this happening as a separate (second) step in the conversion process. North American Aboriginal theologians would probably argue that like salvation, sanctification is a lifelong process of trying to become what the Creator has planned for the individual.

Scriptures

Scriptures are perceived as written forms of Divine direction and guidance. Most world religions have collected forms of scriptural writings, usually made up of essays and less formalized recorded thoughts by respected men and women who were considered to be supernaturally inspired. Sacred writings like the Bible are often the target of attacks by unbelievers who question the authenticity and inspiration of contained writings as well as how the specific collection of writings came into existence. In writing to Timothy, his theological protégé, the Apostle Paul minces no words about the authenticity of Scripture when he says; "All scripture is God-breathed, and is useful for teaching, rebuking, correcting and training in righteousness, so that the servant of God may be thoroughly equipped for every good work" (2 Timothy 3:16, 17).

Societies that functioned before the printed page was in vogue maintained their way of life by relying on the oral tradition. Valued beliefs were transmitted to successive generations, through the enactment of a wide range of ceremonies and rituals, as well as through storytelling. Listening to stories related by elders was part of Aboriginal children's daily routine and provided them with valuable teachings. These teachings were about how things came to be, and how children were expected to behave (Hare, 2011, p. 93). Each facet of Native American culture was safeguarded for future preservation with at least one story.

Second Coming

Christians treasure this expected eschatological happening, because it will signify the end of this age. As Paul writes to the church at Thessalonica:

> For the Lord himself will come down from heaven, with a loud command, with the voice of the archangel and with the trumpet call of God, and the dead in Christ will rise first. After that, we who are still alive and are left will be caught up together with them in the clouds to meet the Lord in the air. And so we will be with the Lord forever (1 Thessalonians 4:16-17).

Although the concept of Second Coming was not part of the traditional Indigenous theological landscape, some tribes *did* hold to the idea that significant divinely safeguarded happenings would occur in the future. For example, the Mi'kmaq people believed that Glooscap (the incarnated being) would appear to help his people whenever they were in need.

Sin

Sin is commonly defined as being guilty of breaking a religious law or moral precept, especially through a willful act. In theological terms, the phrase "missing the mark" is more apt. The writer to the Book of Romans (3:23) is quite blunt on this point: "for all have sinned and fall short of the glory of God."

Use of the word "sin" has virtually disappeared in North American society and this has been so for several decades. American psychiatrist, Karl Menninger (1973, p. 14ff.), lamented this happening, and suggested that disuse of the word had occurred because it has been replaced by a shift in the allocation of responsibility for evil. Menninger defined sin as transgression of the law of God, or disobedience of the Divine will or moral failure. At heart, sin is a refusal of love for others. It appears that few individuals in today's society want to take responsibility for that; hence, sin is redefined as something else or, at best, some anonymous other's doing. Menninger quoted a statement made by President Abraham Lincoln that underscored the necessity to confess sin:

> It is the duty of nations as well as of men to own their dependence upon the overruling power of God, to confess their sins and transgressions in humble sorrow, yet with the second hope that genuine repentance will lead to mercy and pardon (cited in Menninger, 1973, p. 14).

All societies, including Indigenous tribes, traditionally had ways of defining and identifying violations of established norms, and although they might not have been labeled "sin," they were definitely perceived as violations and there were consequences, Divinely or otherwise mandated, for breaking them.

Spirit

Spirit is a term assigned to activities undertaken by an otherworldly Person—in Christianity, the third member of the Trinity, known as the Holy Spirit. When Jesus was preparing His disciples for His ascension into heaven He instructed them concerning God's provision for their spiritual guidance. "But the Advocate, the Holy Spirit, whom the Father will send in my name, will teach you all things and will remind you of everything I have said to you" (John 14:26).

In one way or another, world religions of many persuasions acknowledge the workings of Divine Spirit, and/or of spiritual beings. Spiritually driven happenings are generally believed to have their origin and existence in a transcendental or *noumenal* (Immanuel Kant's word) realm. Genesis, the first book of the Bible, acknowledges the workings of the Holy Spirit in creation: "Now the earth was formless and empty, darkness was over the surface of the deep, and the Spirit of God was hovering over the waters" (Genesis 1:2). Paul cautioned the Corinthian church to realize that the workings of the Holy Spirit would be not be understood nor appreciated by unbelievers. "The person without the Spirit does not accept the things that come from the Spirit of God but considers them foolishness, and cannot understand them because they are discerned only through the Spirit" (1 Corinthians 2:14).

The First People of North America traditionally believed very much in the spirit world. In addition to respecting and honoring the Spirit of the Creator, they also acknowledged the spirit within each created living entity—humans, animals, birds, fish, and plants. This orientation appeared to them as a logical deduction since the origin of things occurred through action of the Ultimate Spirit. Thus the spirits of living phenomena were honored when, for example, the life of an animal was taken for food. On another note, it is helpful to understand that Indigenous people also differentiated carefully between good and evil spirits, believing that individuals could align themselves with either one of these and thereby potentially benefit or harm others through their affiliation.

Spirituality

Spirituality is a closely linked concept to the above (Spirit), and in a Christian context has to do with the realm of "God's wisdom, a mystery that has been hidden" (1 Corinthians 2:7). For the Christian, spiritual knowledge can only be acquired by having faith in the unseen world of God. As Jesus explained to the learned Nicodemus, "The wind blows wherever it pleases. You hear its sound, but you cannot tell where it comes from or where it is going. So it is with everyone born of the Spirit" (John 3:8).

People who used to live in tribal cultures have typically been perceived as spiritually oriented because they acknowledged every living entity in the universe as having a spirit. This meant that spiritual lessons could possibly be learned from any encounter with a living entity. Every human act, including the spoken word, was perceived to have spiritual meaning, making Indigenous peoples a high context culture. This should be interpreted to mean that every situation of everyday life could have spiritual implications.

Trinity

The Trinity is a concept quite unique to Christianity, but not clearly taught in the Scriptures. The notion of Trinity in the Godhead is primarily a necessary inferred doctrine, necessary because faith in it helps make logistical sense of God's redemptive plan for humankind. Christ, as a member of the Trinity, *had* to have equal status with God (Philippians 2:6) if His death of the cross was to satisfy God's requirements for sin. Sin is punishable by death, but faith in Christ (who is equal with God), makes His sacrifice on our behalf qualify as a full representation. Historically, theologians have wrestled long and hard to explain how Jesus Christ could be both human and Divine, with many of them simply accepting the concept by "logical faith" (Placher, 1983, p. 80ff.).

The other member of the Trinity, the Holy Spirit, proceeds from the Father, again as His full representative (John 14:26), and completes the triad of being (Garrigou-Lagrange, 1950, p. 139). Christian logicians sometimes have difficulty with the article "the" that is usually placed before the terms "Holy Spirit," because the word "the" tends to depersonalize God in that Person.

The concepts outlined above are quite germane to most Christian theological discussions, but it is to be expected that the process of writing theology in other than a specifically Christian context requires a broader vocabulary. Now such terms as metaphysics, mysticism, otherworldly, transcendentalism, supernatural, otherworldly, and other terms come into play. An expanded vocabulary is essential to the study of world-views other than European-North American because the validity of related assumptions and beliefs of other view-points is often questioned when approached from a strictly Judeo-Christian perspective. It is not the intension here in any to way diminish the significance of that tradition, but to learn about and appreciate inherent and expressed commonalities. (For further explanation on Trinity, see the section on *Spirit* in this chapter.)

CHAPTER THREE

Divinity: Human Perceptions of Creator God

Attempting to elaborate the rational for believing in a Supreme Power or Force or Being has been a major concern for philosophers since the beginning of time. Theologians call this pursuit the study of Divinity, and it appears to have been a major pastime for nineteenth century philosophers whose ideas will be summarized in subsequent paragraphs. In more recent times, debaters have been less concerned about the existence of a Divine Being. Rather, they have placed more emphasis on what the *nature* of God might be, and whether or not the perceived nature of God has any implications for human behavior. Certainly, the more sophisticated discussions of these questions lie in the past. A brief clarification of the key ideas of notable philosophers from the modern period may serve to substantiate this observation. For most of this information I am indebted to a very fine work, *Four Philosophies and Their Practice in Education and Religion* (Harper & Row, 1968) by the late J. Donald Butler, who for many years served as chair of the department of religion at Macalester College in Minnesota.

Philosophical Concepts of God

As is the case with most philosophical surveys, Butler undertook his journey as far back as Plato (427?—347 BC), and it is also my decision to start there. Following Plato, it is customary to make a quick leap to the modern period. Plato's notion of the doctrine of ideas was probably his most important philosophical contribution and may be summarized as follows. Plato posited that there are in existence certain *universal* (or spiritual?) and enduring ideas, coexistent with the lesser world of images that by contrast, seem fleeting. The primary ideas that belong to the category of eternal truth include absolute beauty, goodness, and essence. Awareness of these concepts arrives in human hearts through the process of remembering from a former existence that preceded the embodiment of individuals in human form. Another universal and moral idea that should be acknowledged is Plato's notion of "the good," to which all people should aspire. This truth is most aptly incorporated in Plato's allegory of the cave (Butler, 1968, pp. 113-114).

Plato did not propose the existence of either a Supreme Being or a powerful supernatural Force; he settled for immutable, nonpersonalized ideas, but his speculations certainly lay the groundwork for assuming that a superior, eternal world exists and serves as the source of universal values and characteristics that should be pursued by human beings. He did state that *Mind* orders everything, but stopped short of identifying *Mind as Being*, or developing a doctrine of creation (Stumpf, 1993, p. 77)

A long historical leap forward brings us to the philosophy of René Descartes (1596-1650). Descartes offered two main ideas that paralleled the direction of Plato's thinking. Descartes suggested that since it was possible for human beings to conceive of perfection, perfection must exist, probably in the form of a Perfect Being, thus God. He also speculated that all-inclusive doubt is the only open road to truth. This speculation made him one of the most famous agnostics in modern history. Descartes doubted the validity of truth obtained by use of sense perception, but was convinced that human intuition could not be dismissed. Hence, the innate notion that perfection is possible led him to conjecture that it must exist in the form of Self

(Butler, 1968, p. 115).

Our survey next takes us to Baruch Spinoza (1632-1677) and his uniquely concocted Doctrine of Substance. Spinoza speculated that the universe is made up of a special Substance that is *not* matter, but is still dependably solid and unchanging. Varying qualities of Substance exist in plants, animals, and humankind, with the highest form properly to be called God. The Divine form of Substance, namely God, is perceived as enduring; it always was, and always will be. Further, God is to be perceived as possessing extension and thought, the former implying that He is capable of creating various forms, and the latter suggesting that He is a thinking Being. Humankind is to be seen as a modification of God—a little island of the essence of God (Butler, 1968, p. 118). This interpretation closely resembles the biblical statement, "So God created man in his own image, in the image of God he created them; male and female he created them" (Genesis 1:27).

A graduate of the University of Altdorf, Gottfried Wilhelm von Leibniz (1646-1716) was a contemporary of Spinoza, but instead of entering the field of philosophy as his father did, he became involved in law and government. Unique to his line of thought, Leibniz invented the term "monad," which he described as a simple, indivisible unit or entity that together with other monads makes up the universe. Not unlike molecules to some extent, Leibniz perceived each monad as unique, and from within constantly changing. Leibniz conjectured that there are several kinds of monads in existence, the most elemental being simple monads that make up the physical properties of matter—both organic as well as inorganic. The second type of monad is more complex in that it enjoys sharper perception and possesses awareness of things about it. The third type of monad is the highest kind and is capable of reason; a collaboration of these monads makes up humankind. The latter type is also seen to possess what Leibniz called "spirit." God is a monad of the last and highest type, but He is unique in having an all-inclusive perception and exists without limits (Butler, 1968, p. 119ff.).

An Irish philosopher, George Berkeley (1685-1753) is next on the list, and is probably best remembered for raising the question, "If a tree falls in the forest and there is no one around to hear it, does it make a noise?" The short answer is "yes," because God, who is everywhere, will hear the tree fall. Berkeley resisted the notion that matter exists, and considered it strange that since no one has ever experienced matter, people generally perceive that it exists. In other words, Berkeley's interpreters bought into the notion that the external physical world exists independently of a greater Mind who made it possible. To Berkeley's way of thinking, the physical world cannot beget itself; it has to have a higher source of origin. Physical matter must be perceived by that higher realm in order to exist. *To be is to be perceived* is a principle that to some extent parallels Descartes' notion that since individuals are able to conceive of perfection, hence it must exist (Butler, 1968, p. 126-127).

A German thinker, Immanuel Kant (1724-1804) has sometimes been described as the greatest philosopher of the nineteenth century. This is no doubt partly due to the fact that his writings are so difficult to decipher! Like his philosophical predecessors, Kant also conjectured two different qualities within the universe—physical (phenomenal) and spiritual (noumenal). True to form, Kant formulated his own vocabulary to describe the two qualities, the one being the physical world in which sensations exist, and the other being the world of *das Ding an sich*, roughly translated to mean, "The Thing-in-Itself." Kant projected that universal moral laws originate within the world of The Thing-in-Itself, a phenomenon, which in his final days he called God. Humankind has an obligation to live in accordance with moral laws, with the possible ultimate reward entering the domain of immortality. Johann Gottlieb Fichte (1762-1814), a disciple of Kant's teachings, postulated that only a true scholar would be able to penetrate the realm of what *he* called, The- Ego-in-Itself, thus personalizing even more Kant's somewhat obscure notion of God.

The last thinker discussed in this section is another German philosopher, Wilhelm Hegel (1770-1831), who followed Johann Gottlieb Fichte to the chair of philosophy at the University of Berlin. Most students of philosophy are probably acquainted with Hegel's notion of the dialectic, namely that social movements, and indeed societies as they evolve, follow a rhythm of movement in three phases—thesis (idea), antithesis (Nature), and synthesis (Mind or Spirit). In other words, dialectic is the pattern by which thought moves. When applied to societal shifts in thought, generally speaking, *thesis* may be perceived as an idea or orientation, which in time is typically followed by an *antithetical* way of thinking, and when the two coalesce, a *synthesis* emerges. In time the synthesis becomes a dominant way of thinking or thesis, thereby giving rise to another antithesis, and so on.

According to Hegel, absolute Mind controls the dialectic process, and Nature is essential to Mind as a means of objectifying and realizing itself (Butler, 1968, p. 136). According to Christian theology, Hegel's approach is a rather complicated way of saying that God created the world and still manifests His will in it. Finally, as an aside, it was Karl Marx who tried to transform Hegel's dialectic into something called dialectic materialism. In other words, he rejected the spiritual element of Hegel's idealism and interpreted the dialectic in strictly materialistic terms.

As we may deduce from the above discussion, traditionally philosophers have tended *not* to accept the existence of God as a given, but instead tried to maneuver their minds towards testing that assumption by constructing what they perceived to be more neutral paradigms by which to approach the original assumption. As we can see, most of them simply ended their speculations by concluding that Deity exists and functions, albeit they preferred to do everything they could to avoid acknowledging the existence of God as a self-evident truth.

Christian Concepts of God

Our next task is to try to decipher what Christian theologians, particularly from a Protestant perspective, have written about the existence of God over the past half century. We begin with Henry Clarence Thiessen's *Introductory Lectures in Systematic Theology* (1959) in which he first introduced the nature and necessity of theology, and the *possibility* of theology. He then launched into a discussion of theism per se. Thiessen reminded his readers that the word "theology" derives from two words, *theos* and *logos*, rendering the meaning that theology is discourse about God—who He is, and what He does. Thiessen claimed that theologizing is a necessary tendency among humans, somewhat following the thinking patterns of René Descartes and George Berkeley. The *possibility* of theology is mandated by two factors—the fact that God has revealed Himself to humankind, and the reality of human endowments, namely that people tend to manifest characteristics that resemble those usually ascribed to God. And why not? After all, God created man in His image (Genesis 1:27).

Thiessen's (1959, pp. 55-63) discussion of theism presents five major arguments to prove the existence of God, the first of which follows Descartes' presupposition that belief in God is intuitive. People generally have a feeling that God exists, even though they may not be able to rationalize why they possess this belief. The second argument is from the Holy Scriptures, which contain numerous assertions about the existence of God. Of course, this argument assumes that the Bible is an authoritative source on which to base theological claims, and critics would argue that this is a circular argument.

Third, Thiessen asserted that the existence of God is corroborated by rational arguments such as the cosmological argument (this is the argument of cause, namely that something cannot come out of nothing); the teleological argument (the argument of design and order); the ontological argument (the very idea of God is proof of His existence); the moral argument (the fact that people seem to have a need to do what is right following Kant's notion of universal moral laws); and, finally, the argument from congruity (this rests on the notion that a postulate which best explains related facts, is probably true). Thiessen concluded the discussion by asserting that there is indeed a personal, extra-mundane, ethical, and self-revealing God (Thiessen, 1959, p. 63).

Christian interpretations of theology have not changed much in the decades that paralleled and immediately followed Thiessen's explications. For example, Augustus Hopkins Strong's 1907 *Systematic Theology: A Compendium* was reprinted for the nineteenth time in 1956, and Thiessen's work was reproduced in 1989. Fitzwater penned a parallel volume in 1953, and in 1958 evangelical theologian, Carl F. Henry edited a volume of readings explaining the same theological arguments and concepts. Theological works published in the last three decades of the twentieth century tend to feature less systematic approaches to the study of theology, perhaps in an effort to attract new readers. Instead they have wrestled with issues pertaining to hermeneutical interpretations and everyday ethical and moral practicalities. Exemplary works include W. T. Purkiser (Ed.), *Exploring Our Christian Faith* (1960); Stanley N. Gundry and Alan F. Johnson (Eds.), *Tensions in Contemporary Theology* (1976); Lawrence O. Richards and Gib Martin, *A Theology of Personal Ministry* (1981); and, Stanley J. Grenz & Roger E. Olson, *20th- Century Theology: God & the World in a Transitional Age* (1992).

Reference to at least one important theological work by a Roman Catholic theologian, Reginald Garrigou-Lagrange (1950) seems appropriate. Writing in the same decade as Thiessen, it is not surprising that Garrigou-Lagrange takes a very similar approach to the subject. Chapter titles and subheadings in *Reality: A Synthesis of Thomistic Thought* are familiar, namely, Intelligible Being and First Principles; Nature of Theological Work; The Proper Object of Theology; Steps in Theological Procedure; and so on. Protestant theologians living in that decade should have been pleased to read this book.

Garrigou-Lagrange differentiates sharply between faith and theology, pointing out that theology is the science of the truths of faith, which truths it explains, defends, and compares. By comparing truths with one another, theologians perceive their mutual relations, and consequences that may transpire. Following the logic of Thomas Aquinas, one should not conclude that God exists on the basis of *a priori* knowledge, because we have no such knowledge. Humankind generally begins with only a nominal definition of God, seeing Him as the first source of all that is real and good in the world. However, God *can* come to be known through sense experience which gradually leads to contemplations of First Cause, and that constitutes a good starting point (Garrigou-Lagrange, 1950, p. 72).

Garrigou-Lagrange posits that the five classical arguments for the existence of God (previously referred to in this discussion following Thiessen's work) essentially rest on the principle of causality. Garrigou-Lagrange explains:

> First: whatever begins, has a cause; Second: every contingent thing, even if it should be *ab aeterno*, depends on a cause that exists of itself; Third: that which has a share in existence depends ultimately on a cause which is existence itself, a cause whose nature is to exist, which alone can say: I am who I am.... Most simply expressed, causality means: the more does not come

from the less, the more perfect cannot be produced by the less perfect (Garrigou-Lagrange, 1950, p. 72).

Based on the above discussion, it would seem that Christian theologians, both Protestants and Roman Catholics, traditionally followed a fairly standard format in delineating the existence of God. Outlining the characteristics of God was considered a logical next step, and here the going has often grown quite complex. Fitzwater (1953, p. 81ff.) lists and elaborates on the following attributes of God, each of them well supported with Scriptural references. These include self-existence, eternal, immutable, infinite, holy, good, truthful, and love—God *is* love. Mickey's (1980, p. 46) list of God's attributes consists of these: omnipresent, all perfect, omnipotent, omniscient, holy, and Spirit.

As the twentieth century came to a close, Christian theologians seemed to have departed from the familiar trail of systematic theology and took to theologizing about more practical themes. Boice (1986, p. 20) tackles the concept that Divine reality may be deduced solely by supposedly impartial reasoning. He emphasizes that the fallacy of this kind of thinking is that a universal interpretation of reason does not exist. In addition, the use of reason cannot provide a code of ethics. It can tell us what *is*, but it cannot tell us what *ought* to be. The new way to approach the problem is to realize that there is a God who created all things, and who Himself gives His creation meaning. This God can be known, and it is through His relationship with us that He *can* be known. In other words, God can be known when humans become aware of their spiritual condition without Him, and earnestly seek his face. As the Old Testament prophet Jeremiah (29:13) put it, "You will seek me and find me when you seek me with all your heart."

Gone are the days when the search for the Omnipotent One had to be directed by leaders of the organized church. The revised theological approach suggests that this is an individual privilege and responsibility.

Grenz and Olson (1992), in a collection of relevant essays include a wide range of opinions on the topic of immanence versus transcendence. Their position is that the view of medieval thinkers who mandated a wide gulf between the two concepts needs to be updated. Grenz and Olson (1992, p. 315) argue that it is no longer acceptable to insist that God's presence (immanence) can only be experienced within the confines of the church. Instead, believers may be assured that our transcendent God—existent beyond the physical level—is immanently available in every human circumstance. This observation substantiates an earlier presupposition in this volume that more recent theological writings have tended to emphasize what the nature of God requires of individuals per se, not necessarily through the medium of corporate Christian institutions.

Anderson (2001, p. 179) follows this line of thinking by suggesting that the role and mission of the Christian church should be to function where people are in greatest need. He accuses the church of abandoning the city which is the place where large numbers of individuals struggle with unemployment, isolation, loneliness, homelessness, substance abuse, and other human maladies. It is Anderson's view that Christians cannot turn away from any form of inhumanity without separating themselves from the humanity of God. God Himself became flesh in Christ so that He could minister to people in the marketplace. Christ's ministry was predominantly to those who hurt—the sick, the poor, and the needy. As Jesus described His own ministry: "It is not the healthy who need a doctor, but the sick. But go and learn what this means: 'I desire mercy, not sacrifice.' For I have not come to call the righteous, but sinners" (Matthew 9:12b-13). James echoes this sentiment when he states, "In the same way, faith by itself, if it is not accompanied by action, is dead" (James 2:17).

Aboriginal Concepts of the Creator

Historians, anthropologists, social scientists, and missionaries, as well as explorers and fur traders who kept diaries when they visited Indigenous communities, tended to shy away from use of the word "theology" when describing the spiritual beliefs and practices of North America's First Peoples. Their choice of words included "spiritualism" or "superstition" and other even less kindly descriptors. This perspective continues to this day, although the practice is slowly changing.

One of the first essential realities to understanding Aboriginal spirituality is to recognize that in pre-contact North America, the various Indigenous communities functioned in accordance with geographically appropriate lifestyles. These lifestyles were often mandated by the availability of food sources. Anthropologists have since designated as many as fifteen distinct cultural areas occupied by North American Indians, and the bands within them often differed somewhat in terms of their cultural practices and spiritual beliefs. The Great Plains area, which is a predominant sub-theme in this volume, extended south from Canada's prairie provinces to Texas and New Mexico. References to other cultural areas and tribal affiliations will be made from time to time as a means of expanding points of discussion.

To begin with, traditionally the North American First People had an ever-present consciousness of the supernatural (Lockwood, 1987, p. 63). The original occupants of the Great Plains particularly viewed the earth as a gift from their parents—the Creator, Father of us all, and Mother Earth. It was the responsibility of their offspring, namely humankind, to appreciate these gifts and live worthily of them (Friesen, 2000a, p. 14). I should mention that although the earth was traditionally respected as a source of sustenance, the concept of Mother Earth per se was likely influenced by imported

Eurocentric thinking.

Further investigations of Aboriginal spirituality beyond the premise of honoring otherworldly parentage, must proceed with attempts to avoid preconceived notions offered by most historical sources. The initial wish to know must begin with a willingness and readiness to learn. A Siksika (Blackfoot) colleague described it this way; there are four essential steps in deciphering First Nations spiritual beliefs, ceremonies, and rituals. The first step is to listen, the second step is to perhaps be invited to observe, and the third step is to participate. The fourth, and final step is to be entrusted to teach the particular sacred truth that has been imparted. Reading emerging literature on the subject, absorbing myself in Indigenous community life, and having considerable contact with Native elders has enhanced my own pursuit. As I indicated earlier, my wife and I have also been recipients of a number of eagle feathers blessed by elders, thereby rendering us the privilege of dealing with this subject.

In my journey to know, following the four steps toward gaining spiritual knowledge, Aboriginal friends have graciously provided guidance and illumination. My goal has been to discover how Plains First Peoples perceive the workings of the Supreme Being, how He reveals Himself, and how He maintains contact with His people. A dear friend, the late Chief John Snow of the Stoney (Nakoda Sioux) First Nation explained that his people believe themselves to have been selected by the Creator to receive the special gift of understanding spiritual phenomena. They have been entrusted by the Creator to hand down spiritual knowledge to succeeding generations (Snow, 2005, p. 4). Much Divine knowledge has been, and is being, derived from observing the working of nature in the environs of animals, birds, flora and fauna, and in the rhythms of natural forces. As indicated in another section of this book, the Siksika (Blackfoot) First Nation has a similar view. They believe that the Creator has a covenant with them, acknowledging them as His people. They symbolize this covenant by braiding their hair.

Fortunately, there are non-Aboriginal students of Plains Indian ways who approach the study of Native spirituality with an open mind. They realize that traditionally grounded Indigenous beliefs and practices comprise a highly developed religious system, full of meanings and sub-meanings (Tooker, 1979, p. 31). These beliefs do not precisely correspond to those of their counterparts in other Indigenous cultural areas, but there are great similarities (Spence, 1994, p. 359). Note, for example, Underhill's (1965, p. 108) description of one aspect of the Sundance still celebrated by many Plains Indian tribes:

> At a Plains Sun Dance, the priest is to lay a rabbit skin at the center pole in memory of a vow. It is a flimsy, grayish, little skin but he holds it in both hands as reverently as a different priest might hold a golden chalice. Three times he gestures towards the center pole and withdraws. The uninstructed visitor grows impatient, for there is no pageantry to mark the importance of this event. But the Indian spectators know that the number four symbolizes perfection.

The specific question driving this discussion is; "Did the Indigenous peoples of the western plains traditionally believe in God?" The answer is a qualified, "yes." Smith (1995, p. 242) suggests that Plains Indians traditionally believed in a Supreme Divine Being, but not in the sense that theologians do who adhere to European-North American interpretations. At its core the European-North American theological perspective focuses on individuality and conjectures that God is a separate, particular Creator Being who exists over against this created universe. God is perceived in a parent role, and is usually elaborated in male form, that is, "God, the Father." According to Smith, in comparison, Indigenous people believe in the Creator as a great Prevailing Force who resides in the sky. All brightness emanates from the firmament above humankind and people's eyes are dazzled by its splendor. Spence (1994, pp. 101-102) observes that the abode of the Creator, the "Great Mystery," is viewed as the source of all life and of all spiritual excellence.

The Plains First Peoples traditionally described God more in terms of a Universal Principle instead of a determinate Being one might call God. This Divine Being may be perceived as an eternal spiritual Force characterized by presence and unity. The Force exists as a vital, energizing part of every living thing including humankind, animals, fowls and plants. Plains First Peoples believed that by honoring the spirits of animals they were acknowledging the universal presence of the Eternal Spirit, but not in any particular form or separate entity. Edwin Thompson Denig (1812-1858), who worked for the American Fur Company, and lived among the Assiniboine people for many years, concurred with this appraisal. In his words:

> All these Indians believe in a Great Power, the First Cause of Creation, though they do not attempt to embody this idea, and call it by name *Wah-con'tun'ga* or Great Medicine. The word "Medicine" in this case has no reference to the use of drugs, but the sense of it is all that is incomprehensible, supernatural, all powerful, etc. Everything that cannot be explained, accounted for by ordinary means, all that is above the comprehension and power of man (Indians) is called *Wah-con* or medicine (cited in Denig, 2000, p. 92).

The concept of interconnectedness is also significant in this context because it implies a connectedness *with* a responsibility *to* all living things. All manners of food were traditionally acknowledged as gifts from the Creator and were consumed only after appropriate prayers of thanks were offered. The first fruits of the berry season were acknowledged by an elder raising a representative sample to the sky with a prayer of thanksgiving, or a portion of meat might be buried in the ground as a symbol of interconnectedness with Mother Earth. The Sioux emphasized the importance of this truth with this statement: "We are all related to all things or, we are all related—we are all relatives" (Champagne, 1994, p. 442; McGaa, 1995, p. 9). Since a very fundamental plank in Plains Indian philosophy mandates caring for one's relatives, and sharing with them whatever resources one has, it also means that humans have a stewardship responsibility to the earth and to *every* living phenomenon, animate or inanimate.

A related concept inherent in Plains Indigenous theology may be illustrated with reference to an Aboriginal interpretation of John 3:16a, "For God so loved the world that He gave . . ." To Plains First Peoples this simply means that God (the Force) created and provides for the earth in all facets as a complete entity. European-North American originated interpretations, on the other hand, interpret this passage to mean that God loves and provides for *people*, but not necessarily for all of the other living entities He has created—at least not in the same sense. As Tinker (1996, p. 156) notes:

> The danger of such privileging of human beings should be obvious. It runs the risk of generating human arrogance, which too easily sees the world in terms of hierarchies of existence, all of which are ultimately subservient to the needs and whims of humans. Designating human forms of life as inferior minimizes responsibility toward them and apparently justifies the abuse of animal life as well as the earth's other resources.

Some Aboriginal teachers conceptualize the workings of the Creator and Mother Earth as a unity. Porterfield (1990, p. 159) suggests that respected Lakota Sioux leader Black Elk ascribed to the workings of the Great Spirit parameters that included all things—

trees, grasses, rivers, mountains, and all the four-legged animals and the winged people. Black Elk viewed the workings of the Creator and Life Force *within* all things.

Until recently, most European-North American theologians viewed the ecological concerns of Indigenous peoples as corollary, but not primary to the obligation of Christian stewardship. For the First Peoples, however, belief in God has always mandated an inherent admonition to respect the earth, which may be perceived as our natural "mother" (Cajete, 1994). The "parents" of humankind, the Great Spirit and Mother Earth are seen to provide their children with the resources needed to sustain and perpetuate life. In light of the many recent incursions into sacred territory that abuse the earth, Native leaders are deeply concerned that the corruptions of Western society will permanently harm Mother Earth. This abuse clearly violates human responsibility and displeases the Creator.

Relating to God

Stolzman (1998, p. 182ff.), a Roman Catholic pastor and theologian, notes that some Indigenous spiritual leaders object to the practice of describing God in anthropomorphisms, that is in terms of human form or attributes. Stolzman claims that Native elders prefer to depict God in abstract, philosophical and theological terms that he calls "third-order abstractions from reality" in the sense that they are always deficient in some reality. Stolzman's view represents the European-North American theological penchant for approaching Native spirituality from the standpoint of a specific Christian model. Stolzman suggests that Aboriginal theologians hold to the assumption that the more simple and abstract a term is, the more spiritual it is. He disagrees with this assumption, arguing that cognitive distinctions function in relation to the materiality of phenomena, rather than their spirituality. This is why cognitive examinations of God always end up in paradoxes. As a Roman Catholic Christian,

Stolzman proposes Jesus Christ as the ultimate anthropomorphiza-tion of God and the model for all Christians. This position is relied on to justify evangelistic efforts among peoples who possess only a "shadow" of the Gospel truth.

Stolzman may be correct that in comparison with European-derived models, Aboriginal conceptualizations of God are abstract and fuzzy. However, as discussed in later chapters, this perspective does not diminish the validity of their belief in incarnation, steward-ship, or discipleship.

Avenues of Revelation (Aboriginal)

All human societies that have transcendental inclinations devise or have devised prescribed means by which to obtain and decipher Divine messages. As Purkiser (1960, p. 103) suggests, it is doubtful that there is a tribe anywhere in the world that does not have some concept of the Divine and tries to make contact with De-ity. This fact demonstrates the universality of the hunger of the hu-man soul for God. Here are some of the principal elements instru-mental to assisting in the quest for Divine revelation.

Elders. The First Peoples of the Plains, as well as those in other cultural areas, had access to a number of established avenues to spiritual knowledge, one being consultation with spiritual elders. As chapter ten will point out, the status of elder varied somewhat among tribes; in societies of the Great Plains, for example, they were apprenticed or appointed, or simply emerged over time. Individuals with issues to discuss could seek out an elder known for his or her wise counsel, and discuss matters with him or her. Certain elders had the authority to preside over spiritual ceremonies and rituals that might also assist individuals in obtaining a Divine message.

Ceremonies, rites, and rituals. Sacraments as an essential part of Christian theology are generally perceived as different from rituals or ordinances, because they are more sacredly regarded. In plain words, sacraments are outward and visible signs of an inward and spiritual grace. Although the New Testament does not speak of sacraments directly, they are regarded by major denominations as means of grace. Denominations that tie their origins to the Reformation developed a sacramental theology based on the covenant principle. This means that sacraments can bear witness to the grace of God, but do not necessarily confer it. Major Christian denominations regard sacraments as effective channels of God's grace including the presence of God in the enactment of them (Douglas, 1991, p. 730). Aboriginal communities do not differentiate between sacraments and rituals because any enactment with divine implications is regarded as sacred.

Vision quest. The concept of having a vision experience with the supernatural is common to all cultures (Harrod, 1992, p. 24). For many generations it was the custom among the First Peoples of the Great Plains that young men (and in some cases young women) might go out to a hillside or mountaintop to seek a spiritual vision. The procedure was actually quite complicated, and there were a great many details to be attended to before the event could take place. The initiation of the vision quest varied slightly among tribes; in some cases young individuals would seek out an elder and share their intentions to go on a vision quest. In other cases, they might be asked to do so by respected spiritual leaders. The ordeal usually lasted four days.

Among the Sioux, when a young man traveled to the location of his intended vision quest he would find the site carefully prepared by elders. Five wooden poles had been placed in the ground, with the four outer shafts facing the four directions. A bundle of sacred items adorned each pole, and a bed of sage lay on the ground near the center pole, stretched eastward, and on this bed the youth would recline. Then the youth was left alone, without food and water, to wait for the *Wakan Tanka*, the Great Spirit, to endow him with a special blessing. When a vision quest was successful, the youth might obtain a guardian spirit who would counsel him and protect him throughout life (Hultkrantz, 1987, p. 30). The vision itself was usually in the form of a creature such as an animal or bird that might appear to the youthful quester with a special message. The vision seeker might take with him a pipe of tobacco that he would raise heavenward and with prayers and loud cries, appeal to the Great Mystery for a special message (Brooks, 1997, pp. 86-87). It was believed that when a young man obtained a vision, the benefits of accrued insights would adhere to the tribe. It could be, for example, that a young man would have a woodpecker appear to him with the message that he should listen carefully as he walked the path of life, always to be attentive to the signs that the Great Mystery provides. Not everyone who went on a vision quest was successful and, as Lowie explained:

> There were several explanations: either the visitant was not strong enough, or his protégé flouted his commands, or a being might maliciously deceive the god-seeker. "Sometimes everything told in a vision is false; perhaps some animal plays the part of another." …There was no way of detecting such trickery beforehand. "They can only find out from what happens later" (Lowie, 1956, p. 238).

Unless tricked into making a false claim about the success of a vision quest, seekers never deliberately lied about making Divine contact. If an individual claimed to have had a vision and it was not later validated through demonstration, that individual would be called a liar or worse, depending on the tribe (Newcombe, 1974, p. 98).

Parallels with this kind of belief and experience exist in the

Holy Scriptures of Christianity. St. Paul, for example, believed that the existence and actions of Divinity were evident in nature, to wit: "For since the creation of the world God's invisible qualities—his eternal power and divine nature—have been clearly seen, being understood from what has been made, so that people are without excuse" (Romans 1:20). Stob (1981, p. 149) points out that humankind often missed Divine messages implanted in nature, because the vanity and darkness of human reasoning was substituted for Divine revelation. Native American theologians cannot easily be accused of this same shortcoming. The question is; can twenty-first century, theologically minded researchers be equally open-minded.

CHAPTER FOUR

Creation: What Do We Know About Our World?

The First Peoples of North America are known nearly the whole world over for their huge repertoire of stories—non-Native researchers often call them myths or legends, but these terms need to be defined. In my interpretation, myths are made up stories, while legends must be differentiated from myths because legends are either believed to be true or believed to *contain* truth. Aboriginal legends cover just about any topic, and there are usually four kinds—entertainment, instructive, moral, and spiritual.

Entertainment stories can be related by just about anyone, and they typically involve a mythical trickster character known by different names (depending on the tribe), but generally called the trickster. The trickster plays tricks on people and animals, and sometimes they play tricks on him. He possesses supernatural powers and even if put to death, can resurrect himself in four days.

Grandparents and elders whose responsibility it is to pass along treasured cultural knowledge usually tell instructional legends. Instructional legends are teaching legends, and are related to inform the young about the workings of nature and culture. Traditionally, among most Aboriginal communities, every cultural entity had at least one legend attached to it pertaining to origin, characteristics, or function. Common instructional legends that explain things include these: why crows are black, why loons are creatures of the sea, why moose has a loose coat, why thrushes sing so sweetly yet are very shy, and so on. In so far as animal life is concerned, most are perceived as having a roster of both male and female characteristics with a related legend explaining each characteristic.

Indigenous moral legends are related so that the hearer will be able to decipher what appropriate behavior might be towards strangers, kinfolk, or members of one's tribal community. Moral legends are much like the parables in the Bible told by Jesus Christ. According to the Indigenous oral tradition, stories about correct behavior would be told so as to avoid confronting an individual who might have made an error in judgment or engaged in wrongful behavior. These stories often involved animal behavior, and it was assumed that on hearing such a story, the offending child or adult would be able to determine where he or she had gone wrong.

Spiritual legends were traditionally told only by elders recognized as having authority to do so. On occasion a request might be made to hear an elder relate a certain legend, a price would be established and paid, and storytelling would commence. Elders responsible for this role made certain to adhere to the established stem of the legend, but they could also choose to embellish parts of it with each telling. They alone had the privilege to do so.

Traditionally, legends about animals were told only during the winter because no one wanted to offend them by telling stories of misbehavior on their part. The animals might be listening and could be offended, depending on what might be told about them. Creation stories, or tribal origins stories used to be regarded as spiritual in nature and for many generations after the appearance of the printed page, only were transmitted orally. More recently, however, many of these legends have appeared in print, thus giving public access to them. A few of them will be summarized in this chapter. Some of these legends bear a remarkable resemblance to the biblical account of creation because a form of Deity is always involved in executing creation.

Creation Legends

It is important to note that before the printed page, every civilization adhered to the oral tradition and passed along vital information via oral teaching and storytelling. Three special categories of information that topped the list of information in this context were accounts of creation, tribal origins, and the workings of selected natural processes, such as the seasons, food getting, and humankind's relationships with other creatures. These sectors will be elaborated through the inclusion of selected Indigenous legends.

The First Peoples of North America endorsed the idea that the universe was created by personal involvement of Deity—sometimes called the Old Man, the Great Mystery, or other respected forms of identity. The Genesis account makes a good parallel: "In the beginning God created the heavens and the earth. Now the earth was formless and empty, darkness was over the surface of the deep, and the Spirit of God was hovering over the waters" (Genesis 1:1-2). Some Aboriginal accounts are quite similar in nature to the biblical account. For example, the Shasta people tell about a dark and formless world covered with ice and snow, so the Old Man bored a hole in the sky and climbed down to the earth. The sun was able to shine down through the hole in the sky which made it possible for the Old Man to plant trees, create animals, and allow humankind to be born (Hungrywolf, 2001, pp. 71-72).

The Hopi Nation has a slightly different version of the creation account. Creation started with the celestial parent, Tawa, the Sun God, and Spider Woman, the earth Goddess. The parents divided themselves so there would be additional beings on earth. "I am Tawa," sang the Sun God, "I am Light, I am Life. I am the Father of all that shall come." Spider Woman also sang, but in a softer voice. "I receive Light and nourish Life. I am Mother of all that shall ever come" (Mullett, 1979, p. 2). According to the Hopi, the first people were created by these parents and divided into clans with women assigned the status of homebuilders and homemakers. Men were assigned the tasks of building special houses of worship (kivas), and paying homage to the Spirit world. Thus the Hopi people were on their way to building a unique culture.

Still another creation story originates with the Blackfoot First Nation. Here is a brief version of that legend.

> One day the Old Man decided to create life on the earth; on it he put animals, birds, and people. He also created grass and forests of trees to provide for the animals and the birds. One day he decided to create a woman and a child—a son. The Old Man shaped the woman and the child out of clay and watched them for four days. On the fourth day he told them to stand up and move around. They did so, and then more people were created, but they had no food. The Old Man taught them to gather certain roots, from which they learned to use for healing, and berries that they could eat. He even showed them how to strip bark off of certain trees and how to eat it. He also told them they could eat animals including the buffalo. Using the gifts of that animal they had everything they needed. Now it was time for the Old Man to rest and he did so. But first he stopped to admire everything he had created (Macfarlan, 1968, pp. 15-21).

The Wyandot people believe that the universe consists of two levels—an upper world, and a lower world. It is believed that their ancestors once occupied the upper world, and this was a world that was not subject to change.

> The people who lived in the upper world did the same thing day after day. They worked and ate and slept in the exact same fashion every day. Each day the women rose to pick a basketful of corn and prepare it for dinner in the exact same fashion.

> The day came when one of the women decided to break the routine by cutting down all the stalks of corn in the garden. She did so, but now there was no food to eat. The woman's brothers were so furious with her that they cast her down to the lower world through a hole in the sky. A flock of geese saw the woman fall and felt sorry for her. Quickly the geese moved into place so that the woman landed on their backs instead of striking the earth.

> As they flew on, the geese began to tire, but were afraid they would drop the woman. Suddenly a giant turtle appeared and offered to hold the woman for a while. Then a toad showed up and dove deep into the waters and came back with a handful of mud that he gave to the woman. He instructed the woman to sprinkle the mud around, and gradually it formed an island that came to be known as Turtle Island. This is another name for the earth. Soon many people from the upper world joined the woman and their descendants now live on the earth (Friesen and Friesen, 2009, pp. 53-54).

The Crow Indians of Montana tell this story of creation.

One day the Old Man, the Creator, looked out over the waters and decided that he was lonely. He saw two male ducks swimming toward him and asked them if they had seen anything interesting in their travels. They assured him that they had not. He suggested that they dive deep into the waters and see if there was anything interesting at the bottom of the waters. They did so, and on their fourth dive brought up a scoop of mud.

The Creator smiled; "Now there is something we can use." Then he made an island from the mud as big as the earth is today. He also created trees, grass, and other plants.

One of the ducks then exclaimed; "It would be good if everything did not look so empty. We need variety." The Old Man agreed, and took some of the mud and created people from it. The ducks were very impressed. Now the Creator would no longer be lonely.

As time went on this duck had another question; "Can you make companions for us too?" The Creator smiled and quickly made two female ducks. Now everything on earth was beautiful and everyone was happy (Hoxie, 1989, pp. 13-15).

Flood Stories

Many Indigenous people, particularly West Coast First Nations, have great flood stories in their repertoire of cultural knowledge. Each tribal version is slightly different from the others, although the storyline remains the same. The flood story of the Cowichan First Nation of British Columbia's West Coast goes like this.

Long ago the various Indian tribes of the earth were numerous in number and began fighting about land space. One of their elders who had the gift of prophecy announced that he had a dream during which much rain fell and covered the earth and everything was be destroyed. Other elders who revealed that they had experienced the same dream supported his claims. Many people laughed at them, but some believed the elders.

Soon a council was called and consensus was reached that a group of individuals would build a huge raft, and after the rains came perhaps float somewhere to safety. Some people agreed with the idea, and in the next few months they managed to assemble a huge raft consisting of many canoes tied together with long ropes made of cedar bark. While construction of the raft was going on, a group of skeptics gathered to watch the work and laugh at the builders.

In due course however, a series of dark clouds formed in the skies, and it began to rain. After several days it seemed as though it would never stop, and those who did not believe the prophecy of a great flood, began to worry. Some of the raindrops were so large that they killed children when they fell. At this point those who had ridiculed the elders stopped laughing.

Tribal leaders and the people who believed the elders took their families and plenty of food and got on the raft. Those who had not believed the elders began to climb up nearby mountains to get away from swollen rivers. However, the rain continued to fall, and the waters rose steadily and swallowed them up. At last the rain stopped and the large raft settled on the top of Mount Cowichan. From there the people who were safe watched the waters subside and witnessed the destruction caused by the flood. Their homes were gone, as were the green forests, and there was mud everywhere.

Gradually the earth dried up and the people were able to leave Mount Cowichan. Eventually, the earth's population greatly increased and the people again began to quarrel among themselves. Sometimes the conflict grew so bitter that some of the people moved away. Some moved in one direction and others moved in another direction. In this way the whole earth became populated with different tribes (Clark, 1971, pp. 20-21).

Not surprisingly, the Haida of the West Coast have a similar story. The story begins in a heavily populated island village.

One day a strange woman appeared in the village, and a child became enamored of her shoes that looked like Chinese slippers. A plant seemed to be growing out of the slippers and soon children were laughing at the woman. The parents of the children told them to stop laughing.

The ocean nearby was at low tide. The woman sat down at the water's edge, and as she did so, the tide began to rise. Slowly she moved back from the water, but it continued to rise. Each time she moved, the water crept up on the shore. Soon the villagers became frightened because they had never seen the water rise so high before. They decided to save themselves and their children from the rising water so they tied a series of logs together to make a huge raft. The waters kept rising until the entire island was covered with water.

In the meanwhile, the strange woman remained seated in the water as it gradually covered the hillsides and the mountains. Many people without rafts were left adrift in the water. Eventually the water abated and the occupants on the huge raft stepped onto dry land. When the people finally reestablished their way of life they were dispersed into many tribes (Erdoes and Ortiz, 1984, pp. 472-473).

Although somewhat unexpected perhaps, the Pima Nation of the American southwest also have a flood story.

It happened many generations ago in the Gila River Valley after heavy rains refused to desist. Swollen rivers overflowed their banks and the people had to scramble to higher places. The event so surprised the tribe that even the elders were flabbergasted and unable to explain the happening. Animals drowned in great numbers and birds flew high up to the sky to escape the flood.

After four days and four nights the water began to subside and the people were able to return to their homes. Everything they owned was washed away or turned to mud, but the determination of the tribe helped them rebuild their way of life (Shaw, 1992, pp. 1-3).

Tribal Origin Stories

An interesting topic related to the telling of creation stories has to do with tribal origins, and each Aboriginal community seems to have one on file. Here is an example from the Lakota Sioux Nation of South Dakota.

At the beginning of time a race of people lived under the waters of a great sea back east. One day, one of the more adventurous members of the tribe climbed out of the water onto the bank. He found himself in bright sunshine with green grass and shady trees nearby. He walked for a while in his new surroundings, and then decided to return into the sea. He was stopped from doing so by a high wall that suddenly appeared. Now a bit worried, he called to his neighbors under the sea, but no one responded. He continued to call, and at last a young maiden answered him. With great effort she managed to climb over the wall, but soon discovered that she also could not return to the sea. Eventually driven by hunger, the two set off to find some food.

After enduring severe hardships, the couple continued to travel until they reached a great river— now known as the mighty Mississippi River. They liked the surrounding region and decided to establish a home. Their new location was kind to them, they found several sources of food, and lived there for a long time. They became the first parents of the Sioux Nation (Workers of the South Dakota Writers'

Project, 1994, pp. 47-48).

The creation story of the Chelan Indians of Washington state contains many subplots, only a few of which can be elaborated here.

Long ago the Creator, the Great Chief, made the world and filled it with creatures of many kinds. He named them all and assigned unique characteristics to the various species. Some of the creatures were not pleased with the names the Great Chief had given them, and said so. Among them, Bluejay, Meadow-lark, and Coyote were particularly displeased with their names. The Creator told them that they would keep their names because His word was law. Coyote was unhappy and did many things to try to change the Creator's law, but to no avail. As a result he was assigned to wear a black coat during the summer time and a white coat in the winter.

The Great Chief created four wolf brothers and named the youngest one of them, Younger Wolf. He was given the authority to perform miracles. He then ordered to kill Beaver and divide him into twelve parts. When he attempted to do so, however, he found that he could only divide Beaver into eleven parts, each of which became a new tribe—Chelan, Nez Perce, Spokane, Methow, Flathead, and so on. At this point someone suggested that Beaver's blood might become a twelfth tribe. Younger Wolf then threw the blood of Beaver across the shining moun-tains and it became the Blackfeet Nation. This meant that the Blackfeet would always be looking for blood.

When all of the twelve tribes had been created, the Chelan people were told to go up to Lake Chelan where they would encounter pictures on rock cliffs made with red paint. These pictures would inform them how to make the things they would need to develop their unique lifestyle including types of clothing and ways to gather food (Edmonds and Clark, 1989, pp. 4-7).

The Mandan Tribe of North Dakota also has an interesting story about its origins.

It seems that the Mandan Tribe once lived in a deep underground cave where there was very little light. One day a Mandan man, out for a walk, found a long vine coming down into the cave from far above. There seemed to be a bright light near a mysterious opening where the vine entered the cave. Curious, the man climbed the vine through the mysterious opening, to the very top, and found himself on the flat earth above. The earth looked bright and beautiful, so the man slid down the vine as fast as possible to share the good news with his family and friends. Everyone was so excited about the news that they began to climb the vine to see the earth above them.

Soon many tribal members had reached the surface of the earth and were very pleased with what they saw. Unfortunately, too many people mounted the vine at once and it broke, leaving some of the people below in the cave. Those on top were delighted with their new surroundings and decided to make their homes there. Naturally, they missed their friends below, but the earth had so much to offer them. The Creator smiled on them and showed them where they could live. There were trees, and grass, and rivers and fields in which to plant corn. Most important of all, there were buffalo! The Mandan people decided that the earth was a good place to live (Friesen and Friesen, 2004a, p. 31).

A little knowledge of Mandan tribal history will quickly reveal that the above legend is not to be taken literally; rather, it is quite likely a metaphoric description of a tribal split and the subsequent relocation of one of the factions.

It is not unusual to encounter claims about being a Divinely-blessed people with regard to tribal origins. As previously mentioned, the Blackfoot, for example, believe that they have a special covenant with the Creator, and they bear the badge of this distinction by braiding their hair. Some Indigenous people have translated their tribal names to mean "the people," implying that their origins are special and unique in the eyes of the Creator.

The writer of the New Testament book of First Peter uses similar language when he addresses the early Christians: "But you are a chosen people, a royal priesthood, a holy nation, God's special possession, that you may declare the praises of him who called you out of darkness into his wonderful light" (1 Peter 2:9). It would seem that every human group promotes some element of identity pride bordering on cultural and/or religious ethnocentrism. If this reality were more globally recognized there might be less intercultural misinterpretation and misunderstanding.

Interconnectedness in Creation

Many Indigenous legends explain the details of the daily lives of earth's various creatures—animals, birds, and fish. These stories include information about the unique characteristics of earth's creatures as well as outlining the interrelationship of all living things. These tales also include teachings for humankind about how to regard one's neighbors and fellow creation. To the Indigenous way of thinking, every aspect and entity within the universe depends to some extent on the others. This is the principle of interconnectedness.

Further, since the Aboriginal people believe that all living things have spiritual competencies, thereby cementing a special relationship with humans, it is not unusual to encounter conversations between humans and animals in Indian legends. It was, and is still widely believed that the creatures of the earth are qualified to deliver messages or teach lessons to people. A biblical example of this relationship is demonstrated in Numbers chapter 22 in which Balaam, an elder of Israel, is asked to put a curse on a neighboring tribe because they were bothersome to the Jewish agenda. However, the enemy camp offers Balaam a bribe if he reverses the curse and puts it on Israel instead, but his donkey stops him. God commissions an angel to reroute the donkey and Balaam's ire is raised. He whips the animal.

After punishing the donkey for not going in the direction that Balaam desires, the animal speaks to Balaam; "What have I done to you to make you beat me these three times?" (Numbers 22:28b). Balaam answers the donkey, accusing the animal of making a fool of him. The donkey responds; "Am I not your own donkey, which you have always ridden, to this day? Have I been in the habit of doing this to you?" (Numbers 22:30b). Ironically, many believers in the biblical record have no difficulty accepting this account in literal fashion, but frown on the Indigenous belief that animals can teach lessons to humankind.

Many Native legends involve discussions between creatures with human characteristics and other animals with both parties exchanging information about moral lessons. For example, consider the Pima legend about Yellow Bird, a young girl who disobeyed her mother. It happened this way.

One day Yellow Bird decided to go berry picking, but her mother told her to wait until someone could go with her. Yellow Bird's mother felt that her daughter was too young to go berry picking alone, but Yellow Bird refused to listen. She really wanted to go berry picking. Yellow Bird watched her mother carefully, and when she noticed that her mother was not looking her way, Yellow Bird sneaked out of the lodge by herself.

While Yellow Bird was picking berries, the weather began to change. Suddenly, a strong whirlwind came along and blew Yellow Bird to the top of a very high mountain. Yellow Bird grew frightened and began calling for her mother. Of course, her mother could not hear her because she was quite far away.

A few hours passed, and Yellow Bird's mother noticed that her daughter was missing. Quickly she went through the village looking for her. She asked her neighbors if they had seen Yellow Bird, and she stopped occasionally to call out to her daughter. It was to no avail. Yellow Bird was nowhere to be found. When Yellow Bird's father came home and discovered that his daughter was missing, he quickly called on his friend, Buzzard, for help. Buzzard agreed to help find Yellow Bird, and so he flew high over all the lakes and rivers and mountain in the area. He came back to report that he had heard someone calling for her mother from the top of a very high mountain.

"That must have been my daughter calling out," said Yellow Bird's father. "We must do something to get her down from the mountain."

"I cannot fly that high," Buzzard informed his friend. "I can be of no help to you. We will have to try something else."

Soon members of the community arrived to help Yellow Bird's father. Someone found some very special gourd seeds that grew very quickly to great heights. The group quickly planted and watered the seeds, which sprouted rapidly. Soon a vine that grew very tall stretched to the very top of the mountain where Yellow Bird was trapped.

Yellow Bird's father cried out in a loud voice so his daughter could hear him; "Yellow Bird, climb down on the vine, and you will soon be home." Yellow Bird did as she was told. She was very happy to finally reach the ground. She hugged her father and promised that she would never disobey her mother again (Friesen and Friesen, 2004b, pp. 51-52).

The Caddo Nation has an interesting story explaining why dogs have long tongues. It seems that long ago, dogs were able to talk, but they abused the privilege by gossiping about everything they heard in the community.

A warrior named Flying Hawk was disturbed about the gossiping habit of the dogs and determined to do something about it. He obtained a young puppy and decided to train the animal, while it was young, never to gossip.

After several months of giving lessons to his dog about the evils of gossiping, Flying Hawk went off one day to hunt, but came home with nothing in his hunting bag. He took his dog with him on the hunt, but at the end of the day the dog was nowhere to be found.

Upon his arrival in his village, Flying Hawk discovered that everyone knew he had hunted unsuccessfully all day. Apparently, his dog had run ahead and told everyone about Flying Hawk's misfortune. Flying Hawk was so annoyed at the news, that he grabbed hold of the dog's tongue and stretched it out as far as he could. Then he ran a stick across the dog's mouth and made it wide. Ever since then, dogs have had long tongues and wide mouths, and they have been unable to talk—only bark.

All dogs learned a valuable lesson that day and so should humans listening to the tale (Brown, 1993, pp. 26-28).

The Sioux have a legend that teaches about a lazy eagle, and the story attaches human characteristics to Beaver Woman, a key figure in the storyline.

One day when Beaver Woman was chopping wood to make a fire and prepare a hot supper, she heard a swooping sound from up in the sky. It was Eagle, flapping his mighty wings and perching himself on a branch above Beaver Woman. He waited until Beaver Woman had finished chopping wood so he could be heard then spoke; "I am hungry, Beaver Woman. Do you have anything for me to eat?" Beaver Woman was a bit annoyed since she was working very hard, and said so. "What right do you have to disturb a woman busy with her daily work? Who do you think you are, Eagle? Why don't you do as everyone else does and work for your food?"

"That is all very well for you to say," said Eagle, "but I am king of the birds. I do not cut down trees and eat bark and weeds or live in a mud-plastered wigwam. I am a warrior, old woman; now, get me something to eat!"

"It is too bad that there are selfish creatures like yourself," said Beaver Woman. "I see no reason why you cannot work for your food just like every one else. I love my work, taking care of my family. You would do well to follow my example." With these words, Beaver Woman dove deep into the water.

Poor Eagle; he waited a long time for Beaver Woman to surface, but she never did. Eagle flew away still hungry, and now he had to hunt for his own food. Eagle learned a valuable lesson that day. (Eastman and Eastman, 2000, pp. 8-9).

In all of these various stories, human and animals appear to be united in an effort to make the world a better place. Lessons taught in and learned from them promote the primary values of North American Indigenous cultures—honesty, kindness, obedience to parents, cooperation, and so on. Both humans and other living creatures seem to have consensus on these values, and both parties are involved in practicing them. The Sioux saying, "All my relations," is to be universally applied to all living entities on the earth. There are no exceptions; the principle of interconnectedness must be fully in play.

Reading or listening to Indigenous stories about working with or living in harmony with nature, provokes a question frequently ignored or dismissed by Christian theologians; Is it not the mandate of humankind to respect the workings of nature? The Christian orientation, instead of working in harmony with nature is to subdue the earth, quite possibly so because the mandate to do so is taken literally from the Holy Scriptures. As the biblical account in Genesis 1:28 has it; "God blessed them, and said to them, "Be fruitful and increase in number; fill the earth, and subdue it. *Rule* over the fish of the sea, and the birds in the sky and over every living creature that moves on the ground" (italics mine). This mandate is reiterated in Psalm 8:6-8; "You made them rulers over the works of your hands; you put everything under their feet: all flocks and herds, and the animals of the wild, the birds in the sky, and the fish in the sea, all that swim the paths of the seas."

The difficulty in reconciling the two primary interpretations of Adam and Eve's responsibilities towards creation—Aboriginal and Christian—stems from the word "subdue" which is often interpreted to mean, "conquer, vanquish, or bring into subjection." This interpretation aligns itself well with North American notions of imperialism, capitalism and free enterprise, and colonialism. These terms do not represent primary value orientations among traditional Indigenous cultures.

It is true that before European contact wars were fought among the First Peoples of North America, however, they were not usually fought as means to expand land holdings. After all, humankind could not own land, so it could not be sold; it was to be respected, often shared, and appreciated. Traditionally, there were no wars fought over land ownership. Wars were sometimes fought because nomadic tribes got in the way of others or they were wrought to show warrior superiority. For example, the Apaches believed that it was their inalienable right to plunder other tribes, because no self respecting Apache would raise cattle or plow the ground in order to plant seeds. Those were responsibilities of lesser nations, and the record shows that some tribes actually grew more corn that they needed because they fully expected the Apaches to demand some of the fruits of their labor and raid their food storage.

The Indigenous interpretation of the human role in the universe appears to render a different definition than the EuroAmerican interpretation. Phrases like "subdue the earth, rule over animals, and subjugate all forms of life" must be juxtaposed against such concepts as caretaker (Genesis 2:15, 19), a man of the soil (Genesis 9:20), and servants of Christ (1 Corinthians 4:1). St. Paul took time to remind his young protégé Timothy that: "For everything God created is good, and nothing is to be rejected if it is received with thanksgiving, because it is consecrated by the word of God and prayer" (1 Timothy 4:4-5).

The Creator is pleased with what He has made, and this includes every living thing in it (Genesis 1:31). Why should humankind think otherwise? Because the Creator is pleased, is the reason why the phrase "All my relations" is theologically significant. It applies to all the living things that God created because they are all interconnected and interdependent by creation. The First Peoples fundamentally agreed with the Psalmist: "the earth is full of his [the Lord's] unfailing love. From heaven the Lord looks down and sees all mankind; from his dwelling place he watches *all* who live on earth" (Psalm 33:5b, 13, 14, italics mine).

CHAPTER FIVE

Revelation: What Do We Know About Divinity?
How Do We Obtain This Knowledge?

Personal knowledge of religious matters, of course, is variable. Navajoes regard religious knowledge as a form of power and a kind of possession, and thus every individual would regard it as beneficial to possess some religious knowledge, however slight. Knowledge could be used for one's own benefit, and in keeping with general Navajo tenets, would not be given away without some form of recompense (Cooper, 1990, p. 72).

Renowned scientist Stephen Hawking announced recently that the notion of heaven is a fairy story—a belief evidently held by less intelligent people. He did admit, however, that his being a victim of amyotrophic lateral multiple sclerosis might be a factor related to his skepticism (or perhaps, bitterness?). Hawking's position is not new; for centuries, individuals of various professional affiliations have tried to discredit belief in God and the various doctrines derived from that presupposition. The Psalmist long ago anticipated these kinds of criticisms; for example, "The fool says in his heart, 'There is no God' " (Psalm 14:1), and "How great are your works, Lord, how profound your thoughts! Senseless people do not know, fools do not understand" (Psalm 92:5-6).

The explanation given by the writer of the Book of Hebrews

is also apt: "By *faith* we understand that the universe was formed at God's command, so that what is seen was not made out of what was visible" (Hebrews 11:3, italics mine). Faith in science has replaced spiritual faith. Jacques Elul agreed, and suggested "The belief in the universal capacity of science is now associated with the faith that science is man's destiny" (Elul, 1973, p. 101).

So the question arises: To what extent have the various elements of religious belief been revealed by otherworldly sources? Given that an otherworldly realm (usually perceived as being more spiritual in nature) exists, what now has to be determined is how knowledge from that realm is transmitted to earth's occupants. The key word in this context is revelation; to what extent, and in what ways is truth from the outer, spiritual realm made available to earthly dwellers?

In the Christian tradition, revelation is a given, starting with faith in the Holy Scriptures as the revelation of God (Klein, Bloomberg and Hubbard, 1993, p. 88; Packer, 1958, pp. 90-92). Other accepted forms of revelation, more specific in nature, include visions and dreams and visits by angelic beings. Sadly, more liberal interpretations of Christian theology have all but eradicated belief in special revelation, and even watered down the mandates of general revelation contained in the Bible.

World religions other than Christianity, including the Indigenous perspective, also suggest various forms of spiritual revelation, but as anthropologists are fond of saying: "Food is hedged by religion in pretty well all cultures. Spirits and magical forces everywhere are thought to determine one's success in obtaining food..."(Friesen, 1997, p. 31). Projected further, it follows that belief in revelation of some kind must have been essential to success in food-getting as well as other means of cultural functioning. The challenge to acknowledge the validity of Indigenous world-views has been equally difficult for anthropologists as for theologians, both having manifested their share of cultural ethnocentrism in the past. As the late Lakota Sioux writer Vine Deloria (1995, p. 47) cautioned:

> Respect for non-Western traditions is exceedingly difficult to achieve. Not only did secular scientists rout the Christian fundamentalists, they placed themselves in the posture of knowing more, on the basis of their own very short-term investigations, than the collective remembrances of the rest of humankind. Social science, in particular anthropology, preserved information about the remnants of tribal cultures around the world, most particularly in North America, but it also promulgated the idea that these tribal cultures were of Stone Age achievement and represented primitive superstitions which could not be believed.

A case in point, attempting to describe First Peoples spirituality emanates from the journals of New Zealand anthropologist, Diamond Jenness (1986, pp. 168-169):

> Spiritual forces akin to those of his own being caused the sun to rise and set, the storms to gather in the sky, the cataracts to leap among the rocks, and the trees to bud in the springtime. A mentality similar in kind to this animated the bird, the animal, and the fish.... The Indian, however, had neither the inclination nor the training for metaphysical speculations.

Anthropologists were not alone in their misunderstanding of and lack of respect for Native spirituality. Governments were no doubt influenced by them to suppress certain forms of religious expression. As Pettipas (1994, p. 215) suggests, this action was partially attributed to contradictions between capitalist philosophy and the Indigenous kinship-based methods of producing, distributing, and consuming goods.

Jenness (1986, p. 168) was generous enough in outlook to admit that many of the pre-civilization tendencies of Canada's First Peoples were paralleled by societies everywhere in the world. However, he *did* give credence to the "superior" Western ways of thinking. Fortunately, as the social sciences continued to develop, its proponents grew more tolerant in their assessments of other cultures. Historian Paul Carlson (1998, pp. 112-113) is quite objective in his assessment of Native spirituality.

> Spiritual activity touched every aspect of their lives, because... sacred and secular were inseparable. Mystic, but not dogmatic, the people called upon a variety of sacred powers for assistance. They felt a shared attachment to the land and its animals and a reverence for nature.... Many Plains Indians recognized the existence of a principal being, or Holy One Above.

More recently theologians have also amended the parameters of their studies by delving into aspects of religious thought before now only glossed over. These include Black liberation theology, Latin American theology, feminist theology, and others. Klein, Bloomberg, and Hubbard (1993, p 457) recommend that these approaches must be examined.

> We must take time to listen to divergent readings of Scripture from our Christian brothers and sisters around the globe, and particularly from women, minorities, and the poor. As we do so, we will both be convinced and renewed.

Hopefully, this new, more open-minded attitude will also extend to studies of the various dimensions of Aboriginal spirituality.

Perceived Avenues of Revelation

All human societies that have transcendental inclinations devise or have devised prescribed means by which to decipher Divine messages. This was very much the case with the First Peoples of North America. While much of traditional Indigenous cultural life was community oriented, a special place for the individual was set-aside in the system, particularly in the context of spirituality. The notion that the Great Spirit or Great Mystery has traditionally been perceived by Indigenous theologians as a universal Force or Presence may lead some observers to conclude that any form of individual contact with the "Grand Force of Being" would be impracticable. However, there is ample evidence to suggest that in Aboriginal thinking individual human contact with the Divine was not only considered a legitimate pursuit, it was both sought after and often realized. Seeking Divine contact through these activities was considered an important part of daily activity.

Ceremonies. Native North American societies still have in place a wide variety of spiritual enactments that they perceive to be mediums of Divine assurance and messaging. Some of the more serious ceremonies hold the same reverence for them, as sacraments do for Christians.

Sacraments are generally perceived to be different from ceremonies, rituals, or ordinances because they are more sacredly regarded. In the Christian tradition, sacraments are viewed as outward and visible signs of inward and spiritual grace. Although the New Testament does not speak of sacraments directly, particularly Holy Baptism and Holy Communion (the Eucharist), they are regarded by major denominations as means of grace. This means that sacraments can bear witness to the grace of God, but do not necessarily confer it. Major Christian denominations regard sacraments as effective channels of God's grace including the presence of God in the enactment of them (Douglas, 1991, p. 730).

If the concept of sacrament primarily encompasses the notion of sacred, there is little doubt but that many Indigenous ceremonies could also fit that category. Among Plains Tribes, for example, the Sundance was regarded as a very sacred ritual, and rules about its enactment were very strict. Among the Cree people it was the practice that the tree placed at the center of the circle in which the event took place, when cut down, was never allowed to touch the ground until it reached its final resting place at the center of the camp. The camp itself was organized around four circles, the innermost of which was reserved for the sacred teepee in which medicine bundles might be opened and/or exchanged. Although medicine bundles, many of which are very old, comprise anything from a few feathers wrapped in animal skins, to objects such as rocks, bones, or roots, each article has special spiritual significance because of the way it was interpreted by the individual who originally assembled the bundle. That individual prepared the bundle as a form of representation of the vision that inspired its creation. Harrod (1992, p. 68) explains the function of medicine bundles.

> Medicine bundles, then, will be interpreted as complex symbolic realities which are associated with various dimensions of transcendent meaning. The ritual that surrounds these objects powerfully evokes a sense of the dimensions of meaning at both the level of individual experience and in the shared experience of the social world.

Some observers have linked the function of medicine bundles to the contemporary parallel need for religious reminders of faith—statues, wall-plaques, or other religious artifacts, but that interpretation falls far short. Medicine bundles, and indeed the enactment of the Sundance itself, represent the most sacred of all entities in Plains First People cultures. Likening this phenomenon to sacramental worship might be a better explanation. After all, the event was accompanied by prayers and even sacrificial activities designed to attract grace from the Creator.

Daily devotions. Traditionally, every aspect of traditional Aboriginal culture was traditionally founded on the principle of spirituality. There were individuals in every community who spent a significant amount of their daily life in some sort of spiritual activity. Spiritual elders provided leadership in this area, mainly by modeling desirable behavior. Consider the following suggestions (Friesen, 1998, pp. 14, 21, 27):

> Always remember the Creator and that He sees everything you do. You can't hide anything from Him. Always remember the Creator.
>
> –Adam Salopree, Dene First Nation.
>
> In the life of the Indian there was only one inevitable duty—the duty of prayer, the daily recognition of the Unseen and Eternal. His daily devotions were more necessary to him than daily food.
>
> –Charles Alexander Eastman Ohiysesa, Santee Sioux Nation.
>
> Always remember the Great Master on high is looking after us at all times. He has saved us time after time. He will look after his children so that no evil will ever come upon them. He has said, "I will spread

my wings over you. I will put you in between my feathers where you will enjoy life in happiness."

–Chief Redsky Mis-quona-queb, Ojibway First Nation.

Elders. The First Peoples of the Plains, as well as those in other cultural areas, had access to a number of established avenues to Spiritual knowledge, a primary one being consultation with elders. As a later chapter will point out, the status of elder varied somewhat among tribes; in some cases they were apprenticed or appointed, or simply emerged over time. Individuals with issues to discuss could seek out an elder known for his or her wise counsel, and discuss the matter with them. Certain elders had the authority to preside over spiritual ceremonies and rituals that might also assist the individual in becoming the recipient of a Divine message.

The pipe. Usually viewed as an intermediary entity through which to make contact with Deity, and perhaps accompanied by a request, there are many versions of legends about how the pipe came to the Indigenous peoples. For example, the pipe came to the Lakota First Peoples by a holy maiden who also gave careful instructions about how to care for the pipe (Brown, 1997, p. 72; Stolzman, 1998, p. 168). When the pipe is smoked, it becomes part of a ritual by which to seek Divine guidance for a variety of purposes, including healing (Eliade, 1974, p. 303ff.). Aboriginal prison chaplains have strongly endorsed the enactment of pipe ceremonies for inmate healing (Waldram, 1997). Pipe smoking is viewed as a preparatory to nearly all events, and no important business can be transacted until pipe smoking is completed. Among the Comanche Nation, pipe smoking represents either a prayer on the part of the smoker, or an oath, a pledge, or a moral commitment (Carlson, 1998, p. 115).

Sacred places. Common to the practices of both Old Testament Israel and the Indigenous peoples of North America was the practice of establishing and revering special places that connected the people with the Great Mystery.

Medicine wheels constitute one of the most significant sacred sites of North America's Indigenous peoples, and they still are frequently used as locations for spiritual exercises (Verslius, 1997, p. 69). There are literally hundreds of medicine wheel remnants spread across the western plains of this continent, many of them still in operation. Medicine wheels are principally made up of a pile of rocks surrounded by four (sometimes more) rock spokes, pointing in the four directions. One of the largest medicine wheels is located at a 10,000 foot (3,048 meters) altitude in the Big Horn Mountains of Wyoming. Probably built by a Cheyenne or Sioux Nation some 500 years ago, this medicine wheel has twenty-eight spokes and six cairns. When first excavated, the cairns yielded some 3,000 artifacts of various kinds. While the precise purpose of the medicine wheel is not known, individual Aboriginals still revere it as a very sacred site and often go there to offer prayers.

The Jewish penchant for establishing scared places is well documented in the Old Testament through the efforts of such patriarchs as Noah, Abraham, Jacob, Moses, and Joshua previously described.

Sacred plants. Incense is created by burning aromatic plant materials that produce a pleasant odor. Incense is often used in religious ceremonies, and this is certainly the case with many Indigenous people. The forms taken by incense differ with the respective culture, and have changed with advances in technology and increasing diversity in the reasons for burning it.

The variety of sacred plants used for incense among North America's First Peoples include cedar, juniper, lavender, mugwort (artemisia), pinion pine, sacred tobacco, sage, and sweet-grass. The four plants used by Plains First Peoples include cedar, juniper, sage, and sweet-grass. These plants produce a desirable aroma, and when utilized in what is called smudging, the smoke arising from their being burned is waved across the various parts of the body—particularly the head and heart, as a symbol of inner cleansing. The ceremony is frequently used as a means of preparing for a gathering of council or other special event.

The purposes for which sacred plants were used included healing, spiritual cleansing, ridding the body of evil spirits, or simply pushing away bad feelings, negative thoughts, or negative energy. As an indication that ceremonies involving sacred plants emphasize Divine approval, individuals participating in them should enter with a positive attitude and goodwill toward others. Those doing otherwise might find themselves concluding the ceremony with negative energy or even physical sickness.

Sweat-lodge. The sweat-lodge used by the Indigenous peoples of North America is essentially a tiny airtight hut, structured by bent willow branches over which buffalo hides or other animal skins have been placed. The willow branches are secured in the ground, then bent over to meet those on the other side to make a dome-shaped, womb-like edifice (Underhill, 1965, p. 109).

The principal parts of the sweat-lodge include the poles, the covering, specially-placed stones, and the pipe. Each part has a special meaning; for example, willow is representative of plant life, and has a special relationship with water since it grows best when near a direct water source. Individuals enact symbolic death when they enter the sweat-lodge because they vow to rid themselves of unclean thoughts and prepare themselves for spiritual and mental regeneration. The number of stones that are heated outside the dome and carefully placed inside may have been envisaged by an elder who now attaches special meaning to each one as it is carefully laid in a particular order (Bruchac, 1993, p. 36). Four endurances of about ten minutes each are observed within the sweat-lodge, and after each period has lapsed, the doorway is opened and participants will take remove themselves from the "steam-room" to take a breath of fresh air outside. The Lakota Sioux also smoke the pipe within the sweat-lodge each of the four times that the flap of the doorway is opened. In the words of Cree elder, Rose Auger (cited in Friesen, 1998, p. 24):

> In the sweat-lodge, when you feel a spirit, you can't deny it. If you have prepared yourself, and the pipe-holder leading the sweat is strong, you can't deny spiritual power. It might come in the form of emotions, but you feel something.

Visions and dreams. As mentioned previously, the vision quest was central to traditional spiritual practices among Plains tribes. When they reached a certain age, depending on their tribal affiliation, young men (and occasionally females) volunteered or were selected to isolate themselves from their communities (usually for four days), during which time they would seek contact with the Great Spirit. During the enactment of the ritual participating youths were supervised by an elder. Should the experience prove successful, the seeker might experience a visit by the spirit of an animal or bird and, if so, could later consult with it whenever he/she felt the need to do so. Such visitations were seen as an awarding of spiritual power, insight or gift that was respected by the community.

The perception that dreams may be classified as valid forms of Divine messages is central to a number of faith persuasions. Traditionally, the Plains Indians viewed dreams as one avenue to interact with the Divine Ground of Being. Chief Red Crow of the Blood (Kainai) First Nation once had a dream in which a gopher spirit came to him and informed him that if he put a blade of grass in his hair every time he went to battle he would never be hurt. Red Crow did as he was advised and although he was engaged in nineteen battles, he was never harmed.

Despite the reluctance of contemporary Christian theologians to validate dreams and visions as legitimate forms of Divine enlightenment, in his address at Pentecost the Apostle Peter felt sufficiently confident to quote the Old Testament prophet, Joel (Joel 2:28).

In the last days, God says, I will pour out my Spirit on all people. Your sons and daughters will prophesy, your young men will see visions, your old men will dream dreams (Acts 2:17).

Contemporary Christian theologians might not wish to be as literal as Saint Peter, backing up their skepticism with allusions to the fact that none of the epistles make mention of either dreams or visions. Indigenous elders are not so easily put off, and they expect the Great Spirit always to find ways to communicate special messages to His children (Friesen and Friesen, 2005, p. 121ff.). I am sure He does.

Conceptualizations of Incarnation

When missionaries from Europe arrived in Indigenous communities, they were often amazed at how quickly the locals appeared to understand their versions of truth. One concept that was quite familiar to the Indigenous people was that the Creator would come to earth in human form to make Himself known at the level of daily understanding. In Christian terms, God would become man so that His creation would be able to understand His will for their lives.

The Blackfeet, for example, have a legend about Poïa, who was sent to earth as Star Boy by the Sun God for the purpose of instructing the Blackfeet in worship. After establishing the Sundance, Poïa returned to the home of the Sun and became Morning Star (McClintock, 1992, p. 491).

Chief John Snow of the Stoney Nakoda Nation, insisted that his people traditionally believed in an incarnate being named "îktomni" or "Thickâ-Yuski," the latter title implying having extraordinary wisdom. It was believed that îktomni was sent to the earth by the Great Spirit to teach the laws of the Creator—laws about medicine, religion and life (Snow, 2005, p. 15).

Most Plains Indian tribes postulated a similar concept of an "incarnate god" like îktomni. The Plains Ojibway called him Nanabush and believed that he came to earth to arrange things in order, that is, the shape of animals and the landscape of the earth. Like most other trickster characters, however, Nanabush served a somewhat ambiguous function, sometimes as a benefactor to people and sometimes as a self-indulgent, aimless wanderer (Miller, 1995, p. 108).

Perhaps the most positive intermediary form was Glooscap, a secondary godlike character of the Mi'kmaq and Maliseet people of the east coast of North America. These tribes considered the Creator the highest form of Deity, and they prayed to him twice a day. Glooscap was a lesser deity who had human form, immortality, and supernatural powers. There are many accounts of the work of Glooscap among the Eastern Woodlands First Nations; some tell how he transformed animals into their present shapes, or maneuvered landscapes to more functional characteristics. When his earthly tasks were completed, he promised to return to his people whenever they needed him (McMillan, 1995, p. 53).

In order to lend credence to the notions of good versus evil among Eastern Woodland tribes, mention must be made of a more negative intermediary being known as Windigo. As McMillan (1995, p. 108) explains:

> He [Windigo] haunted the forests during the dark and cold months of winter, retreating to the north when warmer weather came. His size and supernatural strength made him a dreaded foe, one that could not be killed by ordinary weapons. Only a powerful shaman could destroy a Windigo. An unexplained disappearance of a hunter to return from the forest, would be taken to mean that he had fallen prey to the wiles of Windigo.

Native notions of incarnation to some extent parallel the Christian concept of Jesus Christ as the incarnate Son of God whose task it was to interpret God's will to humankind. Glooscap would be the best example. Aboriginal perceptions of God may have been vague, but there was a measure of exactness about the role of their envisaged intermediary figure. Perhaps these similarities explain why so many Aboriginal people so readily accepted the Christian Gospel when it was first presented to them.

CHAPTER SIX

Anthropology: How Is Human Nature Perceived?

One of the basic considerations in attempting to explain the relationship of Deity to humankind is to attempt a working definition of human nature. To begin, the question might be raised: "If individuals are in need of Divine salvation, what is there about their nature—inherited or carved by free choice—that God has to work with?"

Theologians have wrestled with the challenge of defining human nature from the beginning of time, and an array of perspectives on the subject exists. This chapter will elaborate a series of modern theologies and search out the definitions of human nature that are contained within each of them.

Opinions about human nature are directly related to a discussion of salvation, because its nature, availability, and application will be determined by how people are morally constituted. Are they evil by nature; are they inherently good, but corrupted by society; or should humankind be considered theologically neutral? Our survey begins in the latter part of the twentieth century.

Varying Perspectives

Although somewhat insignificant varying interpretations

may exist, from a purely theological perspective there are essentially three ways to view human nature. People are either morally good, corrupt, or neutral at birth. After conceding this delineation, the conversation becomes more complicated. If at birth babies are perceived to be morally good, what are some of the corrupting influences that later impinge upon them, causing them to become oriented towards evil? John Jacques Rousseau (1712-1778) would have agreed that this happens, blaming negative societal influences for leading the young astray. Conversely, if humankind is to be perceived as fundamentally evil at birth, the question arises: "Is there a way by which individuals can be redeemed?"

The notion that human nature is evil is clearly described in Psalm 51:5 "Surely I was sinful at birth, sinful from the time my mother conceived me." Other Old Testament scriptures confirm this rather blatant reality: "Even from birth the wicked go astray; from the womb they are wayward, spreading lies" (Psalm 58:3), and "We all, like sheep, have gone astray, each of us has turned to our own way; and the Lord has laid on him the iniquity of us all" (Isaiah 53:6). The suggestion that the New Testament views human alienation from God as less pronounced is easily rejected by passages such as these: "Let any one of you who is without sin be the first to throw a stone at her" (John 8:7b); "for all have sinned and fall short of the glory of God" (Romans 3:23); "If we claim to be without sin, we deceive ourselves and the truth is not in us" (1 John 1:8). Traditionally oriented theologians define sin as "the free action of a human being who was created in the image of God to violate that trust" (Fitzwater, 1953, p. 315). God is not the author of sin, but the Creator of beings has allowed human creatures the *option* to sin. This is a necessary theological truth, namely that God created people with the option to sin, and when and if they do, and then renounce their sinful ways, it is because they *chose* to do so—chosen from the options—to continue in sin or to repent from sin. Had people not been created with the option to choose, or if these options were not available to them, they would be reduced to the status of robots. They would therefore not have available to them the ability to exercise free will. The decree to permit sin is therefore not an efficient, but a *permissive* decree on God's part. It is a decree to permit, in distinction from a decree to produce by God's own efficiency (Strong, 1956, p. 353).

More recently the emphasis on humankind as sinful has been subdued, possibly because people are not particularly fond of being labeled sinners, spiritual outcasts, or alienated from God. In many churches today, sermons on repentance have followed suit and replaced condemning treatises with "sharing sessions" about hope, cheer, encouragement, and goodwill. Apparently, people who feel good about themselves are less apt to engage in sinful acts. This continuing trend has so far consumed several generations.

If one assumes the neutral position, namely that people are neither good nor evil at birth, why do these terms even come into play? Rousseau and more liberally minded theologians would likely ascribe the debate to people's need to classify, to find explanations for inerrant behavior. While undertaking this challenge, analysts will take every precaution to remain as objective as possible without committing themselves to any one position.

Boice (1986, pp. 200-201) accepts the observation that there are three basic opinions about human nature, and defines them as follows: humankind is well, humankind is sick, and humankind is dead. Those who hold to the first position argue that the only assistance people need in order to get well is a little exercise, some vitamins, and occasional checkups by a doctor, which, hopefully, result in the professional assessment; "You are OK, Jack!"

Proponents of the notion that people are sick would argue that the situation, while unfortunate, is not without hope; moral and spiritual sickness *can* be cured with the right approach. With proper drugs, personal care, the will to live, and a miracle or two, the patient can soon be good as new. This view represents the contemporary belief that anything can be cured with modern medicine including moral ailments. In some cases, as with diseases that remain immune from cure, it is only a matter of time before cures will be found. According to Boice (1986, pp. 200-201), the biblical view is that humankind is neither unwell nor sick; humankind is spiritually dead through the trespasses and sins that were inherited from Adam, the first man (Ephesians 2:1). Although originally created perfect, Adam, as the representative of humankind, gave in to disobedience to God's law and communication with the Creator was broken. Alienation from God affected human thinking and behavior; in short, humankind was unable to think straight and continually gave in to further disgrace.

The traditional Christian view is straightforward: God created humankind and gave individuals free choice, either to accept His precepts, or go their own way. Adam and Eve, the first people, chose the latter route, after being influenced to do so by the Evil One. This deliberate action on the part of the first parents brought evil into the world of humankind. God then provided a way for the first parents and their successors to redeem themselves, first (in the Old Testament) by offering appropriate sacrifices; then later (in the New Testament) by accepting God's Son, Jesus Christ, as one's personal substitute (Savior). After accepting Christ as one's "stand-in" for sin, believers are expected to live sanctified lives (remaining free from sinful indulgences), and grow in Christ. The result is a guarantee that believers will after death become joint heirs with Christ and be united with loved ones who have gone before (Fitzwater, 1953; Strong, 1956).

Updating Theology

Like other fields that draw academic interest, theology also evolves. This may be surprising to some, because theology is the study of God and His dealings with creation. James contends that God "does not change like shifting shadows" (James 1:17b), but apparently our understanding of His mandates and actions does. As a result new ways of understanding emerge with each new generation of theologians. Here is a summary of the emphases that have arisen in the last half-century.

Secular theology. Not content with the interpretations of traditional fundamentalist theologians, a variety of interpretive schools have emerged over time, some of the most recent being secular theology. Secular theology may be broken down into three emphases— process theology, the theology of hope, and refurbished evangelicalism. Secular theology was essentially a movement of the 1960s, and originated from concerns that liberalism and neo-orthodoxy were no longer holding the attention of religionists. Burgeoning forms of technology were also cited by theologians as areas of address: humankind was suddenly becoming aware that significant aspects of existence could be better controlled by reliance on technology. Conventional Christianity, with its emphasis on the fall of humankind and need for Divine redemption was no longer cutting it. A more up-to-date interpretation of the interrelationship of God and the universe was needed, one that would increasingly blur the lines between sacred and secular (Kuhn, 1978, p. 158). As a result, theology took on the stance of interpreting everyday life without reference to God, emphasizing instead the potentiality of human endeavor. Writers who quickly climbed aboard the express line to abandon reference to God include Thomas J. J. Altizer and William Hamilton (1966), Dietrich Bonhoeffer (1967), Harvey G. Cox (1965), and John A. T. Robinson (1963). These authors elevated the abilities of humankind without significant reference to Divine transcendence, thereby avoiding any reference to God as a caring Creator and Author of redemption. Their portrayals of the person and work of Jesus Christ are, at best, vague.

Process theology. The roots of process theology go back to ancient Greece and the sixth century work of Heraclitus who posited that the universe is in constant change and God Himself is ever unfolding Himself in His revelations to humankind. Philosopher Alfred North Whitehead (1861-1947) promoted this concept with the end result that his perception of Deity was sometimes called developmental pantheism. In this interpretation, human perceptions of God are, at best, temporal, limited to time and space, and as God continues to reveal Himself, perceptions of His Person and work change (Whitehead, 1929). This view was followed up and promulgated by theologians Charles Hartshorne (1941) and John B. Cobb (1965). These thinkers took the concept of relativity seriously, which resulted in the view that perceptions of God were always to be considered transitory, but these perceptions would continue to become more accurate as humankind matured theologically.

Positive contributions of process theologians were these: they emphasized the need to incorporate metaphysical considerations in building theological systems, while at the same time articulating information from the Scriptures, natural revelation, and the incarnation of Jesus Christ (Geisler, 1978, pp. 267-270). This astute observation targets individuals whose concepts of *God* never change; no matter how much new information they receive. At the same time, caution must be exercised with regard to the vagueness of process operation, that is, views of God are continually to be perceived as temporary (Pike, 1970). God cannot be perceived as a timeless Being, which means that the God who is being worshipped may never be the "same" God. This contradicts the assertion made by James (1:17b) that God "does not change like shifting shadows." Some flexibility in theological formation may be commendable, but it is also important not to throw out the baby with the bathwater.

Theology of hope. As interest in the God-is-dead theology of the 1960s quickly dwindled, a new form emerged known as the theology of hope. Key promoters of the new approach to understanding the relationship of God to the universe included Johannes Metz (1972, Roman Catholic). Jürgen Moltmann (1975, Reformed), and Wolfhart Pannenberg (1972, Lutheran). The movement began as a form of protest theology, with its proponents objecting to the presupposition that God is dead. There is hope; God might just be alive in the future!

Metz claimed that the new role of the church in a world of hope is to become critically involved in the political affairs of the world, serving thereby as both conscience and critic. Moltmann encouraged the religions of hope—Judaism and Christianity—to find their action and draw up their lines of battle in the arena where hope was threatened by despair (Moltmann, 1975, p. 29). Pannenberg (1972) found the answer to the contemporary dilemma of despair in history; a study of the past will reveal that only the future can promise absolute answers. Without a study of the past it will be impossible to appreciate the direction that humankind may take.

Refurbished Evangelicalism. Conservative theologians criticized proponents of the theology of hope because they did not go far enough in validating the existence of God. They left the existence of God as an open question (Geisler, 1978, p. 230). While denouncing the God is dead ideology, proponents of the theology of hope did not affirm that God *does* indeed exist. They claimed that only the future would tell if He *does* exist and perhaps define in what ways He relates to people.

Brown (1978, p. 332) criticized conservative Christians for not doing enough to combat this form of creeping atheism. He insisted that too many orthodox Christians have lost the ability of thinking about fundamental issues as Christians; instead they think as the rest of the world does, and then add a Christian comment or criticism as a footnote.

Liberation theologies. Following hard on the heels of the theology of hope came three new emphases that focused on suppressed peoples, namely Black theology, Latin American liberation theology, and feminist theology.

Black theology. To begin with, the civil rights movement of the 1960s spawned a number of related social phenomena such as hippies, Back-to-the-landers, various protest groups, such as those opposed to the Vietnam War, and liberation theologians. Those who descended from Black slaves tended to enjoy a rich spiritual heritage, even though practiced American theology did not take that into account. Grenz and Olson (1992, p. 202ff.) contend that the theological patron of Black theology was Dietrich Bonhoeffer because of his emphasis on social redemption through human effort.

Black theologians emphasized the emancipation of Black people from White domination by endorsing their cultural identity as a foundation from which to oppose domination. Leaders like Martin Luther King, Jr., sought to validate Black spirituality, and the movement quickly targeted related political issues like school integration, injustice in the courts, and the lack of equality in economic opportunity. Black militancy was born out of these concerns. Soon the focus of attention shifted away from the Black church to academic institutions and American religious conservatism. Black leaders sought to align their concerns with neighboring denominations. A small step of success in this area featured a statement against racism issued by the World Council of Churches, but for the most part, many denominational leaders were skeptical of any theological alignments for fear that they were becoming too active in the political arena. Perhaps the most significant theological insight that grew out of the Black theology movement was a renewed emphasis on the immanence of God, which, being interpreted means that "God always encounters us in a situation of historical liberation" (Grenz and Olson, 1992, p. 209).

Latin American liberation theology. In 1968, the bishops of the Roman Catholic Church gathered in Medellin, Columbia, and issued a pronouncement that the church was too closely tied to the political platform of the ruling powers of Latin America. They insisted that this marriage tended to promote the agenda of the rich and left the poor in economic tatters. Reaction to the statement was swift and critical. Many felt that the bishops had wandered too far away from their hierarchical duties and should have maintained their traditional role as sacramental officiators. The bishops were adamant, they wanted to know; what was the church doing for the poor? (Grenz and Olson, 1992, p. 210ff.). If both rich and poor were professing Christians who allegedly believed in caring for one another and sharing their resources, why was there such a huge economic gap between the two levels of economic stratification? Several years earlier Pope John Paul XXIII reminded the church that its first duty is to the poor. After all, the Apostle James posed this warning:

> Listen, my dear brothers and sisters: Has not God chosen those who are poor in the eyes of the world to be rich in faith and to inherit the kingdom he promised those who love him? But you have dishonored the poor. Is it not the rich who are exploiting you? Are they not the ones who are dragging you into court? Are they not the ones who are blaspheming the noble name of him to whom you belong? (James 2:5-7)

Ironically, many Bible-believing evangelicals criticized Black liberation theologians, even though the latter based many of their claims on the Holy Scriptures. A general fear that Black liberationists were proceeding on Marxist grounds pervaded the camp of religious conservatives who apparently preferred to condone economic exploitation unless it could be addressed from purely evangelically-based interpretations of Scripture. Until that happened, conservative

Christians were not prepared to do anything to support the movement.

Feminist theology. Like other liberation movements, feminist theology also grew out of the 1960s civil rights era. It seems to have begun with the 1961 American President's Commission on the Status of Women, and the 1963 publication of Betty Friedan's book, *The Feminist Mystique.* Several religious camps latched onto the theme, quickly concocting interpretations of the need for women to be freed from male domination. Some leaders suggested that it was necessary to examine every religious doctrine and practice for the injustice that was being maintained under the guise of sexual equality. Christian feminists pointed out that the bulk of church practice and belief was founded on the assumption that males were created in the mage of God and this gave them the right to dominate family and church affairs. Feminists rightly pointed out that women were created for *different*, roles, *not* lesser roles. For one thing, their body functions are more closely related to the cycles of nature, and their day-to-day experiences thinking patterns are unique. These new theologians insisted that the male-permeated Scriptures alone cannot be relied upon as the sole authority for theology. Factors such as history, biology, and spirituality must also be taken into account. This insistence quickly motivated biblical literalists to shy away from feminist theology, probably without noting some of its important contributions.

Reformed Roman Catholic Theology. The scenario of Roman Catholic theology just prior to Vatican II was turbulent, focusing as it did on debates about birth control, priestly celibacy, and changes in the celebration of Mass. Thus, by the 1960s, the Catholic Church was in the process of transforming its theology by talking less about eternal truths and more about the process of inquiry as a means of searching for truth, not announcing it. In 1962, Pope John Paul XXIII summoned his bishops to meet in the Second Vatican

Council and issued the statement that "the human race has passed from a rather static concept of reality to a more dynamic, evolutionary one" (Placher, 1983, p, 303). In response Vatican II redefined the church from a hierarchy of pope and bishops to the whole "pilgrim people of God." Latin was removed as the sole language of Mass in order to invite wider participation from believers.

Two Roman Catholic theologians who quickly followed up on Vatican II were Karl Rahner (1978) and Hans Küng (1976). Rahner explained his view of theology in this way:

> I really only want to tell the reader something very simple. Human persons, in every age, always, and everywhere, whether they realize it and reflect upon it or not, are in relationship with the unutterable mystery of human life which we call God. Looking at Jesus Christ the crucified and risen one, we can have the hope that now in our present lives, and finally after earth, we will meet God as our own fulfillment (Grenz and Olson, 1992, p. 240).

So far, so good; here Rahner made a rather orthodox Christian statement, but he then went on to discuss transcendental reflection, which suggests that individuals have an *a priori* concept of God in their hearts. However, this inclination is not intended as proof for the existence of God, but rather an indication that humans possess human capacity for Divine revelation. Their very constitution makes them ready to receive Divine revelation. Rahner's liberalism encouraged him to observe that people of all religious orientations have moments of successful mediation; the nature of God's transcendence makes this possible. This statement quickly motivated conservative Christians to distance themselves from Rahner's discourses. As far as they were concerned, Rahner had more than opened the door for inter-religious dialogue by insisting the equality of world religions in so far as revelation was concerned.

Hans Küng became a controversial Roman Catholic theologian with his announcement in 1979 that only God is infallible, and the Roman Catholic Church can be subject to making theological errors. Küng was immediately declared a non-Catholic theologian and forbidden to teach Catholic ministerial students (Grenz and Olson, 1992, p. 257). Küng's approach to theology was an admixture of rationality and faith, and he accused the Christian church of selling out its rational capacities (Küng, 1976, p. 31). Küng's emphasis on the value of rationality motivated him to criticize the Protestant tendency to esteem the Scriptures as a paper pope. His view was that one must always utilize the God-given gift of mind in formulating theological beliefs. Similarly, rather than accepting Roman Catholic dogma at face value, Küng insisted that some analysis of established doctrines should always take place. Evangelical theologians therefore took him to task for elevating human reason to the level of the Person of Jesus Christ. Küng was accused of portraying Christ as only a special, unique human being, not as God incarnate. Now Küng was welcome in neither camp, but his popularity as a writer and speaker continued to mushroom.

Narrative Theology. Everyone likes a good story, and when individuals begin to relate what happened to them, or what is happening to them, and tie in biblical references and parallels, we have the beginning of narrative theology. The first question in this kind of storytelling is, "What is the situation of being a human being in this world?" The answer to the question is naturally individualistic, and those listening to such discourse will, hopefully, be encouraged to share their own experiences as well. The desired result in such a trusting milieu is that some sort of meaningful theology will emerge.

Originating in the 1970s, narrative theology was essentially a lay movement, emphasizing that merely to quote from the Scriptures is not sufficient. Biblical passages can only come alive when meshed with personal everyday experiences. After all, the Bible is not a static book, but a living resource, in which the central figure is God and in which the underlying concern is to bear testimony to the story of what He has done to save humankind and to bring His kingdom into being on this earth" (Grenz and Olson, 1992, p. 276).

One of the highlights of narrative theology is the open invitation it proffers to participants. Since everyone has a story to tell, everyone is equally qualified to try to tie it to biblical injunctions. No ministerial education is essential to interpreting the Bible, and no reference to biblical commentaries, lexicons, or original languages is necessary. The difficulty that emerges is that the relation between individual stories and biblical truth may be invented on an entirely individual basis, some of which advocates may be quite unequipped to search out hermeneutical interpretations. The other danger is that of developing ethical standards on a purely individual or group basis. Narrative theology is at best community based. Its emphasis is on the search for a transcendent God whose reality is found within informal searches by lay members of the human community.

Neo-evangelicalism. Twentieth century evangelicals may basically be perceived as religious fundamentalists with a flavoring of missionary zeal. While fundamentalists have primarily been involved with "getting things right" in so far as what to believe is concerned, evangelicals like to think that concern about the salvation of the unredeemed is also a priority. In fact, the theological framework driving evangelicals is very similar to fundamentalism, namely that God created a perfect moral world and gave individuals free choice within it. Adam and Eve, the first parents, corrupted that perfect world by disobeying God, therefore, sin entered the world. God arranged for humankind to be freed from the consequences of sin, first through obedience to the law and sacrificial enactments, and then, finally, through the death of His one and only son, Jesus Christ.

"Whoever believes in the Son has eternal life, but whoever rejects the Son will not see life, for God's wrath remains on them (John 3:36). Fundamentalists and evangelicals share consensus on these beliefs.

Evangelicals have traditionally been very eschatologically (study of end things) inclined, leaning heavily towards adopting a pre-millennial stance with minor differences pertaining to pre and post-tribulation interpretations. These variations will be discussed in chapter eleven.

A surprising turn of events took place in the latter half of the twentieth century when various evangelical groups decided to assemble their leaders to share both theological *and* humanitarian concerns. One of the primary concerns pertained to evangelical involvement in social and political endeavors. Humanitarianism was not a traditional evangelical stronghold because it was thought to be a major concern of mainline denominations that greatly emphasized the performing good deeds, but were weak on evangelism. The challenge for evangelicals was to frame a social work program that was based primarily on helping the needy out of genuine concern, not merely as a means by which to add numbers to church rolls. A driving force behind this endeavor was theologian Carl F. H. Henry (1913-2003), founder of a magazine called *Christianity Today*, designed to proclaim his message. In initial and subsequent writings Henry continually reminded his readers that both evangelistic outreach *and* social endeavors must have biblical foundations. After all, "The doctrine of the Bible controls all other doctrines of the Christian faith" (Grenz and Olson, 1992, p. 292). As outlined in his book series, *God, Revelation and Authority* (1976-1983), Henry spelled out the only way for evangelicals to revitalize their theology was by returning to the *reasonableness* of the faith. Henry was predictably criticized for recognizing the efficacy of human reason, but he perceived it to be an essential arm of any program designed to alleviate human suffering. If God is truly perceived to be a transcendent Deity, He must also be viewed as the One who can condescend to the realm of trying to meet all human needs.

Aboriginal Comparisons. Since this topic is discussed or alluded to in other parts of this book, only a summary will be presented in this context. The North American Indigenous position on human nature (if there *is* one) can possibly be inferred from several of the above approaches. To some extent, the Indigenous people of the Great Plains specifically believed in certain fundamentals, but loosely defined. They believed that God, the Great Mystery, created all things, and Mother Earth (a term later ascribed to Aboriginal theology), was the second parent. Together they originated and provide for their creation, including humankind and all other creatures, each with varying but basically similar responsibilities and privileges. The Dakota version suggests that the Sun and the Earth, representing the male and female principles, were the main elements in creation (Laviolette, 1991, p. 26).

A parallel with process theology may also be identified in traditional Aboriginal theology, particularly in the notion that the Creator continues to reveal Himself to individuals who seek Him out in the form of specific rites and ceremonies like the visions quest, or participating in sweat-lodge and Sundance ceremonies. Elders can also be sought out for additional spiritual guidance. The recipient of any new revelations is expected to live out those revelations, and the result of them is always to be shared with the community. Evangelism per se is not a primary concern although strangers are always welcomed. More recently, strains of liberation theology may be identified in Aboriginal thinking as Native leaders continue to seek justice, equality, and fair treatment in North American societies.

CHAPTER SEVEN

Soteriology: On What Basis Can Individuals Negotiate a Peace Treaty With the Great Mystery?

The Lord is not slow in keeping his promise, as some understand slowness. Instead he is patient with you, *not wanting anyone to perish*, but everyone to come to repentance (2 Peter 3:9, italics mine).

The decision for or against Jesus, or for or against being a Christian... whether he is in fact to be the model for me is a wholly personal question. It will depend on my wholly personal decision (Küng, 1976, p. 515, italics mine).

The First People of the Great Plains believed, as Christians also purport to do, that Creator God loves everyone (McGaa, 1995, p. 25). Assuming this premise is mutually acceptable to theologians in both camps, however, this is not to say that unanimity exists with regard to the manner in which God's love may be accessed. Only a limited segment of the more liberally minded Christian community would probably agree with Aboriginal interpretations.

The primary topic of discussion in this chapter is to map out how individuals can find grace in the eyes of the Great Mystery. Evangelical theologians prefer to label the status or process of getting right with God as attaining salvation or "being saved." Other, more liberal Protestant theologians proceed on the assumption that at the time of birth, babies are right with God (hence they are baptized), and it is up to their parents or guardians to assist them in staying on the path of righteousness. Naturally, this topic deserves a much fuller treatment, so we shall begin with a survey of Christian interpretations and then relate the discussion to the theological position of the First Peoples of the Great Plains.

Historical Background

During the various historical epochs following the ascension of Jesus Christ, Christian beliefs pertaining to salvation were well outlined. Believers who aligned themselves with the dominant church of the times, the Roman Catholic Church, simply followed the rules and regulations mandated by that body. Believers attended Mass, went to confession, and regularly donated a portion of their income to the church. They were obedient to the seven Sacraments which include: (a) Baptism (of infants); (b) Confirmation (for children, usually in their early teens); (c) the Eucharist (called Holy Communion or the Lord's Supper by Protestants); (d) Penance (which implies confession of sin, repentance, and willingness to submit to imposed penalties which provides reconciliation with God); (e) extreme unction (anointing of the sick); (f) Holy orders; and, (g) Holy Matrimony.

The first five sacraments may be administered to any Christian, while the last two apply to individuals who choose to join a religious order or who desire to be married by a Catholic priest. Since sacraments are considered acts of God administered by priests who have apostolic succession, theoretically they cannot be broken or evoked. In practice; however, some individuals who have entered Holy Orders have been released from their vows. Similarly, people who have been married by the church and sought divorce and have obtained it are still blessed by the church on the basis of a special procedure informally known as Christian annulment.

Historically, adherents to the Roman Catholic Church found the various behavioral requirements predictable, yet comforting. Families relied on the parish priest for instruction, counseling, and consolation. The priest baptized the children of the families and performed the marriage ceremony when they were grown, heard confessions, and offered parishioners spiritual guidance through sermons and wise counsel. In this way parishioners were assured of salvation and knew that God accepted them, loved them, and forgave them when they did wrong. By following the steps to salvation outlined by the church, Roman Catholic believers could essentially "stay saved."

Protestants sometimes accuse the Roman Catholic Church of proclaiming that salvation can be attained through works, but this is not an accurate assessment. Following the instructions given in the Book of James (chapter two), that good works should be a natural outgrowth of faith, the Catholic Church has always stressed this truth. However, there have also probably been periods in the life of the Roman Catholic Church when this was only more or less the case. Unfortunately, a survey of church history will support this observation. The apostle James is quite specific on the relationship between faith and works:

> What good is it, my brothers and sisters, if someone claims to have faith but has no deeds? Can such faith save them? But someone will say, "You have faith; I have deeds." Show me your faith without deeds, and I will show you my faith by my deeds (James 2:14, 18).

For generations Roman Catholics generally functioned according to the church's interpretation of James' mandate; then came the Protestant Reformation.

Reformers, who instigated the theological insurrection that became known as the Protestant Reformation, targeted what they perceived to be errors within the Roman Catholic Church. Along the way, however, they also originated a few doctrines of their own. "Salvation by faith, not by works and indulgences," became a popular slogan, along with the phrase, "priesthood of all believers." This teaching stressed the significance of the individual Christian against a system that viewed clergy as comprising the Church of God (Richards and Martin, 1981, p. 38). Many of the reformers reduced the number of sacraments to two—Holy Baptism and Holy Communion, although the Church of England (Episcopal) allowed for two fundamental sacraments and five "lesser" sacraments. There were other changes and innovations on the table, but the rapid splintering of church resisters into multiple denominations prohibits the cataloguing of an exhaustive list of the various beliefs and doctrines. The most radical breakaway group was the left wing Anabaptists whose objections included this list:

(a) The Bible, particularly the New Testament, is an open book to all and constitutes the sole guide of faith and practice. This implies the priesthood of all believers, so that anyone, not just a priest, can read, understand, and interpret the Scriptures.

(b) The church is an independent, voluntary group of believers who band together for the purpose of worship and fellowship. This implies a strict separation of church and state. Some Anabaptist groups interpreted this to mean that their adherents should not hold office in a secular, political organization; neither should they vote in state elections.

(c) Infant baptism has no place in a voluntary organization, as it is a sign of initiation into a universal state church. Oddly, although the practice of admitting infants to membership in a state-linked religious institution is no longer the case, Anabaptists still adhere to this line of justification for refusing infant baptism.

(d) The office of magistrate cannot be filled by a Christian. Government, however, is a Divinely approved institution ordained to protect the righteous and punish the wicked. The Christian must be obedient to his rulers, pray for them, and pay taxes to support government.

(e) The Christian cannot take up the sword. Love must be the ruling force in all social relations. It is wrong to kill, either as an individual or by judicial processor military force. Christ taught his disciples that; "...for all who draw the sword will die by the sword" (Matthew 26:52a). This belief obviously did nothing to endear the Anabaptists to state officials.

(f) Christians should live secluded from the outside evil world. Initially, this was the mode of living practiced by all Anabaptist groups, but today there are only a few groups like Amish, Hutterites, and Conservative Mennonites who try to keep themselves "from being polluted by the world" (James 1:27c).

(g) Church discipline should be secured through "the ban," which is used to exclude the disobedient from the rights of fellowship. Its purpose is to bring back dissident members, albeit by continuing to love them from a distance.

(h) The Lord's Supper (Eucharist) is to be regarded

merely as a symbol or memorial of the death and suffering of the Lord Jesus Christ, and should not be seen as containing the Real Presence.

(i) Following the rule of Scripture, it is wrong to take an oath. James underscored this commandment in these words: "Above all, my brothers, do not swear—not by heaven or by earth or by anything else. All you need to say is a simple "Yes" or "No." Otherwise you will be condemned" (James 5:12) (Friesen, 1977, p. 174).

Although the Anabaptist movement served as one influence in getting the Roman Catholic Church back on track, their own subsequent transformation to the point of resembling the state church severely dimmed their credibility as an antithetical institution. Many of their smaller affiliates remained unclear on the doctrine of soteriology, thereby providing material for critics who found ample evidence to attack their gradual religious assimilation. These groups were shy about verbally claiming salvation by faith alone, and the degree to which their religious officials demanded compliance to congregational regulations smacks of salvation by faith and works. However, non-Anabaptist groups, like evangelicals, placed a great deal of emphasis on the verbal proclamation of faith, while at the same time attempting unconvincingly to demonstrate their concern about doing good for others. The attainment of this goal constituted a delicate behavioral balance and related debates among theologians have been going on ever since. Even the exhortation to live an exemplary life of holiness falls short of the expectation to perform good works (Thiessen, 1959, p. 293).

Faith Versus Works

Although theologians sometimes have a way of complicating doctrinal discourse, for our purposes it is beneficial to identify several interpretations in relation to the subject of salvation and good works. It should be noted that there are those who see salvation strictly as a work of God (Wells, 1978, p. 54; Boice, 1986, p. 103), formed in the heart of the willing believer—"not by works, so that no one can boast" (Ephesians 2:9). This is the orthodox evangelical position; beginning with the Genesis account that humankind fell from grace when Adam and Eve disobeyed God in the Garden of Eden. Since then sin has reigned over humankind in a universal fashion, effectively disrupting communication between God and His creation. Evangelical theologians also believe that nothing can save individuals from sin except an act of God Himself. It happens that God has chosen to formulate a way out of this dilemma by sending His own Son, the Lord Jesus Christ, as His true representative, "because he will save his people from their sins" (Matthew 1:21b). As Tanner puts it:

> Here is a God who works unswervingly for our good, who puts no value on death and suffering, and no ultimate value on self-sacrifice for the good, a God of gift giving abundance struggling against the forces of sin and death in the greatest possible solidarity with us—that of incarnation (Tanner, 2010, p. 262).

Those who believe in and accept the gift of God by accepting the Lord Jesus as their personal Savior are saved; that is, having accepted Christ, they now look righteously acceptable in the eyes of God. As St. Paul said to the Philippian jailor, "Believe in the Lord Jesus, and you will be saved—you and your household" (Acts 16:31).

Having believed and received the gift of the new birth, new converts are positioned to receive a Divine title: "Yet to all who did receive him, to those who believed in his name, he gave the right to become children of God—children born not of a natural descent, not of human decision or a husband's will, but born of God" (John 1:12-13). This passage makes it clear that salvation is not of human effort, but it is a gift of God. St. Paul continues on the subject of receiving salvation also without mention of good works; "Therefore, if anyone is in Christ, the new creation has come: The old has gone, the new is here!" (2 Corinthians 5:17). The route to salvation is made abundantly clear in Acts 4:12: "Salvation is found in no one else, for there is no other name under heaven given to mankind by which we must be saved." The reference in this text is clearly to Jesus of Nazareth. The question of works is not approached in any of these contexts; that subject is discussed in other New Testament works, particularly in the Book of James.

The subject of salvation by works does not arise out of a scriptural vacuum, for much of Old Testament religious practice was of that nature. Many of the regulations that the Israelites were expected to heed are contained in the first five books of Moses, particularly Leviticus and Deuteronomy. For example:

> Teach them to your children, talking about them when you sit at home and when you walk along the road, when you lie down and when you get up. Write them on the doorframes of your houses and on your gates…If you carefully observe all these commands I am giving you to follow—to love the Lord your God, to walk in obedience to him and to hold fast to him (Deuteronomy 11:19-20, 22).

Most everyone is familiar with the Ten Commandments (or at *least* some of them), given by God to Moses and then to the Israelites. Their specificity of application, and other related laws and mandated practices contained in the Book of Leviticus, were assigned for several important reasons: (a) the Old Testament laws were intended to show the oneness and sovereignty of Creator God who alone was responsible for delivering them from their Egyptian taskmasters; (b) these laws were originated to provide moral guidelines for individual behavior; and, (c) these laws were intended to show sinners their inadequacy before God and thus motivate them to seek His forgiveness. Individuals who tried to fulfill the law would discover how difficult it was to do so, and thus turn elsewhere—to Christ. As St. Paul wrote to the church at Galatia:

> Before the coming of this faith, we were held in custody under the law, locked up until the faith that was to come would be revealed. So the law was our guardian until Christ came that we might be justified by faith. Now that this faith has come, we are no longer under a guardian (Galatians 3:23-25).

(d) Some Old Testament laws, rituals, and ceremonies were intended to foreshadow various aspects of the New Testament redemption plan, marking them as forms of typology. For example, the tabernacle that Moses was instructed to build in the wilderness was intended to provide a shadow or foretaste of things to come (Hebrews 8:4-5).

Biblical types are generally characterized by three things: a notable resemblance between the type and its antitype; evidence that the type is of Divine appointment; and, a prefigurement of something in the future (Pfeiffer, Vos, and Rea, 1975, p. 1752).

Taking the position that the Old Testament Israelites tried to obtain salvation strictly by obeying the law, is muddied by such passages as Hebrews 11:17-19 (italics mine) that states:

> *By faith* Abraham, when God tested him, offered Isaac as a sacrifice. He who had embraced the promises was about to sacrifice his one and only son, even though God had said to him, "It is through Isaac that

your offspring will be reckoned." Abraham reasoned that God could even raise the dead, and so in a manner of speaking, he did receive Isaac back from death.

St. Paul addresses the same topic in his letter to the Romans 4:1-3:

> What then shall we say that Abraham, our forefather according to the flesh, discovered in this matter? If, in fact, Abraham was justified by works, he had something to boast about—but not before God. What does the Scripture say? "Abraham believed God, and it was credited to him as righteousness."

This point is clear; although the Old Testament saints were expected to comply with a myriad of legalistically based regulations, the intent of those obligations was to show the impossibility of adhering to them. The inevitability of meeting the proposed standard of behavior was supposed to motivate believers to appreciate the grace of God and give birth to personal faith. For many it worked, but there were those who chose to cling tenaciously to keeping the law. One such group was the Pharisees who gave Jesus a great deal of difficulty because He would not always keep to the letter of the law. For example, Jesus occasionally broke rules pertaining to keeping the Sabbath (John 5:16), as two specific instances show. The first example is documented in Mark 2:23-27: "One Sabbath Jesus was going through the grainfields, and as his disciples walked along, they began to pick some heads of grain. The Pharisees said to him, 'Look, why are they doing what is unlawful on the Sabbath?'" (Mark 2:23-24). Jesus reminded the Pharisees that both David (who became king of Israel), and Abiathar (the high priest), had engaged in legally inappropriate behavior in the past because of need. Then Jesus gave His formal theological response: "The Sabbath was made for man, not man for the Sabbath" (Mark 2:27).

The second example is documented in John 5:1-15 where it is recorded that Jesus healed a man who has lain beside the Pool of Bethesda for thirty-eight years, waiting for someone to dip him into the pool whenever the water moved. Jesus commanded the man "Get up! Pick up your mat and walk " (John 5:8), and the man was cured at once. The Pharisees were upset, apparently believing that compliance with the law was more important than seeing the man healed. From time to time, the Pharisees persecuted Jesus for what they believed to be this illegal and outrageous behavior.

The Pharisees were only one of several religious sects who functioned during Jesus' lifetime, and first mention of them is made around 135-104 BC. The Pharisees gradually became the normative expression of Judaism, and because they did not accept Jesus as Messiah, they continued to hope for a Messiah whom they defined in their own terms, namely, a king, the son of David, who would "destroy the godless nations with the word of his mouth" (Pfeiffer, Vos, and Rea, 1975, p. 1327). Their principal occupation was to regard the written law as a summary of the principles and general laws of the Old Testament, as well as accumulated traditions; then impose compliance to those principles and laws on the people. Any deviation from that was regarded with contempt, and individuals who engaged in this kind of behavior, were either severely reprimanded or punished for it.

Remnants of Pharisaical thinking can still be identified in contemporary Christian communities, even though Jesus tried to usher in a new kingdom of behavior based on accepting the grace of God, avoiding the temptation to judge others, and freely offering forgiveness, even to those who do wrong to oneself (Matthew 5:43-44). Jesus insisted that the entire repertoire of Old Testament laws and regulations could be summarized in two commandments:

Jesus replied: "'Love the Lord your God with all your

heart and with all your soul and with all your mind.'
This is the first and greatest commandment. And the
second is like it: 'Love your neighbor as yourself.' All
the Law and the Prophets hang on these two commandments" (Matthew 22:37-40).

Many individuals and religious groups who lived during Jesus' time failed to understand the simplified version of the Christian
faith introduced by Jesus Christ. At least one of the congregations
established by St. Paul had that very difficulty, particularly the Gala-
tian church. St. Paul severely reprimanded this church for their strict
legalism:

You foolish Galatians! Who has bewitched you?...Did
you receive the Spirit by the works of the law, or by
believing what you heard?...does God give you his
Spirit and work miracles among you by the works of
the law, or by your believing what you heard? (Galatians 3:1a-2b, 5).

Paul made it clear that the days of legalism were over; Christ
had fulfilled every aspect of Old Testament law and prophecies. Now
it was up to the church to live by faith, and in the luster of God's
grace. "For it is by grace you have been saved, through faith—and
this not from yourselves, it is the gift of God—not by works, so that
no one can boast" (Ephesians 2:8-9).

St. Paul seems to have picked up on Jesus' attitude of relying
on God's perpetually functioning grace in regard to his own ministry. For example, when writing to the church at Philippi, Paul observed that he willingly endorsed ministries quite different from his
own. As he described it: "It is true that some preach Christ out of
envy and rivalry, but others out of goodwill.... The important thing
is that in every way, whether from false motives or true, Christ is

preached. And because of this I rejoice" (Philippians 1:15, 18b).

The debate, faith versus works may well continue to keep theologians occupied for generations. In an attempt to develop a workable, yet rational synthesis that is in keeping with the mandate of Scripture, we turn again to the Book of James. James makes it clear that if individuals claim to be followers of Jesus, they ought to be able to manifest their faith by doing good works. If it is as simple as that, why is there so much debate on the subject? The answer is that some conservative Christians want to make certain that good works emanate from what *they* perceive to be "genuine" salvation; the occurrence of the new birth has to be traceable to a specific model, time, and place. It cannot be a gradual realization of God's gift to humankind. Moreover, it must meet the specific guidelines outlined by these very theologians. Then, and only then, may good works be identified and considered valid.

Liberally minded theologians reject this legalistic definition of salvation, and are quite willing to concede that when individuals claim to apply the example and teachings of Jesus in their lives, they should be considered "saved." St. Paul seems to be in agreement with this position, based on the first chapter of his letter to the church at Philippi (cited earlier). As Grenz and Olson (1992, p. 56) suggest; "Salvation is not primarily a matter of achieving a state of blessedness in the afterlife; rather it is primarily the full fruition of the benefits of the kingdom of God on earth." Consequently, Christianity is not an otherworldly religion, but a religion of world transformation *through ethical action inspired by love*. This would seem to be quite in keeping with the theology of the First Peoples of the Great Plains.

Contrasting Indigenous Theology

It is easy to categorize cultural phenomena as "primitive" if one is not thoroughly familiar with them. This was basically the practice of the first European visitors to North America when they first encountered Aboriginal cultures. Virtually everyone in these camps—anthropologists, explorers, fur traders, missionaries, and settlers—adopted that stance. A number of anthropologists embarrassed themselves by labeling Aboriginal religions as constituting the fundamental stage of evolutionary religion (Morgan, 1963, p. ii), all the while labeling their own European theological inclinations as comprising an advanced stage in professional development. If indeed, Indigenous faith systems have developed, and they may not have had to do so, so have the perceptions of anthropologists as they have continued to familiarize themselves with Aboriginal belief systems. In essence, the problem is deeper than that; early anthropological descriptions of Native ways, with some exceptions, were soaked in ethnocentrism. Instead of seeking to learn about and understand resident ways when they first arrived in North America, these researchers were quick to compare and judge them from the vantage point of the cultural perspectives back home. The result was that Native American belief systems and practices were misinterpreted, misunderstood, and misconstrued for many generations. Today, the scene is gradually changing, and the good news is that many North Americans, from a variety of professions, are struggling to recast their relationship with the country's Indigenous peoples (Fleras and Elliott, 2007, p. 203).

Robert Lowie was one of the more objective non-Native researchers of Aboriginal cultures, even though one of his books is entitled, *Primitive Religion* (1952). Lowie spent a great deal of time documenting similarities between Native cultures and European models, and noted that Indigenous people had often been decried in literature because of their vicious method of warfare. In Lowie's estimation, whenever war is declared, the cultural origin of those who engage in it makes no difference; all wars are violent. However, it should be noted that traditionally Indian wars were never fought to acquire new lands; they were fought to maintain community, for revenge or horse stealing, or for glory (Lowie, 1963, p. 114). Underhill's (1965) assessment of Aboriginal religions was similarly based, but on a more objective stance.

Tooker (1979, p. 31) notes that outsiders have often labeled Aboriginal religious narratives as "myths", yet they are based on no less acute observations of nature than their European-derived counterparts. Aboriginal narratives reflect no less intellectual effort than do the sacred and secular texts of the "high" civilizations of the Old World. As the discipline of cultural anthropology continues to mature, more objective kinds of observations will increase, so that a more balanced view of Indigenous cultures is made possible.

What was the North American Plains perception of salvation? How did individuals attain peace with the Creator? What kind of action was required on the part of seekers? One can begin with the assumption of both Aboriginals and European Christianity that God created people and He loves them. Again, "He is patient with you, not wanting anyone to perish" (2 Peter 3:9). This implies that God has established for his people a pathway to salvation, which is undoubtedly interpreted differently in various cultural settings.

Based on our discussion of faith and works it would seem that the traditional North American Native view was as follows. Individuals at birth were perceived to be innocent in the eyes of the Creator for they had done nothing wrong simply by virtue of being born—which was not of their own choosing. This position is in direct contrast to the doctrine of original sin. The birth of a new child is always welcomed in Plains Aboriginal societies, even if the child is born out of wedlock (Seton and Seton, 1966, p. 32). This too, is no concern of the child.

The birth of a child was always a joyous event in traditional Indigenous societies because children were seen as gifts from the

Creator (Carlson, 1998, p. 82; Erdoes, 1972, p. 59; Lowie, 1963, p. 83). The arrival of a new baby also underscored the potentiality of tribal existence. As Beck, Walters, and Francisco describe it:

> When a child is born, it is seen by others as having a direction to go in order to survive and live well and long. Needless to say, these patterns and hope for a child are not obvious to that child at the beginning of life or during infancy. However, the child's parents may immediately after the birth of the child, begin the child in established patterns. Because the child is loved and respected as a human being, those close to the child wish him/her a good life and a long life.... The child beginning his road generally held a special place in the tribal world (Beck, Walters, and Francisco, 1990, pp. 190-191).

After an infant is born, it is the responsibility of those caring for the child to provide cultural and spiritual instruction. This is necessary, so the child will have ample knowledge by which to behave morally, as well as to differentiate between right and wrong. Grandparents and elders do much of this training, because they have superior knowledge and experience. They also tend to exercise more patience as they deal with the child (White, 1979, p. 103).

Seneca elder Twylah Nitsch describes the environment in which Native children used to grow up as very nurturing. Natural phenomena world were as active and as responsible for teaching life's lessons as humans were. In her words:

> The native education system of the past recognizes that there must be Love, Truth, and Peace present in all learning. People will recognize it as something that is wonderful for us to be involved in. Because

everything we look at is teaching a lesson; a tree is teaching a lesson; grass is teaching a lesson, everything is teaching a lesson. We need to recognize that we are able to grasp that lesson if it is brought to us in an interesting way. When we can feel comfort we are part of its whole (Nitsch, 1999, p. 87).

Traditionally, pedagogical opportunities in Indigenous families continued as the child matured, and he or she was gradually inducted into a myriad of social and cultural forces, the underlying plank of which was spirituality. Much of the path toward discovering who God is and what His plans for the individual might be was accomplished through storytelling, adult modeling, and imitation. Cultural practices were also learned through hands on practice. Ceremonial knowledge was accumulated and cemented in the mind through four steps: (a) listening to elders describe a particular enactment; (b) being invited to observe that happening; (c) being invited to participate in the ceremony itself; and, (d) perhaps eventually being permitted the honor of providing information about the ceremony or even being chosen to call it into being. The last step was usually reserved for carefully selected, elder-approved individuals.

When a child was born in ancient America, he or she arrived in the world innocent of, but naturally affected by the social and spiritual forces existent in the particular social milieu into which he or she was born. This is why loving care was available to the child at all times, each adult in the immediate community serving in a parental role for the youngster. The child was rarely left alone, always having a caring adult in the immediate vicinity to provide what was needed for the moment. The biblical mandate found in Proverbs 22:6 illustrates this: "Start children off on the way they should go, and even when they are old they will not turn from it." If someone in a traditional Aboriginal culture were to ask the child for a particular time when he or she developed an acute awareness of the existence of God and His personal life plan for the child, he or she would be unable to identify a specific time and place. The term that best describes such a situation would be progressive salvation in that the child, innocent at first, was carefully guided into a gentle awareness of God and then progressively guided to fuller knowledge.

As a children matured in traditional Native cultures they were gradually admitted to more meaningful cultural activities. When they grew older the principle of non-interference was maintained, thereby allowing young people to express themselves in ways that would manifest their individual personalities and gifts. Adults would not interfere with choices made by youthful individuals because they thought it necessary for their children to learn from their mistakes. Since their communities were quite limited in size, the individual even when quite young was never far away from the full pressure of public opinion. This public opinion might induce shame, rather than guilt, which is self originated (Jenness, 1986, p. 152). In addition, it was quite rigorously taught that every member of society, even young children had the responsibility of being contributing members of society (Deloria, 1999a, p. 139), and sanctions were in place for those who engaged in deviant behavior.

The expectation to conform to societal norms is still very much alive in many contemporary Native societies but in a rather unique form. Ross (1992, p. 17) describes a contemporary court scene in which a young Native man is charged for breaking and entering a schoolhouse after hours. The judge asks the youth what his parents had done to him when they learned of his crime. The boy replies that his parents had done nothing, and the non-Native judge was aghast. Ross interprets the event as a case in point for the principle of non-interference. The parents wanted the boy to learn from his own mistakes, and punishing him after the fact would likely accomplish nothing, but would likely incite resentment on the boy's part. There would be no cajolery, no praise or punishment, no withholding of privileges, and no promising of rewards.

Summarizing the Specifics of Salvation

Until European missionaries arrived in North America, local dwellers had no knowledge of the Christian religion, particularly the historical fact of the incarnation of Jesus Christ. The belief that God chose to become a human *and* Divine being in the form of Jesus Christ was unknown to them. However, it *is* important to note that the concept of Divine incarnation per se, *was* contained in their belief system, albeit not in the specific form that Christianity fosters in the person of Jesus Christ.

Old Testament Beliefs. Members of the Old Testament nation of Israel had in store and practice a vast number of rituals and ceremonies through which practice they relied on to obtain grace in the eyes of God. Later, in the New Testament, we discover that many of these enactments were a typology of what God would do for His creation in the redemptive work of His Son, Jesus Christ. This perspective parallels nicely the ceremonial aspect of the Indigenous aspect of spirituality. Indigenous people traditionally also relied on a myriad of spiritual practices and enactments that served to help bridge the gap between the world of humankind and that of the Great Mystery. A vast store of legends was used to inform each child and assist him or her in discovering their unique role in the universe. Since these cultures were solidly spiritual in foundation, every experience was perceived as a possible steppingstone for individual spiritual growth.

New Testament Beliefs. Jesus taught that two things constitute proof that an individual has adopted His redemptive work; first, loving God the Creator with all of one's heart, and second, treating one's neighbor as one would like to be treated. This uncomplicated prescription is not unlike that practiced by the First Peoples of North

America before European contact.

Aboriginal Beliefs. The Indigenous approach to finding favor with the Great Spirit is a curious admixture of both Old and New Testament prescriptions. The primary difference is that the Indigenous people seem to have anticipated the underlying purpose of religious enactments as avenues of Divine connection, in terms of ends-in-view, not as ends-in-themselves. Clearly this position is closely aligned with the attending assumptions of belief in salvation as a progressive process.

CHAPTER EIGHT

Deontology: What Moral Obligations Do Individuals Have to One Another? What Moral Obligations Do Individuals Have To Their Communities?

The Scripture teaches that good works are not optional for the believer. Neither do they come automatically to new creatures in Christ. Good works come through purposeful discipline to witness and deed.... All Christians are called on to do good works as an expression and measure of the good work God through Jesus Christ is doing in them (Mickey, 1980, p. 155).

The etymological definition of deontology requires a discussion of moral duty and obligation to oneself, to others, and to one's community. Related questions include these: do individuals who claim to have a Divine connection *have* such obligations? If so, what is the nature and extent of these duties? Who has the authority to mandate and perhaps oversee that these obligations are fulfilled?

The notion that individuals have moral obligations to one another and/or to the state can easily be documented in the history of human societies, although there are individuals and theorists who from time to time have tried to downplay or question the whole idea. Critics of moral obligation have tried, and do try, to adopt a stance of extreme individuality by suggesting that if humans *do* have any moral obligation, it is to themselves. This perspective was never a reality in traditional Native American communities; theirs were sharing societies. In order to provide a basis for comparison with the Christian tradition, it is necessary first to visit this historical development.

It is universally accepted, at least by sociologists who study religion, that every society with a supernatural orientation, tends to feature four distinct elements in their belief system. The first element is the formulation of a mystical or foundational cosmology that is intended to define the rudimentary structures and limits of the occupied world. This foundational belief seeks to answer such questions as: "Is there such an entity as Divine Deity, and if so, what form does Deity take?" The second element spells out a perceived relationship between cosmic Divinity and human beings. Related to this, is the elaboration of a means of connecting and being regenerated in the pursuit of spiritual perfection. Third, each culture will have elaborated for its membership a series of moral duties and obligations that they will be expected to fulfill in relation to one another and to one's community (Friesen, 1995, p. 77). This mandate is seen to satisfy deontological requirements. The fourth element pertains to spiritual ritual adherence and ceremonial life that is to be practiced as a means of nurturing the connection between Creator God and humankind. This model appears to be applicable to Native American tribal cultures. Their traditional spiritual makeup nicely parallels that of the tribe of Israel as described in the Old Testament.

Old Testament Deontology

It can be a very productive pursuit to compare and contrast the nature of Old Testament society with that of the traditional belief systems of North America's Aboriginal Peoples, and to do so with few limitations. Old Testament society was essentially tribal in nature, as was that of the first North Americans before European contact.

The Old Testament books of Leviticus and Deuteronomy contain a vast store of commandments regarding moral and legal obligations. Leviticus basically deals with the laws of the Levite priests who governed the spiritual affairs of the tribe. The text includes directions for priestly consecration, sacrifices, purification and atonement, as well as directions for preserving holiness, religious feasts, and the sabbatical year. Deuteronomy, on the other hand, contains discourses by Moses pertaining to such topics as forbidding idolatry, establishing the cities of refuge, commandments for daily living, differentiating clean and unclean food, the Feast of Weeks, offerings, and various other laws. Described laws spell out specific behavioral expectations for tribal members complete with lists of taboos, sanctions, and possible punishments for violations. These expectations pertain to virtually all relationships including family, tribe, and foreign relations. Here are a few examples:

> Therefore, watch yourselves very carefully, so that you do not become corrupt and make for yourselves an idol, an image of any shape.... Honor your father and your mother, as the Lord your God has commanded you.... When you have eaten and are satisfied, praise the Lord your God for the good land he has given you.... Do not cut yourselves or shave the front of your heads for the dead, for you are a people holy to the Lord your God.... At the end of every seven years you must cancel debts.... If cases come before your courts that are too difficult for you to judge—whether bloodshed, lawsuits or assaults—take them to the place the Lord your God will choose. Go to the Levitical priests... (Deuteronomy 4:15-16a; 5:16a; 8:10; 14:1a-2b; 15:1; 17:8-9a).

Traditionally Israel's society functioned in alignment with four underlying, spiritually based values. These may be outlined as follows.

First, the Old Testament Israelites, like other tribal societies, viewed their place in the universe as a microcosmic entity in the vast scheme of things. As the Lord reminded Job, the Old Testament patriarch, "Where were you when I laid the earth's foundation?" (Job 38:4). The geographic living areas assigned to each of their twelve tribes were perceived to be the act of a benevolent Deity to whom the dwellers had far reaching obligations. As a result each tribe invented and amassed appropriate rituals and ceremonies of thanksgiving to the Creator for such blessings as food and shelter, benefits of living in family groupings, and indeed for life itself. Until the publication of the first five books of Moses, the tribe of Israel, like North American Indigenous People, functioned according to the oral tradition.

A second key tribal value had to do with responsibility toward kinfolk and family. Obligations to one's relatives were limitless. As Deuteronomy 14:28, 29c, and have it: "At the end of every three years, bring all the tithes of that year's produce and store it in your towns, so that the Levites…the fatherless and the widows who live in your towns may come and eat and be satisfied…" This meant that those with means were expected (and virtually legislated) to share their means. If a family owned a grain field, for example, they were expected to leave some grains fall to the ground so that relatives without food could follow the reapers and pick up the grains left behind.

A third value scheme included generosity towards the tribe, the immediate community, and to strangers. Those who willingly shared their resources with laborers, the fatherless, and widows were to be blessed by the Lord who in return would "open the floodgates of heaven and pour out so much blessing that there will not be room enough to store it" (Malachi 3:10b).

Fourth and finally, was the value of spiritual community with all of God's creation. The nation may have been at war with their enemies from time to time, but they were also cautioned to love strangers (aliens or foreigners) who came into their territory because they themselves were strangers during their 400-year period of slavery in Egypt. The Israelites were reminded that God loves the fatherless, widows, and foreigners and defends their cause (Deuteronomy 10:17-18).

North American Tribal Deontology

> Human kindness was imprinted in our hearts, and the law of the Great Spirit, the Creator, was the only law that we observed. Our society was built around the concept that the Creator is the Supreme Being, the Great Mystery; recognizing Him as the One who provides all things was the very first step and the beginning of our tribal society. The recognition of the Creator in all of life was essential for our survival here on earth and in the hereafter (Chief John Snow, 2005, p. 8).

Chief Snow's statement sets the stage for a discussion of traditional Native American sharing practices. The fundamental belief that drove these practices was this: whoever had resources was expected to share those with others. In fact, the Stoney Nakoda First Nation, near Calgary, Alberta believed that if a family member or relative was known to have resources, those in need could help themselves to those resources without asking. The blessing of the event went to the holder of those resources because it meant that he or she was able to share. Among some Plains First Peoples, it was the custom that if a hunter brought meat from a successful hunt into the camp, it had to be shared with everyone. A special dispensation was that if the "woman of the house" brought the meat into the camp, she could decide with whom she would share it.

Incoming Europeans were flabbergasted by the very informal concept of ownership that the Indigenous peoples practiced and, from their perspective, rightly so. The Plains First Peoples believed that resources or indeed any property was never individually owned; it belonged to the tribe, particularly spiritual materials. Hence, there were such concepts in vogue as "bundle keeper" and "pipe carrier." If someone requested that power, even teepee designs, originally designed in accordance with a dream or vision, could be transferred with the underlying message intact. An elder would be contacted, a price arranged, and a teepee transfer ceremony enacted. Now the "borrower" of the design could share in the original message and power of the design.

In tribal societies, deontological obligations were interpreted by the oral tradition. This was the case in Israel before the written word came into existence. Although the impact of living in alignment with the oral tradition is similar in nature to the written word, the oral tradition offered certain advantages. One of these was that a certain amount of flexibility was built into the system as it was affected by such factors as geographic conditions, changing weather patterns, food source, migrations, and cultural contact and exchange. It was expected that these changes would occur slowly, although there might be circumstances that would enhance the speed of culture change as well.

The content of oral tradition may be thought of as multidimensional, including knowledge and expectations affecting all aspects of tribal life. When the first Europeans arrived in North America, for the most part, they were not aware of, nor interested in deciphering the moral codes of local residents. In fact, they came to conquer, subdue, and transform local cultures and their resources, not study their lifestyles. When they *did* encounter customs and practices different from those they were familiar with in their home country, they judged them harshly. As imperialists, they also squelched Aboriginal practices that they found abhorrent, many of which were kept alive by the Indigenous peoples practice of observing them in secret. Today some Native leaders are not only reviving previously hidden rituals and ceremonies but they are also willing to share knowledge about them with interested non-Natives.

It is probably not well known that traditionally the makeup of North American Native cultural and spiritual practices was very complex. For example, following are some traditional Plains Indian customs and practices that the European newcomers found discomforting.

> When it's time, it will happen; there is little use in trying to schedule everything (Friesen, 1999, pp. 49-50).

> A married man should never speak to his mother-in-law (Jenness, 1986, p. 369).

> Young boys setting out in their first warring group would be given a derogatory name until they had won honor by stealing a horse, or by killing or tagging an enemy (Driver, 1968, p. 463).

> Polygamy was allowed since wars in which men engaged often created an imbalance among the sexes (Lowie, 1963, p. 81).

> Many Plains First Nations celebrated the Sundance ceremony during which they offered sacrifices to the sun (MacLean, 1980, p. 437).

> It was believed that a disease could be "sucked" out of

an individual by a medicine man, using a feather fan
and accompanied by chants and prayers (Hultkrantz,
1987, p. 31).

Among some Plains Indian tribes, the buffalo occupied deity status, and figured in dances, taboos, societies, visions and cures (McHugh, 1972, p. 110).

Adjusting to what were fundamental cultural nuances in Indigenous lifestyles was not on the agenda set by the first Europeans to arrive in North America. Their program of operation was to
substitute their own behavior preferences for traditional Indigenous
ways. As time has passed, it would appear that they were not entirely
successful in this campaign.

Deontology in the New Testament

When Jesus Christ began His Messianic career He announced that an age of grace was being ushered in, and it was no
longer necessary for individuals to heed Old Testament Mosaic laws.
His reductionist approach was uncomplicated; individuals needed
only to love the Lord God with their whole hearts, and love their
neighbors as themselves (Matthew 22:37-40). The Pharisees, leading
religious rulers of the day, were aghast; how could someone claiming to be the Messiah so readily belittle their revered traditions? The
answer they received but did not welcome was that Old Testament
predictions and typologies were being fulfilled and would continue
to be fulfilled in Jesus' ministry. What the Pharisees did *not* envision
was that Jesus would be tried and crucified, and by that means fulfill
the very foundation of Old Testament prophecies. There are ample
Old Testament references that prophesy specifics pertaining to Jesus'
birth (Isaiah 7:14), His announcement of ministry by John the Bap-
tist (Malachi 3:1), the nature of His ministry (Isaiah 61:1), His trium-
phal entry into Jerusalem (Zechariah 9:9), His suffering at the hands

of enemies (Isaiah 53:3), His suffering and death (Daniel 9:26), and His resurrection (Psalm 16:8-10). Each of these was fulfilled in the New Testament.

With such a simple formula by which to attain salvation at hand, Jesus' listeners should have been able to rejoice. No longer was it necessary to try to meet the rigorous requirements of the Old Testament ritualistic moral laws. Now all one had to do was love the Lord God and treat others with the same regard as one had for oneself. Jesus' critics were not happy, probably because they had made a successful business out of legalism. Their refusal to heed Jesus's words was prophesied in Isaiah 6:9-10, and verified in Matthew 13:14-15. Comparing the uncanny resemblance of Old Testament prophecies to New Testament statements of fulfillment certainly lends credence to the claims made by Jesus Christ. The age of grace had indeed been ushered in.

Comparisons

As previously mentioned, storytelling was a highly valued method of teaching in preliterate societies. The practice continued even after the printed word appeared simply because everyone likes to hear a good story. This was also one of Jesus' favorite means by which to impart His moral precepts. One of the best known of Jesus' parables is the story of the Good Samaritan in the Gospel of Luke 10:25-37. This story is an excellent example of Jesus' exhortation to love one another—including one's enemies (Matthew 5:43-44). Here is the story.

An expert in the Pharisaical law, hoping to trap Jesus on a legal point, asks Jesus what he should do to inherit eternal life. Jesus tells him to "love the Lord God with all your heart and with all your soul and with all your strength and with all your might, and love your neighbor as yourself" (Luke 10:27). This raises the inquirer's curiosity as to whom Jesus would identify as his neighbor. Quite equal to the occasion, Jesus tells the story of a Samaritan traveler going through foreign territory who comes upon a Jewish man, beaten up, and lying beside the roadside. The historical fact is that the Jews and Samaritans had long had a strong dislike for one another. The traveling Samaritan is the third individual to come upon the scene; the first two were a Jewish priest, and a Levite or teacher of the Jewish law. These individuals should have known better, but neither of them aided the unfortunate victim of foul play. Although it would not have been expected that the Samaritan would show mercy to the fallen Jew, he does just that. He bandages the victim's wounds, puts him on his donkey, and takes him to the nearest inn. He then gives money to the innkeeper to pay for the wounded man's keep and offers to provide additional sums if needed when he returns to the area.

Undoubtedly, hearers would be surprised by the Samaritan's actions, as told by Jesus, but they would similarly be surprised by the behavior of the priest and Levite. Why did the latter two individuals walk by the ailing man in the ditch? Was their unexpected behavior motivated by fear of corpse or social class contamination? Was Jesus merely differentiating good and bad people regardless of cultural or religious affiliation (Levine, 2006, p. 144ff.)?

After relating the parable, Jesus asked the inquirer which one of the three individuals who came upon the fallen man was neighbor to him. The obvious answer, appropriately acknowledged by Jesus' questioner, was the Samaritan. Rather than indicting the questioner or in any way implicating him, Jesus simply suggests that he "go and do likewise." The underlying implications of the parable were quite clear; it was up to the hearer to decide what he or she wanted to do with the newly encountered truth.

North American Aboriginals were traditionally much given to storytelling, often for the explicit purpose of imparting deonto-logical precepts. The following Cherokee legend is illustrative of that objective.

Two young Native boys were very good friends, and there were also times when they strongly disagreed with one another. One day they were invited to go on their first hunt and they were very excited. If they were successful on the hunt it might mean that they would soon be able to train to be warriors.

The hunting party had not gone very far into the for-est when the boys spied a rabbit and both of them let fly an arrow at the same time. One of the arrows struck its mark and both boys shouted with glee; "I have killed my first rabbit." Unfortunately it was not immediately clear whose arrow struck the rabbit since the boys had made a number of arrows togeth-er and to everyone who examined them, they looked the same.

The boys began to discuss the matter, but soon their voices got louder and louder as they con-tinued to argue about whose arrow had killed the rabbit. Neither one of them would yield. Soon their loud voices bothered other members of the hunting party. Even when one of the seasoned warriors told them boys to stop arguing they found it difficult to do so. Both of them wanted very much to be right.

"Why don't you boys simply say that you killed the rabbit together," their warrior guide said. "All I know is that both of you are as stubborn as elm trees." The boys looked mystified so the warrior added, "Come with me into the woods tomorrow and I will show you what I mean.

The next day the party of three again entered the forest with the seasoned warrior leading the way. As he walked along, the warrior caught hold of various tree branches and broke them off. The boys followed suit; they thought this was a great game.

Suddenly the warrior stopped in front of a great tree. He invited the boys to break off a branch from the tree before them. Immediately they tried to do so, but even after applying all their strength, they were unable to break off a branch.

The warrior watched the boys for a while and then spoke. "This is what I meant when I called you boys stubborn as elm trees. Yesterday you would not give in; both of you wanted to claim having killed the rabbit, and nothing was resolved. You refused to work together because you were stubborn and would not bend—just like this elm tree. It is not always good to be stubborn."

The boys learned a valuable lesson that day.

Obviously Jesus' way of presenting moral precepts by way of relating parables was very effective, and it had a strong historical parallel among the practices of the First Peoples of North America. Their forms of deontological obligation were remarkably similar in nature.

CHAPTER NINE

Sacramentalism: What Were/Are Some of The Sacred Practices of North America's Plains First Peoples?

It is customary in Christian congregations to be familiar with what are regarded as very special sacred practices through which it is believed God works. These practices are called sacraments, and they are regarded as containing the very presence of God when they are enacted. Two of the most universally accepted Christian sacraments are Holy Baptism and Holy Communion (The Eucharist). By contrast, it is not as easy to identify the nature of sacramental belief among North American Aboriginal peoples because their systems are much more complex. However, in the interests of making meaningful comparisons, this chapter will describe a selected number of sacred concepts and ceremonies originated and practiced by the First Peoples of the North American Great Plains. Some similarities to biblical practice, in both Old and New Testaments, will be pointed out. While presented in alphabetical order, this is in no way intended to stratify their importance to these communities.

Circle of Life

The circle of life is a foundational concept that applies to every aspect of the Indigenous lifestyle. Sioux elder Black Elk (cited in Neihardt, 1979, pp. 194-196) explained that the power of the world always works in circles, and everything "tries to be round." The Old

Testament prophet Isaiah would seem to agree. Speaking of the Creator's position in the universe, Isaiah remarks (40:22): "He sits enthroned above the circle of the earth, and its people are like grasshoppers. He stretches out the heavens like a canopy, and spreads them out like a tent to live in."

The circle focuses on life and peace; its center is spiritual. In traditional Sioux country the entire community is viewed as circular with a flowering tree placed in the center. Each of the four directions represents a particular quarter of the circle, with the east providing peace and light, the south giving warmth, the west providing rain, and the north giving wind, which represented strength and endurance. Everything else is also considered to be in a circle, with birds making round nests, the sun and moon perceived as round, and teepees being designed in a circle. Among most Plains First Peoples, teepees were considered human nests in which to raise the young. An individual's life was considered to follow a circular form from helpless infancy to childhood to youth to adulthood to helpless old age.

Dances

Dances are very much a part of Plains culture, and they serve a variety of purposes from sacred to artistic to social to entertainment. In many ways Native dances are like legends; each variation illustrates a story to onlookers. Dances comprise another way of passing along valued beliefs and practices via the oral, and in this case, visual tradition.

Dancing also played an important purpose in biblical times. The Old Testament contains more than a dozen references to Jewish dances, with the fundamental purposes of entertaining or as a form of joyous worship and praise (Psalm 149:3; Jeremiah 31:13, Ecclesiastes 3:4). One quite unique purpose of the dance occurred in Judges 21:21 when men from the tribe of Benjamin, which had an imbalance of males and females, captured women from a different tribe—while they were at a dance! The New Testament records several occasions for dancing with a similar rationale (Matthew 11:17; Mark 6:21, 22; Luke 7:32, and 15:25).

Easily the most recognized kind of Aboriginal dance is the round dance that appears to have originated with the Plains Ojibway First Nation. The dance is usually practiced in connection with a pow-wow and everyone present is invited to participate. The round dance is considered a dance of friendship with dancers forming a large circle and slowly moving in a sun-wise (clock-wise) direction to the rhythm of drums. The round dance is primarily viewed as a fellowship dance.

A pow-wow celebration always includes a variety of specialized dances, with participants being judged for their performance. The repertoire of women's dances at a pow-wow typically includes the traditional dance, fancy shawl dance, jingle dress dance, and team dance. Men perform traditional dances, the grass dance, horse dance, fancy dance, victory dance, and sneak-up dance, the latter representing the poise of a hunter while he pursues his prey. A sacred Cree dance is the prairie chicken dance which will be performed for a special spiritual purpose like a prayer for a sick child to get well. The most sacred dance is the Sundance that will be summarized later.

One of the most misunderstood Plains dances is the give-a-way dance that is sponsored when someone wants to celebrate a family member's formal entry into the dance circle, or wishes to commemorate the death of a loved one. This dance may also be called to give thanks for an individual's recovery from illness or an accident, or simply to share blessings with one's friends. The Plains give-a-way dance is just that, the giving away of items such as quilts or blankets, items of clothing, household goods, beadwork or crafts. Appropriate songs and other dances accompany this event.

Elders

Elders serve in a variety of roles in Indigenous communities across the continent. Their selection, status, and form of office are discussed in the next chapter.

Fasting

Fasting is a time honored practice in many cultures, and is still a respected activity among the Plains Peoples. Fasting is considered a long established way of enhancing one's spirituality. An official fast involves guidance from an elder, who establishes the setting and conditions for the fasting individual. Fasting implies the total renunciation of food and drink for a specified period of time, and here the attending elder will provide special care. Taking health considerations into account is also a responsibility of the accompanying elder for the event. Fasting is often attached to preparation for participation in the Sundance and for vision questing. It is believed that a four-day fast strengthens the senses and opens the heart to a stronger spiritual connection with the Creator.

Feasting

Feasting is often related to ceremonies such as participating in a sweat-lodge ceremony. Afterwards, the participants enjoy a meal of sacred food. The Ojibway regard wild rice, corn, strawberries, and deer meat as sacred, while the Cree people feature bannock (Indian bread), soup, wild game, and fruit (especially blueberries and Saskatoon berries) as sacred food.

Four Powers

Four Powers, just as the number four, are regarded as sacred. The four powers emanate from the four directions and their various characteristics are described in relation to the medicine wheel. Other phenomena that function in fours include things that crawl, those that fly, those that are two-legged, and those that are four legged. There are four solar bodies above the earth—sun, moon, stars, and planets, and there are four divisions of time—day, night, moon, and year. There are four parts to green things—root, stem, leaves, and fruit, and there are four elements—fire, water, air, and earth. Even the human heart is divided into four compartments (McGaa, 1990, p. 33).

The Bible contains more than thirty references to the number four, giving ample evidence that this is not necessarily a coincidence. For example, if a man steals a sheep and is caught, he shall pay back with four sheep (Exodus   22:1); animals that walk on all fours (with certain conditions) may be butchered and eaten (Leviticus 11:27); and, "Under three things the earth trembles, under four it cannot bear up" (Proverbs 30:21). In another context, the Lord sent four kinds of destroyers against the Israelites (Jeremiah 15:3). Many prophecies refer to the number four (Daniel 3:25, 7:17; 11:4; Amos 1:3; Zechariah 1:18; and, Revelation 4:6, 5:14, 9:14, 14:3, and 19:4).

Guardian Spirits

Guardian Spirits are believed to accompany individuals as they make their sojourn through life. This was a fairly universal concept throughout ancient Native America. Some Aboriginal people believe that every individual has a guardian spirit, while others align guardian spirits only with people of specific rank. Human beings who do not have guardian spirits are believed to be weak and ineffective. Those who possess a guardian spirit can often achieve success in a range of endeavors. The names of guardian spirits are usually ancient beings, some of who reside in the world today as animals.

Herbs

Herbs are used for producing incense, and four such plants held sacred by the Plains First Peoples are cedar, sage, sweet-grass, and tobacco. Cedar and sage are used to drive out negative forces, while sweet-grass and tobacco are burned to invite positive forces to enter. Today sweet-grass ceremonies abound, primarily as a vehicle for cleansing before a pow-wow or other ceremony takes place. Often participants use purification rituals to smudge ceremonial objects such as drums before taking part in a pow-wow.

Medicine, Good or Bad

Medicine, good or bad, is believed to exist in individuals, as a source of spiritual power—positive or negative. Individuals who have good medicine are often gifted in the healing arts or in giving counsel. Individuals who possess bad medicine should be avoided, because they can negatively influence the mental or physical health of those whom they want to affect. Negative forces may influence individual states by the way they are looked at, talked to, or thought about. Conversely, four positive individual forces may be identified: (a) the individual who has knowledge of healing herbs; (b) the prophet, who is an individual who can foretell events; (c) the conjurer, who has the ability to eradicate diseases through chants and prayers; and, (d) the scared clown who uses thunder power to heal people. Some tribes combine these roles into one office (Lame Deer and Erdoes, 1972, pp. 154-155).

There are several references to individuals with the spirit of evil power cited in the Bible, the wicked Queen Jezebel being one of them. When Jezebel married King Ahab of Israel, she brought with her prophets from her home country, Sidonia, and then ordered the death of one hundred Jewish prophets (1 Kings 18:4). After a show-down with the prophet, Elijah, about whose God was the stronger—God or Baal, Jezebel tried to kill Elijah (1 Kings 19:1-2). Another reference to the wicked Jezebel occurs in Revelation 2:20, but it is not immediately clear if this reference is actually to the Old Testament Queen Jezebel or metaphoric of a parallel evildoer. In another instance, St. Paul cautions young Timothy not to have anything to do with two individuals—Hymenaeus and Alexander—who have left the Christian faith and now engage in evil blasphemy (1 Timothy 1:20). Conversely, there were also many other individuals whose positive spirits were recognized by the various writers.

Medicine Bundles

Medicine bundles comprise an assemblage of sacred objects kept in a small pouch, the origin of which was revealed to someone in a vision. Bundles are "kept" by bundle keepers, not owned. Band members, who want to have the power of the medicine bundle become theirs, can request this. Then an elder will be invited to perform the necessary ceremony, a price will be paid (determined by the elder), and the transfer will be made. Keeping a bundle means success in life, and a bundle that has been proven to be effective by being in the possession of a prominent individual can bring a high price (Driver, 1968, p. 92). Only authorized elders can add items to an existing bundle. It is important to know that unauthorized individuals should never touch a medicine bundle nor walk directly in front of it. The medicine bundle is considered one of the most sacramental items in Plains Aboriginal communities.

The concept of sacred items can also be identified in the Bible, a notable example being that of the Ark of the Covenant in the Old Testament. This sacred chest was said to contain the original tablets that had the Ten Commandments inscribed on them, and were brought down from Mount Sinai by Moses. At one time the ark was captured by enemies and it was said then that, "The Glory has departed from Israel" (1 Samuel 4:21). Since the ark was viewed as containing the Real Presence of God, any unauthorized individual who touched the ark would be smitten to death (2 Samuel 6:6-7).

Medicine Wheel

The Medicine Wheel is a symbol of the scared circle in the Indigenous belief system. In the medicine wheel, the lives of people as individual harmonious expressions of the power of the world move in, and are nourished by an uninterrupted circular/spiral motion. The medicine wheel is usually constructed as a huge circle of stones with rows of stones emanating from it in all four directions—east, west, north, and south. Participants in a ceremony related to the Medicine Wheel will sit in a circle outside the Medicine Wheel. Sometimes the center of the wheel will be a cairn, possibly containing the bones of a respected deceased individual.

The following chart represents some of the characteristics of the Stoney Nakoda Sioux version of the medicine wheel (Friesen, 1995, p. 120).

	North	East	South	West
Characteristic	models (wisdom)	connectiveness (total illumination)	power (innocence)	introspection (looking within)
Color	white	yellow	red	black
Season	winter	spring	summer	fall
Creature	buffalo	eagle	mouse	bear
Element	fire	sun	earth	night

Naming Practices

Naming Practices, while observed by many Plains Aboriginal people, vary a great deal. Among the Ojibway, a naming ceremony will take place soon after a child is born, and the naming is done by a "name-giver" selected by the parents. This individual serves much the same function as a godparent would in non-Native society. After the ceremony, the parents are expected to gift the name-giver.

In addition to being given a formal name, each individual usually has an everyday name, often representative of something in nature. There are also names of derision or ridicule that are used to tease an individual and bring him or her into line for disobeying community norms. Special names are either assigned or earned through a variety of avenues. For example, an individual might receive a new name after being admitted to a sacred society, or a young man might adopt a new name after a successful vision quest. There are also instances where individuals choose a new name for themselves after a significant life-altering event has taken place. Sometimes the names of respected loved ones might be reserved until a newborn child who appears to have the characteristics of the loved one. In such a case the child would receive that name.

Naming practices are usually accompanied by appropriate ceremonies. To illustrate: the Chippewa recognize six distinct kinds of names, namely; (a) a "dream name," assigned by a namer in a special ceremony; (b) a dream name acquired by an individual usually received while engaged in fasting; (c) a namesake name given a child by his/her parents without ceremony or assigned power; (d) a common name or humorous nick name used daily; (e) a kinship name; and (f) a euphonious name that has no significance (Densmore, 1979, pp. 52-53).

A parallel to the Indigenous practice of treasuring individual names can be identified in the Scriptures. There are countless examples of name changes in the Bible, and one's name was usually intended to describe a person's character, position, function, some circumstance affecting him or her, or some hope or sorrow concerning that individual. Here are three examples. Abram (meaning *exalted father*) became Abraham (meaning *father of a multitude*) after he established a covenant with God to become the father of many nations (Genesis 17:3-5). When Naomi (meaning *pleasant*), returned to her homeland from Moab where her husband and her two sons had died, she insisted in being called Mara (meaning *bitter*) (Ruth 1:20).

Pipe

The Sacred Pipe is made up of several significant parts, which are joined together only during ceremonies. Otherwise they are kept apart. Every Aboriginal individual has potentially the right to hold a pipe, but this privilege is usually earned. Like other sacred items, a pipe is never actually "owned" by an individual. An individual who has a pipe in his or her possession is called a pipe-carrier.

A pipe is made up of three major components—the bowl, the stem, and the design. The design that has been carved into the bowl is made to face the smoker, not the onlooker. This is intended so the holder of the pipe will be reminded of the message of the carving while using the pipe.

Pipe stems comprise the male part of the item, and when the male stem is connected to the bowl, which is symbolically the female part, the Sacred Pipe becomes ritually active and powerful. Pipe bowls are often carved to represent different creatures and are therefore used for different purposes. The bowl itself represents the life-giving, life-sustaining figure of a woman and the earth. Its shapes, colors, and other features are designed to link to this symbolism.

Contrary to what might be public opinion, the Indigenous people of North America did not use tobacco in the way that non-Native smokers do today. They did not become addicted to tobacco through habitual smoking. Since tobacco was regarded as one of the sacred plants, smoking was not to be abused, but reserved for special ceremonies. As one elder informed me, when the pipe was smoked, only 1/10th of the pipe filling was actually tobacco; the rest of the content was made up of sweet-grass and herbs.

Pipe ceremonies, which are usually held for special purposes, involve rather intricate enactments. To begin with, a braid of sweet-grass will be lit and fanned to make smoke, then passed around to all participants in a container. Usually an elder will walk around the circle and offer the sweet-grass to each participant. In some Aboriginal communities, the practice is that participants will be careful to wave the smoke onto their head and chest only four times, while other tribal practices vary in this respect. After the sweet-grass ceremony, the presiding the elder will light the content of the pipe and offer the pipe to the four directions. When the pipe is passed around it is usually done in a sun-wise direction, and there are participants who will puff the pipe only four times. Appropriate songs often accompany pipe ceremonies.

Use of the pipe among most Aboriginal people still comprises a sacramental event, and most tribes have stories that detail the story of the origin of the pipe virtually back to the time of creation. The Lakota Sioux insist that a mysterious woman, Buffalo Calf Woman, gave the scared pipe to them when she appeared to two young men looking for food. She instructed the men to respect the pipe she was giving them, and to pray with it whenever they were in need. Then she vanished and turned into a white buffalo (Stolzman, 1998, pp. 166-167). Various versions of the story exist among factions of the Sioux Nations, but all agree that it was Buffalo Calf Woman who originally gave them the pipe.

The burning of incense was a fairly widespread practice among tribal nations in the past, and if the Sacred Pipe, so respected by North American Aboriginal people, may be viewed as a vessel for incense burning then we can identify an easy parallel in the Bible. In fact, incense ceremonies were very much a part of the Israelite tradition in the land of promise. Their priests frequently offered incense (1 Kings 13:1 KJV). Incense was to be burned on the altar of incense in the holy place of the tabernacle in the morning and in the evening (Exodus 30:7-8). In addition, the high priest was to burn incense annually on the Day of Atonement (Leviticus 16:12-14).

Pow-wow

The pow-wow was traditionally a religious event, but has more recently adopted a largely social theme. Pow-wows are still sponsored to honor individuals, and they include many traditional elements such as the grand entry, invocation, honor songs, eagle staff, flag songs, drums and eagle whistles. Dance competitions, celebrations, and feasting are still part of a pow-wow celebration. Elders support these activities by declaring that a pow-wow is a coming together in a unifying, joyous manner.

Each pow-wow begins with a grand entry led by elders, chief and council, and specially invited guests. This group, followed by other participants, form a circle around the hall in which the event is being held. After the fourth round, they stop and the invocation is offered. One of the members of the grand entry party will carry the eagle staff that symbolizes the characteristics of farsightedness, strength, speed, beauty, and kindness. Honor songs are sung at a pow-wow, if someone special is to be honored. Flag songs used to be sung to honor warriors who engaged in war for their tribe. Today, flag songs are sung to honor veterans who fought in the two World Wars; they are honored with a gift of eagle feathers. It is important to note that if an eagle feather is dropped during a ceremony, it must be carefully retrieved by an elder and four prayers will be said.

The drum is a vital part of any pow-wow because it is perceived to be the heartbeat of Mother Earth. Sometimes drum groups perform in competition at a pow-wow. The eagle whistle is blown four times to honor the drums present, the dancers, and the spirit of the eagle. Rattles are shaken to call up the spirit of life when someone is sick. Elders also use rattles to summon the spirits of the four directions to provide cleansing for someone planning to participate in a sweat-lodge ceremony.

Visitors are always welcome at a pow-wow; it is a very joyful and colorful event with individual dancers competing with their skills and showing off their fancy and brightly colored costumes. At a pow-wow food is always shared with everyone present.

Sacred Fire

The Sacred Fire is sometimes lit with two logs placed in the form of a cross and the ends pointing in the four directions. Sacred events, like the annual Indian Ecumenical Council that began in 1970 on the Crow Agency in Montana, will feature a sacred fire scheduled to burn throughout the entire ten-day event. The fire symbolizes the maintenance of a unifying spirit throughout the on goings of an important occasion.

Words for fire occur 450 times in the Bible with both literal and figurative meanings. Many uses of fire could be considered domestic, but fire also had figurative or spiritual uses such as Divine presence, holiness, glory, guidance, and protection (Ezekiel 1:4, 13, 27; 8:2). The prophet, Isaiah (29:6), employed the term in connection with purification and testing, Jeremiah (20:9) referred to its prophetic and inspirational use, and Job (5:7) used fire as symbolic in relation to trouble, suffering, and affliction.

Sacred Objects

Sacred Objects often originate in a dream or vision, and usually symbolize an animal, bird, plant, fish, or other life form. The symbols are also realized in the form of animal parts such as feathers, claws, beaks, hides, quills, bones, or shells. Some of the objects that are important to the carrying out of special ceremonies include plants such as tobacco, sage, and cedar, as well as other objects like eagle feathers, medicine bags, crystals and stones (Ross and Gould, 2006, p. 154).

There are often restrictions in place as to what constitutes appropriate behavior in the presence of sacred objects. This practice easily finds a parallel in Old Testament history as depicted in the Ark of the Covenant described earlier.

Sacred Sites

Sacred sites are places where spiritual events took place, or take place, such as a successful vision quest. Sacred sites can be located on mountains, in lakes, piles of rocks, unusually shaped mounds, burial grounds, ceremonial grounds, and even caves. These are places where it is believed that spirits visit. The Sundance site is always regarded as sacred and there are restrictions in place as to required behavior on the site when it is visited. Spirit visitations are rare at times when the Sundance is not being celebrated.

It was very much customary in Old Testament times to establish sacred sites by building altars to commemorate sacred happenings. Noah was probably the first to build an altar, which he did after the Great Flood had subsided (Genesis 8:20), and Abraham followed suit after God called him to the "promised land" (Genesis 12:7). Jacob established a scared site at Bethel after successfully wrestling with an angel (Genesis 28:19-22). Moses built an altar after he received confirmation of his covenant with God (Exodus 24:4-6), and his successor, Joshua did the same a little later on (Joshua 8:30-32). Archaeologists have identified many altar objects in Palestine, built by the generations that followed Moses and Joshua, indicating that the practice of building altars was widespread.

Shaman

Shaman is a rather unfortunate label invented by non-Native explorers and researchers to describe the role of spiritual leaders in Indigenous communities (see chapter ten on *ecclesiastical offices*).

Sundance

The Sundance, also called the Thirst Dance, is the most sacred of Plains Aboriginal ceremonies, and was traditionally held during the summer months when nomadic tribes of the same kin met to celebrate, exchange news, and perform the sacred event. Among member tribes of the Blackfoot Confederacy, a highly respected woman sponsored the Sundance. The Sundance grounds consist of four concentric circles, with the scared lodge in the very center. It was, and sometimes still is in this sacred lodge that respected elders preside, and open scared medicine bundles. Although tribal perceptions vary, it might be safe to say that essentially the Sundance is considered to be a celebration of life and thanksgiving.

The Sundance was outlawed by Canada' federal government in the latter part of the 19th century because the piercing ceremony that was practiced by some tribes, was considered cruel and barbaric. As a result a great deal of public misunderstanding of the event occurred. Informed perceptions of the Sundance are gradually increasing, but because Indigenous people are reluctant to talk about the various sacred activities associated with the Sundance, this situation will probably continue for a while.

Sweat-lodge

The sweat-lodge is basically a cleansing ritual, usually conducted before participating in a Sundance or other important event. Some individuals regularly "bathe" in a sweat-lodge as a means of enjoying perpetual cleansing of the body, mind, and spirit. A typical Cree sweat-lodge ceremony consists of four rounds lasting about ten minutes each. Water is poured over hot rocks to make steam, and participants will experience a vigorous cleansing process. Four prayers are said in each segment of the four rounds, the first, as thanksgiving for life; the second, for all participants in the ceremony; the third, for oneself only; and, the fourth again for thanksgiving and a request that all participants have a safe journey home.

The sweat-lodge itself consists of quite complex symbolism (Bruchac, 1993). The lodge, which represents the womb of Mother Earth, is made of bent willow branches, covered with animal hide. The number and shape of the rocks that are heated outside the lodge and carefully located inside the lodge itself in a special order, that may have appeared to the builder of the sweat-lodge in a dream or vision. Each rock may represent a particular characteristic and must therefore be placed in the order in which the dream indicated. It is commonly believed that when individuals engage in a sweat-lodge ceremony with pure hearts, they will feel renewed and uplifted. On the other hand, if they enter the lodge with negative feelings or ill will towards anyone, they may leave the ceremony and become ill.

Teepee Designs

Teepee Designs, which often feature various creatures, have or had their origin from a dream or vision that the originator perceived. The power of the designs can be transferred to another individual provided an authorized elder preforms an appropriate ceremony and related protocol is followed.

Vision Quest

Vision Quest is a ritual still practiced by young men among Plains Aboriginal Nations, and in some communities it is now permitted for young women to participate. As described elsewhere in this book, a vision quest consists of an ordeal of testing during which the individual spends four days and four nights on a hillside or other similar site, without food or water, and through prayer seeks a vision from the Creator. Elders play a significant role in the planning, and execution of a vision quest in preparing, pre-briefing, and debriefing the seeker.

Both the Old and New Testaments include records of individuals being recipients of visions and/or spiritual dreams, although these appear to have occurred without a great deal of preparation or protocol.

It is important to understand that cultural parallels drawn here are just that—they are parallels. They imply nothing by way of historical connection or causality, but they can assist serious researchers in understanding and perhaps appreciating the deep spiritual orientation of North America's Indigenous peoples.

The purpose of this discussion has been simply to show that traditional spiritual practices of North America's First Peoples were in essence similar to those introduced by North America's first European visitors. Unfortunately, the newcomers were not trained to understand cultural similarities and/or differences, or perhaps they were too much in a hurry to exploit local resources that they did not take time to note the similarities outlined above. Today, a real opportunity is available to correct a serious error in unwarranted cultural assessment.

CHAPTER TEN

Ecclesiology: What Is the Nature of
Spiritual Leadership?

The New Testament makes it clear that there is a distinct difference between secular forms of leadership and that exercised in the church (Richards and Martin, 1981, p. 297). Secular rulers reign over nations and states and boldly exercise authority over them, while Christian leaders are supposed to follow the model of servanthood. To illustrate: in the 25th chapter of Matthew's Gospel, the mother of Jesus' disciples, James and John, comes to the Lord and asks a special favor. This eager mother wants Jesus to assure her that after the resurrection, Jesus will grant her sons a special privilege when they get to heaven. She asks that one of her sons be seated to the left of Jesus' throne, and the other on the right. In response to the request, Jesus quickly calls his twelve disciples together and explains His position on servanthood:

> You know that the rulers of the Gentiles lord it over them, and their high officials exercise authority over them. Not so with you. Instead, whoever wants to be great among you must be your servant, and whoever wants to be first must be your slave—just as the Son of Man did not come to be served, but to serve, and to give his life as a ransom for many (Matthew 20:25b-28).

Based on this Scripture passage, church leaders are not to function by exerting power, but rather by acting as servants to the people they have been charged to govern. In short, church leaders are to spend their lives ministering to others, and their role is to be accentuated by humility, obedience, gracious modeling, and submission. In addition, the Apostle James makes it clear that those who *do* choose to take up a form of church leadership may be subject to harsh criticism. In his words;

> Not many of you should become teachers, my fellow
> believers, because you know that we who teach will
> be judged more strictly. We all stumble in many ways.
> Anyone who is never at fault in what they say is perfect,
> able to keep their whole body in check (James 3:1-2).

James does not seem to hold out much hope that perfection in leadership roles will occur, and points out that the human tongue has the potential to be a vital negative ingredient in this context. This is potentially a real challenge for leaders since they are frequently expected to speak out, model ideal behavior, and propose exemplary forms of behavior. James warns that words spoken at the wrong time or misinterpreted can cause damage analogous to an immense fire. He also likens the tongue to a horse's bridle, a small instrument that can sway the direction of a two thousand pound animal. Similarly, like a tiny spark at first, the tongue can ignite an entire forest fire that may burn millions of acres of forestland to the ground.

Old Testament Examples

One of Israel's Old Testament leaders, Nehemiah, knew whereof he spoke. Nehemiah had the task of leading a group of Israelites back to their homeland in 536 BC, after the seventy-year Babylonian captivity ended. A major challenge for the returnees was to rebuild the city of Jerusalem, particularly the temple. On arrival in the homeland, Nehemiah and his followers immediately experienced a great deal of opposition from Samaritan Jews who were Jews that were somehow missed by the invading Babylonians and had not been taken into captivity. These individuals, now called Samaritans, had remained in the motherland. After seventy years of being left alone to develop a separate identity and lifestyle, they strongly resented the return of their former brothers and sisters (Malphurs, 2004, p. 177). With this mindset, the Samaritans determined to scuttle everything that Nehemiah and his colleagues tried to do. They used tactics such as ridicule (Nehemiah 2:19; 4:1-6), conspiracy (4:7-10), spreading false rumors (4:11-12), and intimidation (6:13). Despite these various forms of opposition, Nehemiah and his cohorts persisted in rebuilding their former homes and temple, and in due course celebrated their success in a public ceremony (Nehemiah 8:1). The Bible describes the service of thanksgiving that was finally possible:

> All the people came together as one in the square before the Water Gate. They told Ezra the teacher of the Law to bring out the Book of the Law of Moses, which the Lord had commanded for Israel…. Ezra praised the Lord, the great God; and all the people lifted their hands and responded, "Amen! Amen!"… Then Nehemiah the governor, Ezra the priest and teacher of the Law, and the Levites who were instructing the people said to them all, "This day is holy to the Lord your God" (Nehemiah 8:1, 6a, 9a).

It seems somewhat ironic that the two communities—Jews and Samaritans, once closely related by blood, could demonstrate such intense dislike one toward one other. A unique form of sibling jealousy had evolved, but quite characteristic of human nature in other contexts. Nehemiah, as leader became a special object of attack. Based on this incident it would seem that in biblical times religious leadership was not necessarily something to be sought after.

Poor Moses, the well-known Israelite leader, suffered a similar unfortunate experience when his brother Aaron, and his sister Miriam, verbally attacked him for having married outside the faith (Numbers 12:1-2). In this example, Moses had just led the tribe safely through another section of the desert, having successfully appealed to God to provide the nation with needed food (quail). Later, he had to deal with two individuals who were prophesying without authorization. At that point his siblings, Miriam and Aaron attacked his leadership, and there were consequences. For her part in the affair, Moses' sister Miriam was stricken with a disease and banished from the camp for seven days (Numbers 12:15).

The concept of leadership has many synonyms, depending on context; for example, consider the following terms—administrator, chief, commander, director, elder, foreman, guide, guru, head, judge, manager, master, mentor, peacemaker, pathfinder, prophet, supervisor, trailblazer, and so on. The Old Testament seems to prefer the terms "judge, prophet," or "elder" in a spiritual context, while North American Aboriginal communities traditionally settled for the term elder. Analysis will show that the office of Aboriginal elder can further be broken down into several sub-classifications.

In the Old Testament, the office of judge was often seen to be a temporary post, depending on the political or economic status of the community. Many judges were deliverers in times of war, while others administered justice to the people from special places at the gates of cities (Exodus 18:13-14). Although Moses initially served his people as a lone judge at the city gates, eventually a council of seventy was appointed which met regularly to decide on tribal matters (Numbers 11:16). Of greater interest, however, is the role that individual judges and prophets played in the Old Testament.

Following the career of a number of Old Testament judges (or elders) may be accomplished alphabetically, as well as by any other approach, basically, because their mandates were so diverse, often depending on personality traits. The Book of Judges chronicles many of their deeds and misdeeds, although others are described in 1 and 2 Samuel, 1 and 2 Kings, and 1 and 2 Chronicles. The list of leaders includes: Abimelech, Balaam (previously mentioned), Barak, Deborah, Ehud, Eli, Elijah, Elisha, Gideon, Jair, Jephthah, Micah, Nathan, Othniel, Samson, Samuel, Shamgar, and Tola. When Saul, the first King of Israel was anointed, the role of elder diminished somewhat in status, but there were some religious leaders who still exercised judgment at the risk of being banished by regal authorities. The list would include Elijah, Elisha, and Nathan. A brief survey of the more important elders should set the stage for a similar explication of the role of Native American elders. The following discourse will expand on the professional activities of Elijah, Elisha, Nathan, Gideon, Samuel, and Samson.

Elijah held office during the reign of kings Ahab and Ahaziah, 875 to 850 BC, and was probably best known for his theological disagreements with King Ahab and his wicked wife, Jezebel. At one point, Jezebel influenced Ahab to seize the vineyard of a certain landowner named Naboth, who was then falsely accused of blasphemy and summarily executed (1 Kings 21). Elijah bravely took up this matter with King Ahab. On another occasion Elijah also faced Ahab about an impending drought (1 Kings 18:2), and a battle of religious loyalties ensued—Jehovah against Baal, a god whom Jezebel introduced. Whose God would ignite an altar fire to prove ultimate power—Jehovah or Baal? Not surprisingly, Jehovah triumphed, yet Elijah was forced to flee for his life. Being human, at one point he felt so despondent that he asked the Lord to take his life (1 Kings 19:4-5). He was subsequently instructed to appoint Elisha as his successor, and reminded by God that he was not alone in his faith. God informed him that there were still seven thousand people in Israel who had not bowed down to Baal (1 Kings 19:18). Typical of his career, Elijah faithfully served the Lord and confronted anyone in authority who ignored or disobeyed the word of the Lord God.

Elisha's career also involved dealing with political authorities, this time with Naaman, a foreign leader who had contracted the dreaded disease of leprosy. Probably best known for working miracles, at one point Elisha was approached by the servant of Naaman, commissioner-in-chief of the Syrian army about possible healing for his superior (2 Kings 5). Naaman had heard about Elisha's gift of healing from an un-named Jewish servant girl, and decided to seek him out. When Naaman's servant reported Elisha's recommended form of cure for Naaman, that is, to dip seven times in the muddy Jordan River, Naaman became annoyed and went off in a rage. His servant begged him to reconsider, and when Naaman reluctantly chose to follow Elisha's advice, he was healed, and promptly wanted to reward Elisha. Elisha refused, of course, making certain that Naaman understood that his healing was a gift from Jehovah God, not from Elisha personally. Gehazi, Elisha's servant, felt differently, and she arranged to receive gifts for Elisha, allegedly on Elisha's behalf. When Elisha discovered this, and confronted his disobedient servant, Gehazi himself was stricken with leprosy. After faithfully serving his office for sixty-six years, Elisha died in his own house (2 Kings 13:14-20).

Nathan was still another Israelite prophet/elder, who found himself tangling with regal authority. This time it was with King David. It seems King David had fallen in love with another man's wife—the beguiling Bathsheba who one day took a bath within view of David's palace window (2 Samuel 11:1-14). David took Bathsheba in, then arranged for Bathsheba's husband, Uriah, to die by having him placed at the front of the Israeli army. Uriah conveniently died, and David added Bathsheba to his harem. In due course, David and Bathsheba had a son, and at that point Nathan the prophet took a risk and confronted the evil-doing king. He began by telling the king a story about a rich man who owned herds of sheep but still insisted on taking his neighbor's only lamb from him. David immediately became angry with the man in the tale and threatened to make the evil-doer pay four times for his misdeed. At that point Nathan pointed his finger at King David and uttered the accusing words, "You are the man!" (2 Samuel 12:7). He then informed the king that the child he had with Bathsheba would die, and although David very sorrowfully repented of his sin, the child *did* die.

Another religious Israelite leader, Gideon, essentially served the Israeli nation as a war leader, although he did not necessarily desire to take on that role. One day Gideon was secretly threshing grain when an angel appeared to him and asked him to defend the Israelites against the Midianites, the dreaded enemy of Israel (Judges 6:11). Gideon reluctantly did so, but not before he put God to the test. He wanted to be certain that he was being called to the role of war chief, so he asked that his request for a miracle or two be granted. The miracles were granted and so Gideon gathered an army of three hundred men who subsequently defeated the much larger Midian army. Then there was peace in the land for forty years. At one point the Israelites asked Gideon to rule over them (Judges 8:22), but he steadfastly refused. Israel enjoyed peaceful living conditions during Gideon's entire lifetime.

The prophet Samuel, chosen to his office while still a young boy, probably had the toughest job of them all when his peers told him they were weary of being guided by tribal elders and they now wanted a king to rule over them. One of the reasons for the desire to have a king may have stemmed from the fact that Samuel appointed two of his sons, Joel and Abijah as judges, and they did not walk in his ways (1 Samuel 8:3). After committing the matter to prayer, Samuel rested in the thought that the nation was rejecting God, not himself as prophet. Samuel tried to talk the people out of wanting a king to rule over them, but they insisted. This is part of what Samuel's argument against appointing a king.

> This is what the king who will reign over you will claim as his rights: He will take your sons and make them serve with his chariots and horses, and they will run in front of his chariots. Some he will assign to be commanders of thousands and commanders of fifties, and others to plow his ground and reap his harvest, and still others to make weapons of war and equipment for his chariots. He will take your daughters to be perfumers and cooks and bakers. When that day comes, you will cry out for relief from the king you have chosen, but the Lord will not answer you in that day (1 Samuel 8:10-13, 18).

Despite Samuel's warning, the people were in no mood to accept his advice, and somehow Samuel got the idea that God was permitting Israel to have a king, perhaps as a means of teaching them a lesson about leadership.

As it turned out, Israel was no more obedient to God under the leadership of a king than they were under the guidance of elders, judges, or prophets. In the meantime, Samuel anointed Saul, a tall Benjamite, as king. Saul could hardly believe his good fortune. He protested, of course, but gradually learned to enjoy his new role. When he later felt more confident and powerful, he began to disobey God's voice, and Samuel was instructed by God to anoint David, a shepherd boy as the next king. Saul became very angry when he heard about this, and eventually pursued David with the intent to put him to death. Samuel passed on while Saul was hunting down David. The scripture records his death as follows: "Now Samuel died, and *all Israel assembled and mourned for him*; and they buried him at his home in Ramah" (1 Samuel 25:1, italics mine). Saul did not fare as well; in fact, he died at his own hand when he threw himself on his sword in battle (1 Samuel 31:4).

Last, but not least, our survey takes us to the life of Samson who served as a judge in Israel for twenty years (Judges 15:20). Samson possessed special spiritual gifts (Judges 13:5), and proved himself to be victorious against his enemies even as his life ended (Judges 16:23-31). Even though he was a capable leader, Samson's downfall was to fall in love with Delilah, a prostitute from an enemy camp. Delilah eventually sold Samson out to the Philistines, Israel's seemingly perpetual enemy (Judges 16:18).

Samson's extraordinary powers originated with a Nazirite vow he had taken never to cut his hair. When Delilah inquired as to Samson's unusual strength, he kept putting her off with jokes and fibs, but she persisted on knowing the truth. When Samson finally gave in to Delilah's pestering and told her the truth, she cut off his hair while he was sleeping and then alerted his enemies. Samson was imprisoned and ridiculed, but prevailed against the enemy in his final days. Like other leaders, spiritual, legal, or judicial, Samson proved that giving in to human weaknesses is a perpetual threat to men and women of any status.

Although our survey has featured only men in the role of spiritual and judicial leaders, Israel also honored women in that office. A case in point is Deborah, who served primarily as a prophetess (Judges 4:4). She was preceded in that role by Aaron's sister, Miriam (Exodus 15:20), and succeeded by Huldah (2 Kings 22:14; 2 Chronicles 34:22), and an unnamed prophetess cited in Isaiah 8:3.

New Testament Examples

It is important to note that the entire Old Testament prophetic movement must be viewed as preparatory to the coming of the

Messiah. With the arrival of Jesus the Christ, many Old Testament prophecies were fulfilled. The New Testament role of prophet basically appears to have been assigned to the writer of the Apocalypse— the Book of Revelation. A number of references to prophets appear, for example in Ephesians 2:20, 3:5, and 4:11. In terms of church hierarchy, they ranked second, next to apostles (1 Corinthians 12:28). In addition, the Book of Acts refers to prophets (Acts 11:27-30; 13:1-4, and 15:32). Prophetesses are specifically mentioned with regard to Anna, who worked in the temple when Jesus was dedicated (Luke 2:36) and the four daughters of Philip the Evangelist who had the gift of prophesy (Acts 21:9).

Indigenous Orientation

The office of elder in its various dimensions was held in very high esteem in traditional Indigenous societies, although a variety of other leadership positions were also in place. Many Aboriginal Nations functioned with hereditary chiefs, male or female, while others had clan mothers who had power to assign and/or depose of chiefs and band council members. In some tribes the office of temporary chief was established, those individuals operating in a special capacity "until the job was done." These included war chiefs, hunting chiefs or, as the Plateau First People had it, temporary salmon chiefs who functioned in that capacity until the fishing season was over. The late Joseph Couture described the status of the various kinds of elders:

> I am of the opinion that elders are the superb embodiments of highly developed human potential. They exemplify the kind of person which a traditional, culturally-based learning environment can and does form and mold.... Further signs of elderhood are found in their level of trust of both life itself and their own experiences, by being into true feelings (i.e., into the spiritual side of things, without sentimen-

tality), by the art of being still, unafraid of darkness and nothingness, by the ability to laugh at one another, as well as at self (Couture, 1991a, pp. 207-208).

When the European explorers arrived in North America they encountered a variety of Indigenous people with well-developed cultures whose participants had resided on the continent for centuries. During that time, Indigenous people had invented and maintained finely tuned political institutions that were quite successful in keeping order and promoting social harmony. The arrival of the Europeans posed a new kind of challenge and greatly affected locally formulated social structures and organization. Like most Indigenous cultures in other lands, various Native North American Nations had in place a system of hereditary leadership with built-in checks and balances to provide for any glitch in operation. Training for leadership positions, like most other important roles, was done by elders—men and women who were recognized in their communities for their wisdom and knowledge, or who had handed down to them the right to perform special ceremonies through an apprentice system. As Macfarlan (1968, p. 50) observes;

> Like other Native political institutions, the process of anointing leaders drew much of its strength from its flexibility. If the youth showed that he did not have the mettle for the job, he could be passed over and someone else would be found to fill the role.

Traditionally, there were elders who predominantly filled the role of teachers because of their experience and knowledge and their symbolic link to the past. This role has never been completely abandoned, but when the Europeans arrived, the pressures of yielding to imported institutional practices and value systems compelled the system of eldership to go underground. Some public rituals and ceremonies traditionally presided over by elders were banned by governments and forced these leaders to practice their skills in secret. As a result, many valued beliefs and practices were lost and respect afforded the office of elder dissipated.

Today the scene is slowly changing, and both Aboriginals and non-Aboriginals are seeking out ways to reactivate and access Indigenous wisdom. Couture (1991a, p. 202) noted that elders are making a comeback and are being "hammered back into the woodwork" of Indigenous spiritual life. The good news is that although elders have been reticent and most discreet about sharing and teaching their knowledge, today those same elders point to an unfolding prophecy, which states that "...the time has come to share the secrets" (Couture, 1991a, p. 202). As Joe Crowshoe, a Piikani elder observed; "Some tribes say they don't want white people at ceremonies. Well, that's not sharing or communicating. The world is changing, and now is the time to reveal much of what was once considered secret" (as cited in Couture, 1991a, p. 201).

Some Aboriginal spokespersons, like Pam Colorado, a Wisconsin Oneida of the Iroquois Confederacy, are actively promoting a synthesis of Indigenous and EuroAmerican scientific knowledge (Colorado, 1988, p. 57). This would suggest that Native elders and EuroAmerican scientists try to collaborate. Success in this pursuit could provide science with a much-needed spiritual base. According to the Indigenous tradition, the search for truth and learning is essentially a spiritual relationship between an individual and the Great Spirit. Some Aboriginal educators think otherwise. Marie Battiste, a Mi'kmaq educator, and James Henderson, a Chickasaw educator, argue that indigenous knowledge is intellectual property and belongs solely to the Aboriginal community. They suggest that:

> ...the first concern of Indigenous peoples is their
> right not to sell, commoditize, or have expropriated
> from them certain domains of knowledge and cer-

tain sacred knowledge of current use, previous use, and/or potential use of plant and animal species, as well as soil and minerals; knowledge of preparation, processing, or storage of useful species... (Battiste & Henderson, 2000, p. 70).

Perhaps Battiste and Henderson are overly cautious about exclusive ownership of spiritual knowledge since the concept of exclusivity was never entrenched in traditional Aboriginal societies. Historically, if anyone had access to resources of any kind—spiritual or otherwise, they would be expected to share them with their community. This was particularly true of the resources and benefits of Mother Earth. The resources of Mother Earth could not be owned and her bestowals were for everyone to enjoy. As Nez Perce Chief Joseph put it, "All men were made by the same Great Spirit Chief. They are all brothers. The earth is the mother of us all, and all people should have equal rights upon it" (as cited in Friesen, 1998, p. 45).

The Elder Phenomenon

It appears to be standard procedure that every religious configuration features a leadership stratum occupied by individuals who are respected because they possess vital knowledge of their cultural workings and therefore have authorization to lead or perform related rituals and ceremonies. In certain contexts these individuals are also considered experts on life. Generally known as elders, these selected individuals were traditionally charged with the complex responsibility of carrying forth to the next generation the valued beliefs, traditions, and practices of their respective tribes.

Today elderly people per se are generally treated with respect in many Native American communities, but not all are regarded as spiritual elders. Native cultures fully realize that elderly people commonly have valuable knowledge to share about their life experiences, but only a few have specialized knowledge about the workings of the cosmos that uniquely equips them to provide counsel to their communities (Knudtson and Suzuki, 1992, pp. 179-180). These individuals usually have a deep abiding humility and reverence for life and the natural world. They generally fulfill their teaching roles as facilitators and guides. Today, as historically, these individuals see their mandate as one of guiding their people toward a better knowledge of their rituals and growth processes. That knowledge might then help their people become more aware of themselves as well as the natural world, its workings, and their place within it.

Indigenous spiritual rituals are presided over by elders who are recognized to have the proper authority. They have also received a kind of formalized community approval, but differ from other elders who possess other gifts. Consistent with the "vagueness" or elusiveness of the oral tradition, some elders, like "wisdom elders," are not elected or appointed, nor do they have special training for their task. They simply "emerge over time" and their community informally recognizes their role, particularly their talent for giving guidance, when it is sought. A certain generalization often pervades Native communities when they make reference to the observation, "our elders have told us" (Retzlaff, 2008, p. 337).

In some tribes, there is an observable, definite process by which certain individuals become elders. An individual's motivation to take up that role could have been sparked by a personal, spiritual, or political event or events that turned them back to the traditional way. As Stiegelbauer (1996, p. 47) points out, such experiences may motivate individuals to take up the task of learning tribal teachings and ceremonies in an active and involved way by practicing them. The community may in turn call upon these individuals to "give those teachings back." It is through that process become recognized as teaching elders. However, their corollary experiences, outside of learning those teachings, may also contribute to their ability to help others rediscover their culture and regain the "good life of health."

The identification and verification of eldership rests with each local Aboriginal community, although elders may develop their stature through interaction with their neighbors. The people who respect them and come to them for guidance reinforce their status and gifts. The current resurgence of interest in seeking direction from this special source is evident among many North American tribes today and comprises a strong indication of the increasing importance of the role and the vitality of these individuals (Lincoln, 1985; Couture, 1991b). In recent years elders have been invited to participate in Aboriginal organizational structures while continuing to counsel troubled youth on an individual basis (Medicine, 1987, p. 148). It might be too much to hope, but it would be encouraging to discover a genuine intrigue on the part of both Native and non-Native observers to share in this revival.

When the Europeans first became acquainted with the various cultural configurations of Native North American Nations, they did not appreciate the nuances of the office of shamans (as they were called by incoming observers), particularly the belief that some shamans were perceived as having strong supernatural powers. Also dubbed "medicine men" or "medicine women" by the newcomers, locals believed that elders' powers went far beyond the arena of healing. They were seen as being able to establish direct contact with the spirit world or themselves be possessed by the spirit. Individuals in the tribe approached these elders about such matters as seeking success on a hunt, determining time for planting crops, or seeking good fortune in war. A related position in some tribes was the office of counseling elder held by certain senior members of the community. These individuals had lived long, full lives, learned the way of Mother Earth, and survived a myriad of experiences valued by the tribe. They were viewed as sources of tribal knowledge and wisdom. They were consulted for advice on matters, listened to, and usually heeded, even though their wisdom was not imposed on anyone.

In some tribes elders held memberships in what have been called sacred (or secret) societies, dedicated to specific spiritual purposes within the tribe. These operated much like the religious orders committed to specific purposes within certain Christian denominations. Members of sacred societies, like the Horn Society in the Blackfoot (Kainai) First Nation, were believed to have special spiritual powers and they were feared and respected by their compatriots. Even today, for example, individuals, even elders, are not to walk in front of a Horn member, lest the power of the Horn members affect them (Taylor, 1989).

At one point in the mid nineteenth century the Montana Blackfeet had seven age-graded men's societies in their religious structure, the youngest being called the "Mosquitos," and the oldest, the "Buffalo Bulls" (Ewers, 1989, p. 105). When the older members of the latter group passed away their secrets died with them and a new society, the "Pigeons" (or "Doves") was organized. As a new society, however, it held the lowest rank among the seven. To make things more complicated, the members of these societies also belonged to different hunting bands that were only active during the summer months. At times, the head chief of the summer camp would call on one or two of the societies to police the camp and the summer hunt. Each society performed its unique ceremony during the Sundance.

Arrangements regarding spiritual structuring were not unique to the Blackfoot Confederacy. Many Woodland First Nations also operated sodalities or secret societies whose members (elders) were holders of special spiritual knowledge involving charms, rituals, prayers, and songs. The Great Lakes Ojibway region was home to one such organization known as the "Midewiwin" (Underhill, 1965, p. 92). Nanabush (the trickster), by order of the Great Spirit, apparently started the society. The Midewiwin was somewhat unique to the Ojibway, the Menomini, and the Winnibego. Basically, it was a society of wonder workers and an individual could be admitted to membership only if he had been recipient of a vision. After being apprenticed, the initiate would be instructed by a chosen member in herbal lore and spiritual traditions.

The Midewiwin was organized in eight ranked levels. The higher an individual ascended in the ranks, the greater the cost of membership. Few individuals ever achieved the highest rank, but if they did they were seen to possess extraordinary spiritual powers and were greatly respected. A special function of the Midewiwin was to sponsor healing services. If an individual became ill, he or she might request help from the society (Taylor, 1994, pp. 332-333). At that point the individual became a member of the society and rendered remuneration for the privilege.

The formal societies of the Native North American Nations played an important role in preserving and passing on ceremonial and spiritual knowledge. During the years when governments banned certain religious practices, these societies took them underground until it was safe to reveal them again. Today, a revival of these practices has fairly well spread throughout all Native North American communities.

Classifications of Eldership

There are self-proclaimed Aboriginal prophets who claim that the Native Way holds a key, if not *the* key to the future survival of mankind (Couture, 1991a). Elders are definitely the most important link in this formula because they alone have access to the knowledge that may save Mother Earth from being extinguished. Fortunately, elders are currently being sought out for healing and inspiration, and the interpretation of past and present events. Battiste (2000, p. 201) emphasizes that elders are a critical link to Aboriginal epistemology primarily through their knowledge of Indigenous languages. The last vestiges of Aboriginal languages exist in the hearts and minds of Indigenous elders.

In the days before European contact, an individual's role in the community had to be recognized and affirmed by elders. Indian males, for example, were often recognized for their talents as hunters, warriors, or guides, but before they could be formally executed these enterprises required a form of spiritual confirmation. This enactment was the responsibility of the elder whose office was not one of appointment but of informal recognition. The late Beatrice Medicine (1987, p. 141), herself a Lakota Sioux elder, explained that elders are "... those people who have earned the respect of their own community and who are looked upon as elders in their own society."

As previously indicated, it is important to differentiate several kinds of functions fulfilled by elders in traditional Aboriginal societies. A wide range of gifts was recognized in relation to that office. Elders were generally perceived as individuals who had special insights pertaining to medicines, leadership, spiritual knowledge, or other areas. In order to maintain cultural and spiritual continuity, some elders, particularly those who had special knowledge about the healing arts or ritualistic practice, might apprentice to themselves young people who would hopefully inculcate this special knowledge through an unspecified period of time, on a one-to-one basis. That way the unique gift of knowledge held by the elder would safely be transmitted to the next generation. The elders referred to by Medicine (1987) were men and women of wisdom or counselors, so designated because they demonstrated unique insights, and could offer relevant, insightful prophetic utterances. Meili (1992, p. xi) describes her experiences in consulting with such elders:

> I was impressed by their prophetic vision. They taught me that I am part of God, so I could stop my

search in trying to find Him/Her in someone else.... the Great Spirit, or life, or God (whatever you consider to be the highest), is love and always says yes if we seek it and try to live good lives. The elders collectively taught me that things have a spirit and gently influenced me to give up the search for personal enlightenment and gain. I need to love, trust, and learn from all my relations.

Since the office of elder is being revived and strengthened, the functions of the office have recently been magnified and expanded. Today elders are being called upon to help communities with decisions regarding everything from education and health issues to community development and self-government (O'Brien, 1989, p. 26). Others are involved in developing "culture-based" programs, language instruction, and locally approved school curricula. Still others have become active planners and decision-makers in education (Castellano, Davis, and Lahache, 2000, p. 98). It has been concluded that elders can offer input that takes the minds of their apprentices beyond the walls of the classroom. "Such strategy provides the community with contact with tradition, traditional beliefs, ceremonies and experiences, and a philosophy unique to First Nations cultures" (Stiegelbauer, 1996, p. 40).

Today, rapid changes are affecting the role of elders, as large numbers of Indigenous people leave their reserves and relocate to urban areas. Many elders have moved to cities and towns along with their families. There they have carved out a unique niche for themselves as ritualists, healers, consultants, and counselors. Some elders even make house calls in response to individual or family requests for counseling or prayers. Once again, as is typical of their history, elders have demonstrated an ingenious ability to change with the times. These changes, however, have only affected their geographic location, not their spirituality. Perhaps the time will come when the non-Native world seeks out the kind of advice that Aboriginal elders can offer to a needy world.

Elder Sayings

Psychologist and Cree elder, the late Joseph Couture (1991a, p. 205ff.), pointed out that elders often serve as mediaries or spiritual therapists in assisting seekers to grasp the Divinely designated roles they should play in this life. In some capacities and appropriate contexts, elders today engage in humor or metaphor as a means of getting their point across. For example, consider the following elder sayings (Friesen, 1998).

> Don't worry. Take it easy. Do your best. It will all work out. Respect life. Respect your elders. It's up to you. You have all the answers within you…. Listen to what Mother Earth tells you. Speak with her. She will speak to you (Couture, 1991a, p. 205).

> It just seems to a lot of Indians that this continent was a lot better off when we were running it. --Vine Deloria, Jr., Lakota Sioux First Nation.

> And then we started to learn about money. People kill for that. A lot of Indians spend money the day they get it...it makes us do things we're not supposed to do. I always say, Indians were not born with money. We were born with animals. —Maggie Black Kettle, Siksika (Blackfoot) First Nation.

> I am proud to be an Eskimo, but I think we can improve on the igloo as a permanent dwelling. —Abraham Okip, Inuit First Nation.

Believe it or not, the Indian had to learn the white man's language to break the first commandment. In the Indian language we have no profane words. --Chief Dan Kennedy (Ochankuhahe), Assiniboine First Nation.

I am not as American as those whose ancestors came over on the Mayflower, but we met them at the boat when they landed. --Will Rogers, Cherokee Nation.

If the Great Spirit wanted man to stay in one place he would have made the world stand still. --Chief Flying Hawk, Oglala Sioux Nation.

Native elders often also play an interpretive role as the following recommendation by the late Charlie Blackman, an elder of the Chipewyan Nation, reveals (Couture, 1991a, p. 205).

On a given day, if you ask me where you might go to find a moose, I will say, "If you go that way you won't find a moose. But, if you go that way, you will." So now, you younger ones, think about that. Come back once in a while and show us what you've got. And we'll tell you if what you think you have found is a moose. -- Charlie Blackman, Chipewyan elder.

In pondering the latter saying, it becomes evident that the pursuit of the "moose" metaphorically represents the individual's search for personal meaning, purpose, and destiny. Initially, an individual may seek out an elder for guidance regarding a potential direction to undertake in seeking personal fulfillment regarding a life goal. The elder invites seekers to check in from time to time in order to help them evaluate whether or not they are indeed "on the moose's trail."

Perhaps the most appropriate way to end this chapter is with an elder saying by Chief John Snow outlining the potentiality of Native wisdom.

> And so I say to you, the EuroCanadians, you have discovered our land and its resources, but you have not yet discovered my people, nor our teachings, nor the spiritual basis of our teachings (cited in Friesen, 1998, p. 60).

Today many Plains Aboriginal communities continue to revive their traditional spiritual beliefs and practices. Many of them finding strength through a renewed sense of cultural awareness. Their perception of the Great Spirit includes the provision of a warm reception to those who wish to decipher their perspectives.

I count myself blessed in being part of that company.

CHAPTER ELEVEN

Eschatology: What Happens After Death?
Is There a Future Life?

For God so loved the world that he gave his one and only Son, that whoever believes in him shall not perish but have eternal life –John 3:16

But whoever lives by the truth comes into the light, so that it may be seen plainly that what they have done has been done in the sight of God—John 3:21

The time came when the beggar died and the angels carried him to Abraham's side—Luke 16:22

Christian Perceptions of the Afterlife

Death is an inevitable part of human existence, and every nation and culture has in place a series of enactments appropriate to commemorating human passing. While the ceremonies and rituals pertaining to death often vary in format and intensity, no one really knows what happens after an individual dies. This fact has not hindered some theologians from speculating about the hereafter, and indeed some have worked out quite elaborate schemes outlining the various activities they perceive will occur after death.

There are basically two views in Christian theology as to what occurs when individuals die, one being that if these individuals have lived a righteous Christian life, they will immediately be admitted to heaven (Philippians 1:23). Conversely, after death, the wicked will immediately migrate to the gates of hell.

The second view postulates that after death individuals remain in soul sleep until the end of the age when Jesus Christ returns to earth and awakens the righteous dead and admits them to heaven (1 Thessalonians 4:17).

For further debate on soul sleep, one might look at thoughts by some Evangelical theologians who are opposed to this view. Evangelical theologians like Fitzwater (1953), Thiessen (1959), and Strong (1956) denounced soul sleep on the basis that God's judgment occurs immediately after death.

More liberal theologians have always left the question open as to God's judgment of human behavior after death. Some nineteenth century liberal theologians acknowledged apocalyptic references in the New Testament, but dismissed those statements as unimportant appendages to the true message of Jesus. Instead, they concentrated on the eternal truths that Jesus taught, as well as His impressive personage. Crossan (2007, p. 78) argues that notions about the end of the world predicted in the Bible may actually be misunderstood. He points out that the passages in Matthew 13:39 and Matthew 13:49, and Matthew 24:3 and Matthew 24:20, which refer to the "end of the world," actually have reference to a specified period of time. Following Crossan's logic, it is easy to imagine the destruction of the earth, but those passages cannot be used to prove this.

As the twentieth century dawned, apocalyptic passages in the New Testament were rediscovered, and fundamentalist-oriented clergymen once again preached sermons about the importance of preparing for the afterlife. Liberal theologians, like Johannes Weiss, Albert Schweitzer, and Rudolf Bultmann, argued that speculations about the afterlife were peripheral to Jesus' ministry (Grenz and Olson, 1992, p. 89). Evangelicals and fundamentalists remained unconvinced and continued to pound the pavement with their messages of warning, slowly gathering audiences made up of individuals who took their words seriously.

Twentieth century theologians who adopted a pre-millennial eschatological view, like Fitzwater (1953, pp. 523-528), formulated one of the more detailed outlines of events that are alleged to occur when Jesus Christ returns to earth and the physical world as we know it would end. First, Fitzwater prophesied that as soon as Christ returns to earth there will be a resurrection of the dead who will be assigned new bodies. This implies that the dead in Christ are actually in a state of soul sleep, literally in the arms of Jesus. The difficulty with this position has to do with the concept of soul sleep, that is to say, if the deceased individuals are *not* in a state of soul sleep, why are they being resurrected? The second plank in Fitzwater's fundamentalist eschatology is that the righteous will be caught up in the air and taken to heaven. Third, with the Christians now gone from the earth, a preaching campaign to those left behind will occur, but we are not exactly sure who will undertake that task. Fourth, a great tribulation will happen on earth, probably affecting those who repented when they responded positively to the preaching campaign. Fifth, will be the gathering of the elect—the chosen few. Sixth, all nations will be gathered together for a general Divine judgment, and divided into good or evil sections. Seventh, God will establish a righteous kingdom on earth for those nations that passed the test just outlined. During this time the Evil One will be bound, and Christ will reign on the earth for one thousand years. Another fundamentalist theologian, Augustus Hopkins Strong (1956, p. 1023), added that at the end of Christ's thousand years reign there will be a final judgment. At this judgment, the wicked will be assigned to hell and believers will be assigned to eternal life.

Thiessen (1959, pp. 499-501) offers a slightly more complicated treatment of these events, for example, with regard to final judgments. He identifies seven judgments: judgment of (a) believers; (b) the Nation Israel; (c) Babylon; (d) the beast and the false prophets, and their armies; (e) all Nations; (f) the Evil One (Satan) and his angels; and, (g) the wicked dead. Is everyone still with me?

In summary, while some biblical scholars would like to think that the Bible is explicit about the nature of life after death, and what will occur after the world ends, unanimity on the subject among biblical scholars does not exist. Lay people can only marvel at the complexity of schemes concocted by these scholars, and hopefully will take faith in the Biblical exposition, "But about that day or hour no one knows, not even the angels in heaven, nor the Son, but only the Father" (Matthew 24:36).

Aboriginal Concepts of the Afterlife

Although anthropologists have generally described Native American conceptualizations of the afterlife as vague and undefined, there is some evidence that these perceptions may have missed the target. Hultkrantz (1987, p. 33) speculated that the question of an individual's survival after his or her demise was not a prominent theme in Aboriginal theology, and that statement appears to have validity. Cree elder Joseph Dion (1979, p. 55) expressed it this way:

> It can readily be understood that when an Indian prayed he prayed for something in this world instead of the next, which he believed would take care of itself. The present was too close at hand, too pressing to be set aside to any second place. His material welfare was always uppermost in his mind. He asked

for health, long life, and for achievement of his ambitions.

Further study will reveal that is inaccurate to suggest that the Native North American Nations completely ignored the subject of the afterlife. While they may primarily have been concerned about living righteously in this life, they did keep one eye on the phenomenon of life after death. Father Gontran Laviolette was an Oblate missionary to the Dakota of Saskatchewan and Manitoba who was convinced that Indigenous perceptions of the existence of the soul and the afterlife were quite specific. In his words, "The Dakota belief in the existence and the survival of the soul is clearly expressed by the word, *Nagi* (spirit)" (Laviolette, 1991, p. 21).

On a related matter, it must be mentioned that generally the First Peoples of the Great Plains did not specifically fear death but saw it as an essential and expected link in the circle of life. This view contrasts sharply with the Old Testament Christian version that death was originally an aversion to creation and resulted from the disobedience of the original occupants in the Garden of Eden. As a result, fundamentalist evangelists have employed fear of death as an incentive for nonbelievers to endorse their version of the Christian faith. In their theological view, physical death is considered as unnatural to creation, and an evil resulting from Adam and Eve's disobedience in the Garden of Eden (Deloria, 1995, p. 167). By contrast, in Indigenous society, death is not necessarily considered the enemy. When an elderly person dies, for example, this is nothing to be deplored; it is expected. What was traditionally feared more was what a warrior might expect to experience if he was captured and tortured by the enemy. Many tribes believed that it was important not to molest the body of the dead, even that of an enemy, because that individual would take those disfigurements into the spirit world (White, 1979, pp. 170-174).

It is intriguing to note that in the New Testament death is treated with a milder form of anguish. Here is the reason. In the first letter to the Corinthians, St. Paul describes death as a normal part of the life cycle, and not to be feared because Jesus Christ negated it by His own resurrection from the dead. In St. Paul's words:

> Death has been swallowed up in victory. Where, O death, is your victory? Where O death, is your sting? The sting of death is sin, and the power of sin is the law. But thanks be to God! He gives us the victory through our Lord Jesus Christ. Therefore, my dear brothers and sisters, stand firm. Let nothing move you (1 Corinthians 15:54b-58a).

Anthropologist, Ruth Underhill (1965, pp. 74-75) suggested that Aboriginal concepts of the afterlife were not expected to be a shadowy replica of the present world, but rather a land of improved status, and a land of plenty, filled with joyous dancing. Jenness (1986, p. 165), Maclean (1980, p. 100), and Kasprycki (2000, p. 134) disagreed somewhat with Underhill's assessment, describing the Native North American Nations' perceptions of death as a future abode of happiness that could be attained only by completing a long and dangerous spiritual journey. This is why many Aboriginal tribes placed items such as food and hunting tools in graves to assist the departed in making that journey. The Ojibway, for example, kindled a fire four days after a loved one had departed in order to light the way for the departed wayfarer. Many Algonquian tribes believed that the journey after death lasted only four days.

According to Jenness (1986, p. 165), some tribes also conceived of a special hereafter for spiritual elders and great warriors, and another for common people. Still another perception was the existence of two "heavens," one for those individuals who had lived uprightly, and another one for those who eschewed evil ways. If this version is correctly understood, it seems to parallel certain aspects of Christian perceptions of the hereafter. According to MacLean (1980, p. 446), the concepts of resurrection and immortality were also identifiable in some tribal belief systems. Therefore, it may be conjectured that this reality gave incoming Christian missionaries a useful conceptual connection when they introduced the Christian Gospel.

As suggested, conceptualizations about life in the hereafter varied somewhat from one tribe to another. For example, an important characteristic of the Chipewyan concept of the hereafter was possible reunion with loved ones after someone passed away. To illustrate this, we refer to Jenness' (1986, p. 166) personal experience in researching this topic. Jenness met an Aboriginal woman whose very young son died, an event that was accompanied with heavy mourning. When Jenness inquired about this situation he was informed that the most regrettable part was that the woman's young son would have no one to meet him in the next world. Six months later, Jenness met the same woman, only to find her quite content about the unfortunate event. He was informed that the boy's father had recently passed on and now the woman's son would have someone to communicate with in the new world. She was no longer a sorrowing woman.

Lowie (1963, pp. 180-181) noted that members of the Winnebago tribe were very concerned about the afterlife, and although there was not much concern about rewards and punishments after an individual passed on, the primary perception was that people would live in the hereafter in much the way that they had lived on earth. Time would be spent in earning a living, maintaining family life, and generally enjoying these and related activities. The Winnebago also expected to be reunited with their loved ones after death. These observations were gleaned from reports of individuals who had visited the spirit world, but were somehow revived and came back to life. The Blackfoot held a similar view, insisting that deceased individuals would live a lifestyle in the hereafter patterned after their life on earth (Ewers, 1989, p. 184).

The Comanche Nation had an unwavering faith in a hereafter that would emulate the imperfect reality of their daily lifestyle, but without all the disagreeable aspects; in their conception of heaven, all things would be perfect. Wallace and Hoebel (1986, p. 186) called it a "valley ten thousand fold longer and wider" than the valley which the Comanches called home. There would be no rain or wind, and the climate would always be mild, the air fresh, and the water cool.

Algonquian First Nations, which both Blackfoot and Cree peoples are part of, believed that individuals could occasionally be sent back to earth from their heavenly abode, possibly to inform their counterparts about the nature of their potential status in the afterlife. These tribes also believed, that no one need fear any form of judgment in the afterlife no matter how they had lived, because the Creator received everyone equally (Kasprycki, 2000, p. 134).

It was probably nomenclature invented by European missionaries to label the Native concept of the afterlife as "the happy hunting ground," which Deloria (1995, pp. 167-168) denounces as a mistranslation from the European perception that heaven will consist of a city with streets paved of gold occupied by a heavenly choir who will spend eternity singing the same worshipful songs that they sang on earth. A few television evangelists may even suggest that they will be appointed to govern large groups of humankind and judge the deeds that their peers performed on earth before their deaths. In any event, nothing is to be gained by a hasty mislabeling of one another's belief systems. A more fruitful route is to seek understanding and as a meaningful by product, try to gain a measure of appreciation for diversity of belief.

CHAPTER TWELVE

Missiology: Is There a Concern About the Spiritual Welfare of Others?

A study of contemporary Christian perspective indicates that dramatic changes in belief have occurred since nineteenth century theologians admonished Christians literally to "Go into all the world and preach the gospel to all creation. Whoever believes and is baptized will be saved, but whoever does not believe will be condemned" (Mark 16:15-16). As memberships in major Christian denominations continue to dwindle, evangelistic efforts in those churches have been replaced by concerns about social issues and institutional maintenance.

Looking back, it is easy to identify the names of zealous missionaries whose efforts ear-marked the era of missionary endeavor as encased in church history. These are some of the most well-known Protestant examples: William Carey (1761-1834) missionary to India; Jonathan Goforth (1859-1936), missionary to China; Adoniram Judson (1788-1850), missionary to Burma; David Livingston (1813-1873), missionary to South Africa; Samuel Marsden (1765-1838), missionary to New Zealand; Robert Moffat (1795-1883), missionary to South Africa; and, Hudson Taylor (1832-1905), missionary to China. Many institutions, like church denominational structures and colleges in North America, commemorate the efforts of these individuals in their naming practices—for example, William Carey

Library, Judson Press, Taylor University, and so on.

Contemporary Christian Perspectives

Often propelled by missionary zeal, the origin of many new Christian denominations occurred in the 19th century. Following Karl Marx' (1818-1883) interpretation of Wilhelm Hegel's (1770-1831) theory of dialectic, sociologist Ernst Troeltsch (1865-1923) developed a theory that church origins tend to follow a cyclical pattern in practice, going from break-a-way sect to state church (Friesen, 1972, p. 31). Troeltsch argued that as mainline church structures gradually adopt state-liked characteristics, new and more fundamentalist-oriented sects develop, and decry mainline beliefs and practices. However, as time goes on, these groups gradually adopt a similar, more open orientation, and new sects therefore originate from within *their* ranks. Troeltsch labeled this unique migration process, sect-to-church, and noted that as society continues to develop more liberal tendencies, new and more evangelically zealous denominations arise out of the ashes of their liberalism. For example, the Church of England (also known as the Anglican Church or Episcopal Church) originated in the Roman Catholic tradition, and Methodism came from the ranks of Anglicanism. Later the Salvation Army burst forth from Methodism, allegedly in an attempt to reach the ranks of the working class that the Methodist church was bypassing.

As the world moved towards the midpoint of the twentieth century, most major denominations were rapidly losing members, and only a few Pentecostal-like or charismatic denominations flourished. With the theological faltering of mainline church denominational zeal, the tenacity of personal faith and missionary outlook also withered. Now the emphasis was on church mergers that, if nothing else, grabbed a few newspaper headlines. The United Church of Canada, almost two million strong, resulted from a merger of

Methodists, Congregationalists, and two-thirds of the Presbyterians in the country. Since then the denomination has lost at least three-fourths of its membership. In the United States the Evangelical Association and the United Brethren Church merged in 1946 to become the Evangelical United Brethren Church. This body then joined the Methodist Church in 1968 to become the United Methodist Church. That denomination has decreased in membership ever since. These two examples only represent the tip of the iceberg of church mergers.

In October 2011, *The United Church Observer* (p. 6) reported that only 76% of United Church of Canada clergy even believe in God. At this writing, the denomination is closing down churches at the rate of more than one per week. This, among other startling statistics about membership loss may be just cause for concern. Unless a workable formula for membership growth is quickly discovered, in a generation or two there will be no Anglican or United Church congregations in Canada. It is doubtful that smaller evangelical denominations can pick up the slack, partly because they tend to avoid sociopolitical concerns, and therefore have a limited national presence, and partly because their involvement in social welfare and social justice movements is dismal at best.

Twenty-first century North American Christians demand more than that from religious organizations. Those individuals who *do* align themselves with a local church tend to prefer one of three kinds of personal fulfillment: (a) a comfortable pew, good preaching, first rate music, a strong youth program, and someone to have lunch with after the morning worship service is over; (b) evangelical zeal and Biblical lingo, enclasped in charismatic emotion; or, (c) not too much theology, but lots of discussion about social concerns and some action on the social justice front.

Missionary Platforms. Evangelicals tend to view people of God as joyous, separated from worldly practices, truth-rooted, and missionary minded. Jesus explained the first characteristic when He said: "I am coming to you now, but I say these things while I am still in the world, so that they may have the full measure of my joy within them"(John 17:13, italics mine). One would like to believe that this Divine source of joy could readily be identified in the lives of believers.

Second, it would appear that separation from worldly practices among Christians is less distinguishable today than it was in biblical times.

Third, the concept of being biblically rooted is less popular today than it was a century or two ago, probably because the exhortations of the Bible appear to be unduly harsh. For example, the Apostle Paul insisted that every aspect of daily living should be affected by and measured according to the biblical principle. "All Scripture is God-breathed and is useful for *teaching, rebuking, correcting and training in righteousness*, so that the servant of God may be thoroughly equipped for *every* good work" (2 Timothy 3:16-17, italics mine). Most believers today are quite interested in teaching and training, but being rebuked or corrected appear to be significantly less appealing (Boice, 1986, pp. 577-582).

Fourth, and finally, the propulsion to win "the lost" emanates from a literal interpretation of Mark 16:15: "Go into all the world and preach the gospel to all creation." Evangelical Christians have traditionally interpreted the mission of the church in somewhat imperialistic terms—trying hard to convince nonbelievers to accept Jesus Christ as the Son of God, accept Him as their personal Savior, and then join their particular denomination. In this context, Jesus established a parallel between *His* purpose in coming into the world and that of His followers because *they* are now commanded to go into the world. In His words: "As you sent me into the world, I have sent them into the world" (John 17:18). After making a firm decision to accept Jesus' substitutionary death and resurrection, at a definite time and place, new disciples are expected to commit their lives to following His lifestyle. The specific evangelical missionary mandate of the church is perceived as the following: (a) to reveal the presence of God in daily living; (b) make known God's wisdom to principalities and powers; (c) witness of Christ's saving grace; and, (d) help new believers to grow spiritually (Fitzwater, 1953, pp. 500-501). One of the corollary requirements of this responsibility is to learn how to be in the world, but not of the world. "Religion that God our Father accepts as pure and faultless is this: to look after orphans and widows in their distress and *to keep oneself from being polluted by the world*" (James 1:27, italics mine).

For the most part, conservative evangelicals today still believe that those who do not hear or heed the Gospel when it is presented to them will suffer eternal damnation after death. One again, the words of Jesus ring out the warning: "Whoever believes in the Son has eternal life, but whoever rejects the Son will not see life, for God's wrath remains on them" (John 3:36). The wrath of God is literally translated into these words: "But the cowardly, the unbelieving, the vile, the murderers, the sexually immoral, those who practice magic arts, the idolaters and all liars—they will be consigned to the fiery lake of burning sulfur" (Revelation 21:8).

The more liberal view of the mandate to evangelize nonbelievers emphasizes mission programs that combine concerns of salvation with the necessity of becoming politically involved, then combining these concerns with social welfare programs. Küng (1976, p. 555) pointed out that this should be made clear—the Christian message must be perceived as interdependent with mankind's social situation. Thus the tension between the two positions—evangelical and liberal, continues today with the latter view tending increasingly to dominate the scenario. Theologically speaking, more liberal minded thinkers are interested in reconstructing Christian beliefs in light of modern knowledge. They promote the idea that after conversion individual believers should retain the right to analyze, criticize, and reconstruct traditional beliefs. Christians should particularly stay focused on the practical or ethical dimension of Christianity, and try to replace empty speculations with moral doctrines that center on the kingdom of God as a whole (Grenz and Olson, 1992, p. 52).

Perhaps the most unsettling premise of liberalism, at least to evangelicals, has been their attempt to base theological speculations on a foundation other than the absolute authority of the Bible. Evangelicals have condemned the move, suggesting that once the theological gate has been opened to spiritual authority other than the Bible, who decides what is to be included or excluded? What are the criteria by which such judgments can be made and who has the right to formulate them? Liberals respond to this criticism by claiming to preserve the essence of Christianity, by unlocking it from its husk of cultural underpinnings, and replacing those with more recent scientific and philosophical knowledge. The "husk" includes Divine miracles, belief in supernatural beings such as angels and demons, and valuing the efficacy of apocalyptic events. Projected further, this also implies that theological beliefs and practices of religious systems other than Christian could beneficially fuel related conversations. Such an open acceptance of religious inclusiveness essentially voids the necessity of trying to win the lost for Christ. Now the efforts of believing Christians are to be directed to learning about and gleaning insights from neighboring world religions. Evangelicals complain that reference to cultural values can be used as an excuse to lull believers into a false sense of what God expects of them. The end result is that Christians can console themselves by claiming that God simply smiles on them no matter what beliefs they cling to or how they behave (Klein, Bloomberg, and Hubbard, 1993, p. 393).

Finally, and this is the nail that closes the coffin of meaningful dialogue between evangelical and liberal theologians is that liberal theologians downplay the immanence of a loving God through the sacrificial death and resurrection of His Son, Jesus Christ, and substitute emphasis on the transcendence of God whose character was best revealed in the exemplary behavior of Jesus Christ (Grenz and Olson, 1992, pp. 52-53).

Change is everywhere present in human society, and concern about Christian world missions is no exception. Today, except for the zealous efforts of a few fundamentalist Christian church denominations, the era of missionary zeal appears to be over. Jürgen Moltmann (1975, p. 172), a promoter of the theology of hope, used to reprimand evangelicals for perceiving world peace strictly in biblical terms, namely, delivering the "peace of God, which transcends all understanding" (Philippians 4:7). His view was that the message of the hope of faith had to be interpreted in political terms. This is not an entirely unrealistic position in light of the fact that missions of any kind are so often fraught with political involvements emanating from government restrictions in countries where missions are undertaken.

Anderson (2001, pp. 320-321) cautions that theology is in danger of losing contact with its object of study when it is no longer interested in studying the interaction of spiritual practice and revealed truth. As a result, orthodoxy appears to have triumphed, by influencing contemporary theologians to separate theology from missions, leaving the study of missions to cultural anthropology. The new emphasis in orthodoxy in the church has therefore left the study of missions without a solid Christology. Fundamentally the theological task of evangelism belongs to the church, not to those who value scholarly concerns above practice. It is unfortunate that individuals, who *do* teach in the area, are usually university trained and have little or no experience in leading the mission of the church.

To sum up the array of contemporary theological positions

representing Christendom is no easy task because the rift continues between relentless biblicism and theological inclusiveness. Conservative theologians will continue to argue that a loving, transcendent Creator God has chosen to disclose Himself in carefully delineated immanent ways; that is, through the work of His Son, Jesus Christ, the Savior, and through the Holy Bible. Liberals may admit that this is all well and good, but may ask: Are these rather restrictive parameters able to incorporate modern scientific findings and new philosophical insights? Does this juxtaposition foster the creativity that is needed to clarify the various aspects of the complexity of modern theological deliberations? (Tanner, 1997, p. 157).

The academic debate continues, while Christian practice follows a path long ago described by Canadian humorist, the late Stephen Leacock (1869-1944): "He flung himself upon his horse and rode madly off in all directions."

Aboriginal Missionary Mandate

Missionary endeavors on the part of the Aboriginal nations of the Great Plains did not traditionally exist, but that is not to say that the Indigenous peoples were entirely provincial in their thinking. Like nations of every background, Native North American tribes traditionally engaged in war, mainly to protect their own economic or geographic interests. However, on occasion they also engaged in friendly interaction with other Aboriginal nations for trade and other purposes. Even though most tribes did not have an abundance of material articles, bartering among tribes often enabled both parties to supplement their own economy with products of the other's labor (Ewers, 1988, pp. 19-20). Jenness (1986, p. 156; McMillan, 1995, p. 3) indicate that there were tribes who sometimes sought wives from neighboring communities because they considered them more desirable. There were also instances where captives obtained through war efforts were made full members of the community in which they were adopted. In so far as religious imperialism per se was concerned, however, it simply did not exist. McGaa (1995, p. 55) suggests that "Indigenous tribes were content to remain as distinct tribal entities," with no intention of expanding their cultural or spiritual holdings. Deloria (1999b, p. 321) concurs, and cautions that "A warning light should flash when the Indian practitioners say that their elders told them to go into the world and teach the traditional ceremonies." The Indigenous people of North America traditionally respected each other's spiritual beliefs and practices, a perspective that was partially feasible because many of their perspectives were similar.

It is possible to identify four significant concepts central to this discussion that may help to differentiate the Native North American nations theological orientation from that of incoming Europeans. These are: (a) the concept of sharing; (b) the concept of ownership; (c) ecumenical outlook; and, (d) confrontation with Christian Imperialism.

Aboriginal Sharing. A primary difference between traditional Indigenous societies and that of their new European neighbors, having to do with individual and community welfare, was the Indigenous dedication to socialism versus capitalism, and communalism (in the good sense), versus free enterprise. A Jesuit missionary working among the Sioux in 1936 made a telling comment about Aboriginal welfare. In his words:

> Hospitals for the poor would be useless among them, because there are no beggars; those who have are so liberal to those who are in want, that everything is enjoyed in common. The whole village must be distress before any individual is left in necessity (as cited in Seton and Seton, 1966, p. 36).

Captain John G. Bourke, who spent many years as an Indian fighter, was eventually overwhelmed with the magnanimous nature of Sioux culture and felt compelled to observe:

The American Indian, born free as the eagle, would not tolerate restraint, would not brook injustice; therefore, the restraint imposed must be manifestly for his benefit.... The American Indian is the most generous of mortals; at all his dances and feasts, the widow and the orphan are the first to be remembered (Seton and Seton, 1966, p. 40).

The arrangement regarding sharing among Native North American peoples was traditionally quite the opposite of that practiced in Europe mainly because the privilege of sharing lay with the recipient, rather then the giver. It was generally the case among Plains Nations that those who had access to resources were expected to share them, and anyone of kin to the "keeper" of goods could take them if he or she had need. As the late Siksika elder Russell Wright stated: "Material culture is interesting to look at... our traditional concept of possessions is not to hoard them, but to use them. *If anybody can find a better use for what I have, let him take it*" (cited in Friesen, 1998, p. 5, italics mine).

In the traditional world of Native North American Nations, sharing did not mean that that an individual who possessed resources was expected to give them out, but rather that those in need could avail themselves of those resources without asking for them. In this sense, sharing was *taking*, rather then necessarily *giving*. In fact, it was considered to be an honor for an individual to have goods, like food supplies, taken by someone of kin; it was considered an honor to be able to provide in this fashion (Friesen, 1995, p. 49ff.). The give-a-way dance, sponsored by many Plains tribes was a more formalized approach to sharing. If an individual wished to celebrate a special event, he or she might sponsor a dance in which all kinds of goods would literally be given away.

Despite these complimentary appraisals, the question must be raised, "If the Native North American people were so kind and sympathetic to their own, what was their attitude towards strangers?" The truth lies in history, and these questions must be raised; "Were Native American tribes traditionally always mean to one another? Were incoming European invaders always taken prisoner, tortured, and put to death by local Native people?" The answers are unequivocally negative, first of all, because many tribes had in place mutually beneficial trading practices. Second, if every missionary and "would-be culture changer "was disposed of by resident tribes, how did Christianity so easily become assimilated into Aboriginal theology? By comparison, the Old Testament Deuteronomy mandate nicely parallels traditional Aboriginal philosophy:

> For the Lord your God is God of gods and the Lord of lords, the great God, mighty and awesome, who shows no partiality and accepts no bribes. He defends the cause of the fatherless and the widow, and loves the foreigner residing among you, *giving them food and clothing* (10:17-18, italics mine).

The Concept of Ownership. As pointed out earlier, the Aboriginal approach to sharing found an easy parallel in relation to spiritual possessions in that no one actually *owned* them. An individual might be a pipe carrier or a bundle keeper, but that honor was considered temporal and then only for the benefit of the community. Similarly, if someone wished to have the power of a particular of a teepee design that someone had originally received from a dream or vision, that design *had* to be shared, albeit the transfer was made through a special ceremony overseen by a respected elder.

Few things are more near and dear to Native communities than the subject of reverence for the land, later named Mother Earth. To the Indigenous way of thinking, no one can actually *own* land; it is a gift from the Creator or, better put, the land is our Mother whose resources should be available to all humankind (Weeks, 1990, p. 219). This outlook was quite foreign to the first European visitors who soon after their arrival in North America began negotiating for land ownership with local tribes. No one properly explained to Aboriginal people that land was considered salable. In fact, when some of the treaties were signed, Indigenous leaders sometimes thought they were signing peace treaties, not documents pertaining to land purchases (Treaty 7 Elders and Tribal Council, 1996, pp. 77-78).

Today, because of its ever-increasing value, Indigenous lands are being sought after by both individual farmers and ranchers, as well as by farming corporations. Many tribal councils are leasing land as a means of generating much needed capital. However, as Deloria (1999b, p. 314) points out: "Leasing of tribal lands involves selling the major object of tribal religion for funds to solve problems that are ultimately religious in nature." Plowing up land or employing strip-mining techniques that permanently harm the earth clearly violates the traditional belief that land is an eternal gift from the Creator. No one is creating any more land.

Because land is perceived as a special spiritual gift, many Native North American people designate specific areas as sacred sites. This practice also has been cause for controversy, because land hungry groups of various kinds—ranging from government to land developers—often desire access to said lands. The assortment of Aboriginal sacred lands range from the Gettysburg National Cemetery in Pennsylvania and the Lincoln Memorial in Washington, DC, to mountaintops and hillsides across North America, were vision quests were once and still are held.

History will show that Native North American people were not alone in identifying sacred places. As the Old Testament records, Judaism, which is the foundation of the Christian religion, greatly valued sacred places. Moses, the Israelite leader, saw a vision when he was tending a flock of sheep owned by his father-in-law, Jethro. Moses saw a bush and though it was on fire, it did not burn up. God spoke to Moses and warned him to take off his shoes because the ground on which he was standing was holy or sacred (Exodus 3:1-14). Acting on God's words to him, Moses subsequently returned to Egypt, the land of his birthplace, and proceeded to free Israel from Pharaoh's dictatorship. Later, when the Israelites crossed the river Jordan under the leadership of Joshua, into what would become the Promised Land, they placed twelve stones in a commemorative memorial, to represent their twelve tribes (Joshua 4:1-24).

Today, the reality is that we live in an age when the sacred is no longer strongly regarded, and as a result sacred sites are often disregarded and sometimes even abused. As Deloria (1999c, p. 337) cautions:

> Sacred places are the foundation of all other beliefs and practices because they represent the presence of the sacred in our lives. They properly inform us that we are not larger than nature and that we have responsibilities to the rest of the natural world that transcend our own personal desires and wishes.

Ecumenical Outlook. Although international travel was not much of a practice in pre-contact days, there is evidence that Indigenous spiritual leaders did not work in isolation. For example, Black Elk (1863-1950), one of the most remembered elders of the Lakota Sioux, held frequent conferences with spiritual elders from his tribe. This included spiritual elders who were living on different reservations (Deloria, 1999b, p. 309). Even today, many Native leaders spend a great deal of travel time and money in seeking out collegial spiritual leaders to participate in similar events. This kind of concern took on a more formal tack in 1969 at the occasion of the first Indian Ecumenical Conference held at the Crow Agency in Montana. After that, and for the next two decades the conference convened on the Stoney Nakoda Reserve west of Calgary, Alberta. These conferences had excellent attendance by Indigenous spiritual leaders from all across the continent including Seminoles from the Florida everglades, Mi'kmaq from Nova Scotia, and Dogrib people from the Northwest Territories. A key conference concern was the maintenance of Aboriginal languages and cultural and spiritual heritage (Snow, 2005, pp. 198-199). As was traditionally always the case, these leaders were interested in more than religious expansion; they also emphasized appreciation of the past, nurture of the whole person, and intertribal cooperation.

Confrontation with Imperialist Christianity. As a Christian, this is a difficult section to write because in many ways it reflects negatively on my own background and religious perspective. Let me hasten to say that I believe we have learned as lot about intercultural appreciation and sensitivity in the past few generations, although this in no way can excuse what has been done in the past.

To begin with it is necessary to understand and appreciate the mindset of the first Europeans who arrived in North America—explorers, fur traders, nation builders, settlers, and missionaries from England, France, and Spain. Although the bulk of the first visitors came from these three countries, there were other representatives as well. Generally, all these first visitors shared in the same value system of imperialistic expansion and national supremacy (Smith, 1994, p. 419). Hindsight affords an easy condemnation of their initial tactics, and resident Aboriginals made them susceptible for takeover with their attitude of listening to anyone who made claims within a spiritual context. Often Indigenous leaders listened politely as missionaries told them that their ways of living should be set aside and new ways adopted. Red Jacket, a Seneca orator, told missionaries that he would listen to them, but he wanted an opportunity to respond (Noley, 1998, p. 55). The nature of this approach sharply differentiates those missionaries who primarily sought souls, from nationalistic inclined imperialists who had other goals. The latter wanted to expand what they perceived to be superior civilizations, but they were willing to include religious concerns as a vital component in that package (Peers, 1994, p. 131). For example, Jesuit missions in North America dated to the arrival of Jacques Cartier in 1534 and Samuel de Champlain in 1608, were intricately tied to colonization. One Jesuit priest, Father Jean Brébeuf, in 1632 worked closely with the colonizing philosophy of Samuel de Champlain, the latter deeply involved in a trade agreement with the Huron people. There is, however, some difference in interpretation about the exact nature of missionary roles. Bowden (1981, p. 77), for example, suggests that Franciscan missionaries were distant in their approach and refused to live in Indian villages; in addition, the trading companies they worked with did not encourage permanent European settlements. Underhill (1963, p. 27), on the other hand, observed that the Franciscans were devoted missionaries, and strongly committed to vows of poverty and service. They fully integrated with locals by settling in villages around a mission that consisted of a church, a school, and local shops.

There are essentially four perspectives on what happened when the two cultures, European and Aboriginal, first clashed. First of all there are critics, both Native and non-Native, who out rightly condemn everything that newcomers (especially missionaries) did when they first met resident Aboriginal Nations. Unfortunately, this attitude coincides with the intolerance and lack of understanding that their incoming European forebears manifested. Second, there are those who believe that the invaders did nothing wrong; after all, the Indigenous people *needed* saving. These interpreters of history usually hold to a more fundamentalist view of Christianity. Third, there are those who look back from a more modern liberalist stance and try to apologize for virtually everything their imperialist ancestors did, but offer little by way of substantial sustenance. Fourth, there are those students of history, both Indigenous and non-Indigenous writers, who take a more balanced view and even try to synthesize insights from both camps.

Two individuals who stand out in this fourth identified group are the late Chief John Snow of the Stoney First Nation, and the late Vine Deloria, Jr. of Lakota Sioux background. I can speak personally about my friendship with Chief John Snow for some forty years, and I have long been a student of Professor Deloria's works. Both leaders tended to exhibit a more sympathetic tone of historical understanding when they addressed the cultural clash between Native and non-Native theologies. It was my privilege for many years to conduct weekend field trips to the Stoney community with students from the University of Calgary, and Chief John Snow was always ready to address and interact with the students without remuneration of any kind. He answered many sometimes embarrassing questions from uninformed students, and always did so with kindness and patience. His personal view was that the differences between Christian beliefs and Stoney spirituality were minor, and what differences there were did not seem very important (Snow, 2005, p. 22; Waldram, 1997, p. 165). Spiritual leaders of other tribes often agreed with Chief Snow, because missionaries who lived among them adopted the local lifestyle of living off the land, learned local languages, and respected tribal authorities (Dickason, 1984, pp. 256-257; Ryan, 1995, p. 59). One Methodist missionary to the Cree, the Reverend James Evans (1801-1846), even developed a form of writing in a syllabary that the tribe adopted (Dickason, 1993, p. 241). Chief John Snow believed that personal energy was better spent in trying to learn from one another than out rightly condemning one another before examining each other's views. Many Native spiritual leaders, like Chief Snow, never completely discarded the traditional ways of their forebears and often practiced Christianity and Indigenous spirituality in an integrated way (Carlson, 1998, 165; Powers, 1977, p. 124). Herring (1990, p. 150) points out that during the days following the arrival of European missionaries, there were many Aboriginal people who continued to practice their traditional sacred ceremonies, deceiving onlookers by carefully camouflaging them as Christian rites. Others, like the Dakota people, one day decided that they would surrender no more of their traditional ways—spiritual or otherwise—nor any longer grovel at the door of the Indian agent's warehouse (Elias, 2002, p. 17).

The passing of time has appeared to change official attitudes towards Indigenous spiritualty. Dickason (2009, pp. 458-459) suggests that the recent renaissance of Native spirituality has even influenced the Roman Catholic Church to incorporate elements of Aboriginal spirituality into their rituals. Vine Deloria, Jr., (1995, p. 36) was often a critic of both Christianity and "born again" Indians, but he rarely engaged in theological analysis without also offering meaningful insights for readers to ponder. Deloria (1999b, p. 308) told it like it was when he observed that Chief Joseph of the Nez Perce Nation "refused to have missionaries around, fearing that they would teach the people to quarrel about God." On the other hand, Deloria (1999b, p. 307) also observed "some Christian missionaries successfully bridged the cultural gap and became more important to the tribes than most of their own members." He satirically criticized one particular Christian denomination (Deloria, 1999d, p. 276) whose spokesmen became ecstatic when they were informed by Indians that they were guilty of America's sins against their Native brothers; this provided denominational leaders with added incentive to embark on a massive program of fund-raising to pay for their alleged sins. Deloria also castigated theologians Martin Buber, Theodore Gaster, and Johannes Pederson (Deloria 1999e, pp. 346-348) for their inability to understand the value of Indigenous mythology and historical accounts that paralleled those offered by Old Testament Jewish writers. Deloria suggested that these writers probably did not likely familiarize themselves with the oral tradition practiced by Aboriginal societies. On the positive side, Deloria praised the efforts of Immanuel Velikovsky (1895–1979) who believed that the Old Testament Book of Exodus should be viewed as an historical record because so much of it can be verified by other accounts. Unlike his three colleagues mentioned above, Velikovsky spent countless numbers of years amassing mounds of evidence from many different sources before he made his pronouncement on the Book of Exodus (Deloria, 1999e, p. 345). Deloria was at once thorough, honest, and objective in making his assessments. This is the legacy of a hard-hitting, yet not unkind, thorough academic scholar.

The history of Aboriginal relations with their new European neighbors was basically unfortunate from the start. Missionary objections to the practice of Indigenous practices such as warfare, slavery, plural marriage, shamanism, witchcraft, and certain ceremonies like the Sundance and the potlatch are well documented (Fassett, 1996, p. 178; Pettipas, 1994, p. 115; Price, 1979, p. 208). Vogel (1990, p. 35) contends that Christian missionaries were especially hostile towards Native spiritual leaders, and Alfred (2005, p. 104) uses terms such as the following to describe the result of early missionary legalism among local Natives—hypocrisy, guilt-ridden, condescending, and inauthentic.

Negative condemnations notwithstanding, there is another side to the story that may be illustrated with reference to residential schools in Canada. Denominational leaders of several kinds have in recent years been severely criticized for taking Indian children away from their nomadic families and incarcerating them in boarding schools for years at a time (Bull, 1991; Dyck, 1997; Furniss, 1995; Grant, 1996; Haig-Brown, 1993; Hookimaw-Witt, 1998; Knockwood, 1994, Schissel and Wotherspoon, 2003; Steckley and Cummins, 2008; and, Warry, 2007). Historians Miller (1997) and Milloy (1999) have estimated that only 30-35 percent of Native children attended residential schools while most, but not all of the others, were enrolled in day schools. There were small numbers of Native children who managed to avoid church sponsored education entirely, and were educated solely in tribal ways. Staff in both residential schools and day schools essentially followed the same curriculum and equally downplayed the integrity of Aboriginal culture and spirituality. Agnes Grant (2004, p. 95), herself a product of residential schooling, has observed that attitudes about residential schools are diverse. One student claimed that she very much enjoyed being in residential school because it freed her from excessive childcare responsibilities at home. She was also very proud of her high marks.

As Grant (2004) has indicated, personal experiences in residential schools were not all negative. Today there are respected elders who were enjoyed their experience at residential school and remain active in congregations that sponsored residential schools. Since much of the literature about these church sponsored institutions is so negative, one wonders, have these individuals forgotten the extent of their sufferings, or are they just naturally forgiving people? Have they blacked out these unfortunate experiences or, since many of them are now elders, do they proclaim that forgiveness is better than bitterness? The answer to this question remains somewhat of an enigma, although it is well documented that Aboriginal elders tend to be very positive thinkers (Garnier, 1990; Meili, 1992; Cardinal and Hildebrandt, 2000).

A band conducted interview survey with 272 Blackfoot or Blood elders on the Kainai reserve in southern Alberta revealed that more than half the interviewees reported positive impressions of their school experiences in one of two local residential schools. One of these schools was run by the Roman Catholic Church and the other by the Anglican Church of Canada (Friesen and Friesen, 2008, pp. 110-119). The elders who reported enjoying their schooling expressed appreciation for attaining domestic and life skills, developing a functional faith, engaging in recreational activities, and learning useful vocational skills. There are also First Nations leaders who testify that skills they learned in residential schools have aided them in negotiating effectively with governmental officials.

By contrast with the above, there are many former residential school survivors who report very negative experiences about harsh treatment, strict discipline, sexual abuse, and too many rules. It is difficult to understand how these variances of opinion have developed, but perhaps they must be interpreted with reference to differential treatment or differences in personal perception. At this point, it may be useful to question the assumption that every individual who was enrolled in a residential school, or their offspring, suffered irreparable damage. Thus the query; was the interaction of Indigenous peoples with missionary-minded Christian emissaries always detrimental to Aboriginal ways? Even more importantly, is there a way we can resolve the past devastation and move beyond suffering and blame to a new form of mutual resolution? This is more than a study of history or poetry; it is a serious responsibility on the part of every Christian, regardless of orientation. Chances are there will be kind, accepting Indigenous elders waiting to engage in meaningful collaboration.

CHAPTER THIRTEEN

Toward Reconciliation

How can the two theological belief systems, Aboriginal and non-Aboriginal, be reconciled or even be synthesized into some sort of meaningful whole? Perhaps this is not plausible, but it should at least be possible for believers of the two systems of thought to develop a measure of respect for one another. Since this book is primarily aimed at adherents to Eurocentric theology, it might be appropriate to start there. After some analysis is undertaken, a few practical suggestions toward that end are offered at the end of this chapter.

Indigenous identity in North America is swiftly being strengthened, particularly by more favorable media exposures as well as increasing numbers of publications produced by Indigenous academics. Unfortunately, this positive development appears to have a flipside in that it is becoming increasingly unpopular for non-Aboriginal scholars to investigate and research topics pertaining to traditional Native cultures.

Some publications appearing on the market, written by Aboriginal scholars tend to adopt an antithetical stance and decry work done by their non-Indigenous colleagues. Two recent publications that exemplify an exclusive stance are *Kaandossiwin: How We Come to Know* by Kathleen E. Absolon (2011), and *Racism, Colonialism, and Indigeneity in Canada* edited by Martin J. Cannon and Lina Sunseri

(2011). The first book cites works written exclusively by Aboriginal scholars, while the second, a book of readings, includes essays written exclusively by Native academics. The implication of both works is that "finally the truth is being told about Native North American history and culture." It is easy to understand why these writers wish to put their ideas into the public domain, thereby attempting to set the record straight by correcting errors and misinterpretations made in the past by uninformed but well-meaning non-Native writers. Perhaps a defensive stance is a necessary step in the long climb towards rectifying what promoters of Eurocentric thinking have inflicted on an unsuspecting North American public for so many generations. On the other hand, it would seem that a more conciliatory approach might be fruitful on the chance that *some* non-Aboriginal scholars might also have valid insights to share, particularly if respected Indigenous elders have mentored these writers. As a result, non-Aboriginal scholars take a risk in writing about Native matters, even though they might hope that some form of networking might occur with Indigenous scholars. Perhaps, together, the viewpoints of both Aboriginal and non-Aboriginal scholars might yield a more comprehensive picture of Indigenous cultures and belief systems. At the very least, it is always academically beneficial to exchange ideas.

To set the stage for our final discussion, it is useful to direct attention to four Eurocentric assumptions about the natural world and contrast these against Aboriginal theological premises. In the past these key outlooks of the two views made it virtually impossible to navigate meaningful discussions between Eurocentric-minded theologians and Indigenous theologians in the past. Hopefully, we can make a fresh start.

The New Approach

The description of the four assumptions is available in an article by noted Mi'kmaq scholars, Marie Battiste and James Sakej

Henderson (2011, p. 13) entitled, "Eurocentrism and the European Ethnographic Tradition." The four Eurocentric assumptions identified by these writers are: (a) the natural world exists independent of any beliefs about it; (b) perceptions may provide an accurate impression of the natural world; (c) linguistic concepts may describe the natural world; and, (d) certain rules of inference are reliable means for arriving at new truths about the natural world.

To begin with, EuroCanadian theologians generally take for granted that the essence and workings of the natural world can be attained through empiricism, that is, through human experience. The problem is intensified simply because these premises cannot be proven by *any* means. Following Indigenous thinking, one has to accept the notion that there is no dichotomy between the natural world and humankind. They are one and the same, not separate or distinct from one another in kind. Thus humans have an obligation to respect the workings of nature because they are one with it.

A similar notation may be observed with regard to the notion that perceptions about the natural order can provide an accurate assessment. In Eurocentric thinking, it is believed that people can never experience reality per se, but only in terms of their characteristics like appearance, sound, or smell. This is analogous to Immanuel Kant's notion of two worlds, the one of human experience, and the other consisting of absolute truth. Indigenous perceptions of the natural world are that its reality can be experienced as "intelligible essences," that is to say, everything in the world can be known to the human mind" (Battiste and Henderson, 2011, p. 13).

A further difference between Eurocentric thought and that of North America's Indigenous peoples has to do with the notion that linguistic conceptualizations are adequate to explain the natural world. Aboriginal theologians would argue that since there is no difference in essence between the constitution of the natural world and humankind, and the latter can effectively utilize their five senses in arriving at functional perceptions of the natural world. "Since people enter into language through their sensory relationships with the natural world, languages cannot be understood in isolation from the ecologies that give rise to them" (Battiste and Henderson, 2011, p. 13).

Finally, Battiste and Henderson (2011) point out that in Eurocentric thought a series of conventional codes are entrenched in language, and these must be used in order to decipher truths about the natural world. They contend that the workings of the natural world are not subject to these rules, and function independently of them. Indigenous people recognize this reality and are prepared to adjust to the cycles and changes within the natural world without resistance. "Life is to be lived not in accordance to universal abstract theories about the way things work but as an interactive relationship in a particular time and place" (Battiste and Henderson, 2011, p. 14). Eurocentric thinking fosters an "us versus them" attitude, humankind versus nature, with the end goal of wanting to captivate and even exploit the natural world. This stance has ecological implications because our European ancestors did not typically arrive in North America with a plan to work in conjunction with the natural world. They came to conquer, dominate, and exploit resources—including people, if necessary.

The above assumptions are significant in explaining the difference between the way mainline North Americans view life and the way this continent's First Peoples do. They are also important in terms of contrasting theological differences, but that is not the major difficulty. Studying these differences with a view to understanding and appreciating them is important; otherwise there is no common ground on which any move towards theological reconciliation can occur. The steps towards attaining mutual understanding and possibly even theological reconciliation are really quite simple.

Steps Toward Reconciliation

Having studied and lived in a variety of Aboriginal communities over several decades, I am delighted to be able to say that I have met many very friendly Indigenous leaders and elders who have been willing to share information with me. On that basis, I offer the following advice to my fellow North Americans who may be interested in knowing more about Aboriginal cultural beliefs and practices.

First, it is always advisable to become knowledgeable about new avenues of interest and a good starting point is to research reliable literature. For starters, this may be undertaken by using the reference list located at the end of this book. All of the books in the reference list have been cited and described in previous discussions.

Second, it is now possible in virtually every major city in North America to visit public institutions (like museums) that feature Native art, music, drama, and/or history, many of them hosted by Indigenous people. Many conferences featuring Indigenous themes are available across the continent, and participants of virtually any background may enroll. At these occasions, polite questions, respectfully posed, are always welcomed.

Third, many North American universities, particularly those located near Aboriginal communities, offer relevant courses on Indigenous topics, both for credit and non-credit. One does not have to become a fulltime university student to avail oneself of this fruitful opportunity.

Fourth, it is often possible to visit Native American communities so long as visitors follow proper protocol. A good starting place is the local reserve/reservation headquarters or band office. Alternately if the opportunity lends itself, it may be possible to seek advice from a member of an Aboriginal community about undertaking such a visit. Here too, only efforts undertaken with a respectful and sensitive attitude will be mutually beneficial to both parties. When planning to involve oneself in these kinds of endeavors, it would be advisable to keep in mind the words of Chief Joseph of the Nez Perce Nation:

> All men were created by the same Great Spirit Chief. They are all brothers. The earth is the mother of us all, and all people should have equal rights upon it (as cited in Friesen, 1998, p. 45).

ABOUT THE AUTHOR

A graduate of seven postsecondary education institutions, John W. Friesen, Ph.D., D.Min., D.R.S., is the author, co-author, or editor of more than 50 books on education, religion, ethnicity, and Indigenous studies. A Professor in the Werklund School of Education at the University of Calgary, he currently teaches courses in Aboriginal studies and teacher education. An ordained clergyman with 50 years of ministerial experience, he is affiliated with the All Tribes Presbytery of the All Native Circle Conference in the United Church of Canada, and serves as pastor of Morley United Church on the Stoney (Nakoda Sioux) Indian Reservation.

Friesen grew up in northern Saskatchewan where he attended school with Native students, and it was then that he began to pursue Indigenous studies as a lifetime interest. He and his wife, Dr. Virginia Lyons Friesen, have worked in several Western Canadian First Nations communities and visited many others in the American Southwest. In recognition of his many contributions, Friesen has been honored as a recipient of four eagle feathers, one of which authorizes him the privilege of teaching about Aboriginal spirituality.

REFERENCES

Absolon, K. E. (Minogiizhigokwe), *Kaandossiwin: How We Come To Know* (Halifax, NS: Fernwood Publishing, 2011)

Alfred, T., *Wasáse: Indigenous Pathways of Action and Freedom* (Peterborough, ON: Broadview Press, 2005)

Altizer, T. J. J. and W. Hamilton, *Radical Theology and The Death of God* (New York: Abingdon-Cokesbury, 1966)

Anderson, R. S., *The Shape of Practical Theology* (Downers Grove, IL: InterVarsity Press, 2001)

Andrist, R. K., *Long Death: The Last Days of the Plains Indian* (Don Mills, ON: Macmillan, 1993)

Archambault, W. G., Imprisonment and American Indian Medicine Ways: A Comparative Analysis of Conflicting Cultural Beliefs, Values, and Practices. In J. I. Ross, and L. Gould, eds, *Native Americans and the Criminal Justice System* (pp. 161-178) (Boulder, CO: Paradigm Publishers, 2006)

Battiste, M., Maintaining Aboriginal Identity, Language, and Culture. In M. Battiste, ed, *Reclaiming Indigenous Voice and Vision* (pp. 192-208) (Vancouver, BC: UBC Press, 2000)

Battiste, M. and J. S. Youngblood Henderson, Ethnocentrism and the European Ethnographic Tradition. In M. J. Cannon and L. Sunseri, eds, *Racism, Colonialism, and Indigeneity in Canada: A Reader* (pp. 11-19) (Toronto, ON: Oxford University Press, 2011)

_____. *Protecting Indigenous Knowledge and Heritage* (Saskatoon, SK: Purich Publishing, 2000)

Bayles, E. E., *Pragmatism in Education* (New York: Harper & Row, 1966)

Beck, P.V., A. L. Walters and N. Francisco, *The Sacred Ways of Knowledge, Sources Of Life* (Flagstaff, AZ: Northland Publishing, 1990)

Boice, J. M., *Foundations of the Christian faith: A Comprehensive & Readable Theology* (Downers Grove, IL: InterVarsity Press, 1986)

Boldt, M., *Surviving as Indians: The Challenge of Self-Government* (Toronto, ON: University of Toronto Press, 1992)

Bonhoeffer, D., *Letters and Papers From Prison*, rev. edn (New York: Macmillan, 1967)

Bonvillain, N., The Iroquois and the Jesuits: Strategies of Influence and Resistance. *American Indian Culture and Research Journal*, vol. 10 (1) (pp. 29-42) (1986)

Bordewich, F. M., *Killing The White Man's Burden: Reinventing Native Americans at The End of The Twentieth Century* (New York: Anchor Books, 1996)

Bowden, H. W., *American Indians and Christian Missions: Studies in Cultural Conflict* (Chicago, IL: University of Chicago Press, 1981)

Brooks, T., *The Way Of The Spirit: Nature, Myth, And Magic In Native American Life* (New York: Time-Life Books Inc., 1997)

Brown, D., *Dee Brown's Folktales Of The Native American* (New York: Henry Holt and Company, 1993)

Brown, H. O. J., The Conservative Option. In S. N. Gundry and A. F. Johnson, eds, *Tensions in Contemporary Theology* (pp. 327-360) (Chicago, IL: Moody Press, 1978)

Brown, J. E., *Animals of the Soul: Sacred Animals of the Oglala Sioux* (Rockport, MA: Element, 1997)

_____. *The Spiritual Legacy of The American Indian* (New York: Crossroads, 1992)

Bruchac, J., *The Native American Sweat Lodge: History and Legends* (Freedom, CA: The Crossing Press, 1993)

Buckley, H., *From Wooden Ploughs To Welfare: Why Indian Policy Failed in The Prairie Provinces* (Montreal, PQ: McGill-Queen's University Press, 1993)

Bull, L. R., Indian Residential Schooling: The Native Perspective. *Canadian Journal of Native Education*, vol. 18 (pp. 1-64) (1991 Supplement)

Butler, J. D., *Four Philosophies and Their Practice In Education And Religion* (New York: Harper and Row, 1968)

Cajete, G., *Look to the Mountain: An Ecology of Indigenous Education* (Durango, CO: Kivakí Press, 1994)

____. Indigenous Knowledge: The Pueblo Metaphor of Indigenous Education. In M. Battiste, ed, *Reclaiming Indigenous Voice and Vision* (pp. 181-191) (Vancouver, BC: University of British Columbia Press, 2000)

Campbell, M., *Halfbreed* (Toronto, ON: McCelland and Stewart, 1973)

Canada, *Annual Report of The Department of Indian Affairs* (Ottawa, ON: Queen's Printer, 1895)

Cannon, M. J. and L. Sunseri, eds, *Racism, Colonialism, and Indigeneity in Canada: A Reader* (Toronto, ON: Oxford University Press, 2011)

Cardinal, H. and W. Hildebrandt, *Treaty Elders Of Saskatchewan* (Calgary, AB: University of Calgary Press, 2000)

Carlson, P. H., *The Plains Indians* (College Station, Texas: Texas A & M University Press, 1998)

Castellano, M. B., L. Davis and L. Lahache, Innovations in Education Practice. In M. Castellano, M. Brant, L. Davis, and L. Lahache, eds, *Aboriginal Education: Fulfilling the Promise* (pp. 97-100). (Vancouver, BC: UBC Press, 2000)

Chalmers, F. G., European Ways of Talking About The Art of the Northwest Coast First Nations. *The Canadian Journal of Native Studies*, vol. XV (1) (pp. 113-127) (1995)

Champagne, D., *Native America: Portrait of The Peoples* (Detroit, MI:

Visible Ink Press, 1994)

Churchill, W., *A Little Matter Of Genocide: Holocaust and Denial in The Americas: 1492 to the Present* (Winnipeg, MB: Arbeiter Ring Publishing, 1998)

Clark, E. E., *Indian Legends from the Northern Rockies* (Norman: University of Oklahoma Press, 1989)

____. *Indian Legends of Canada* (Toronto, ON: McClelland and Stewart, 1971)

Cobb, J. B., *A Christian Natural Theology* (Philadelphia, PA: Westminster, 1965)

Coffer, W. E., *Spirits of the Sacred Mountains: Creation Stories of the American Indian* (New York: Van Nostrand Reinhold Company, 1978)

Colorado, P., Bridging Native and Western Science. *Convergence*, vol. XXI (2-3) (pp. 49-68) (1988)

Cooper, G. H., Individualism and Integration in Navajo Religion. In Christopher Vecsey, ed, *Religion in Native North America* (pp. 67-82) (Moscow, ID: University of Idaho, 1990)

Couture, J. E., Where Are the Stories? In R. Couture and V. McGowan, eds, *A Metaphoric Mind: Selected Writings of Joseph Couture* (pp. 91-93) (Edmonton, AB: Athabasca University, 2013)

____. The Role of Elders: Emergent Issues. In J. W. Friesen, ed, *The Cultural Maze: Complex Questions on Native Destiny in Western Canada* (pp. 201-218) (Calgary, AB: Detselig Enterprises,

1991a)

_____. Explorations in Native Knowing. In J. W. Friesen, ed, *The Cultural Maze: Complex Questions on Native Destiny in Western Canada* (pp. 53-73) (Calgary, AB: Detselig Enterprises, 1991b)

Cox, H. G., *The Secular City* (New York: Macmillan, 1965)

Crossan, J. D., *God and Empire: Jesus Against Rome, Then and Now* (San Francisco, CA: HarperSanFrancisco, 2007)

Cumming, P. A. and N.H. Mickenberg, *Native Rights in Canada*, 2nd edn (Toronto, ON: The Indian-Eskimo Association of Canada, in association with General Publishing Co., 1971)

Deloria, V., Jr., Knowing and Understanding: Traditional Education in the Modern World. In B. Deloria, K. Foehner and S. Scinta, eds, *Spirit and Reason: The Vine Deloria, Jr., Reader* (pp. 137-143) (Golden, CO: Fulcrum Publishing, 1999a)

_____. Tribal Religions and Contemporary American Culture. In B. Deloria, K. Foehner and S. Scinta, eds, *Spirit and Reason: The Vine Deloria, Jr., Reader* (pp. 305-322) (Golden, CO: Fulcrum Publishing, 1999b)

_____. Sacred Places and Moral Responsibility. In B. Deloria, K. Foehner and S. Scinta, eds, *Spirit and Reason: The Vine Deloria, Jr., Reader* (pp. 323-338) (Golden, CO: Fulcrum Publishing, 1999c)

_____. The Religious Challenge. In B. Deloria, K. Foehner and S. Scinta, eds, *Spirit and Reason: The Vine Deloria, Jr., Reader* (pp. 275-289) (Golden, CO: Fulcrum Publishing, 1999d)

____. Myth and the Origin of Religion. In B. Deloria, K. Foehner and S. Scinta, eds, *Spirit and Reason: The Vine Deloria, Jr., Reader* (pp. 339-353) (Golden, CO: Fulcrum Publishing, 1999e)

____. *Red Earth, White Lies: Native Americans and the Myth of Scientific Fact* (New York: Scribner, 1995)

Deloria, V., Jr., and C. M. Lytle, *American Indians: American Justice* (Austin, TX: University of Texas Press, 1983)

Denig, E. T., *The Assiniboine*, J. N. B. Hewitt, ed, (Regina, SK: The Canadian Plains Research Center, 2000)

Densmore, F., *Chippewa Customs* (St. Paul, MN: Minnesota Historical Society Press, 1979)

Dewey, J., *Human Nature and Conduct* (New York: Modern Library, 1957)

Dewey, J., and J. H. Tufts, *Ethics* (New York: Henry Holt and Company, 1908)

Dickason, O. P. and W. Newbigging, *A Concise History of Canada's First Nations*, 2nd edn (Don Mills, ON: Oxford University Press, 2010)

Dickason, O. P. with D. T. McNab, *Canada's First Nations: A History of Founding Peoples From Earliest Times*, 4th edn (Don Mills, ON: Oxford University Press, 2009)

Dickason, O. P., *Canada's First Nations: A History of Founding Peoples From Earliest Times* (Toronto, ON: McClelland and Stewart, 1993)

_____. *The Myth of the Savage: And the Beginnings of French Colonialism in the Americas* (Edmonton, AB: University of Alberta Press, 1984)

Dion, J F., *My Tribe, the Crees* (Calgary, AB: Glenbow-Alberta Institute, 1979)

Douglas, J. D., ed, *New 20th Century Encyclopedia of Religious Knowledge*, 2nd edn (Grand Rapids, MI: Baker Book House, 1991)

Driver, H. E., *Indians of North America* (Chicago, IL: The University of Chicago Press, 1968)

Dyck, N., *Differing Visions: Administrating Indian Residential Schooling in Prince Alberta, 1867-1995* (Halifax, NS: Fernwood Publishing, and Prince Albert, SK: The Prince Albert Grand Council, 1997)

Eastman, C. A. and E. G. Eastman, *Wigwam Evenings: 27 Sioux Folk Tales* (Mineola, NY: Dover Publications, 2000)

Edmonds, M. and E. E. Clark, eds, *Voices of the Winds: Native American Legends* (New York: Facts on File, 1989)

Eliade, M., *Shamanism: Archaic Techniques of Ecstasy* (Princeton, NJ: Princeton University Press, 1974)

Elias, P. D., *The Dakota of the Canadian Northwest* (Regina, SK: Canadian Plains Research Center, 2002)

Elul, J., *The Ethics of Freedom*, translated and edited by G. W. Bromiley (Grand Rapids, MI: W. B. Eerdmans Publishing Company, 1976)

____. *The New Demons*, translated by C. E. Hopkin (New York: The Seabury Press 1973)

Erdoes, R., *The Sun Dance People: The Plains Indians, Their Past and Present* (New York: Random House, 1972)

Erdoes, R. and A. Ortiz, eds, *American Indian Myths and Legends* (New York: Pantheon Books, 1984)

Ewers, J. C., *The Blackfeet: Raiders on the Northwestern Plains* (Norman, OK: University of Oklahoma Press, 1989)

____. *Indian Life on the Upper Missouri* (Norman, OK: University of Oklahoma Press, 1988)

Fassett, T. White Wolf, Afterword: Where Do We Go From Here? In Jace Weaver, ed, *Defending Mother Earth: Native Perspectives on Environmental Justice* (pp. 177-192) (Maryknoll, NY: Orbis Books, 1996)

Fitzwater, P. B., *Christian Theology: A Systematic Presentation* (Grand Rapids, MI: Wm. B. Eerdmans Publishing Company, 1953)

Fleras, A. and J. L. Elliott, *Unequal Relations: An Introduction to Race, Ethnic, and Aboriginal Dynamics in Canada*, 5th edn (Toronto, ON: Pearson Prentice-Hall, 2007)

Francis, D., *The Imaginary Indian: The Image of the Indian in Canadian Culture* (Vancouver, BC: Arsenal Pulp Press, 1992)

Friedan, B., *The Feminist Mystique* (New York: W. W. Norton & Company, 1963)

Friesen, J. W., *Aboriginal Spirituality and Biblical Theology: Closer*

Than You Think (Calgary, AB: Detselig Enterprises, 2000a)

____. _Legends of the Elders_ (Calgary, AB: Detselig Enterprises, 2000b)

____. _First Nations of the Plains: Creative, Adaptable, and Enduring_ (Calgary, AB: Detselig Enterprises, 1999)

____. _Sayings of the Elders: An Anthology of First Nation's Wisdom_ (Calgary, AB: Detselig Enterprises, 1998)

____. _Rediscovering the First Nations of Canada_ (Calgary, AB: Detselig Enterprises, 1997)

____. _You Can't Get There From Here: The Mystique Of North American Plains Indians Culture & Philosophy_ (Dubuque, IA: Kendall/Hunt, 1995)

____. _Pick One: A User-Friendly Guide to Religion_ (Calgary, AB: Detselig Enterprises. 1995)

____. _People, Culture and Learning_ (Calgary, AB: Detselig Enterprises, 1977)

____. _Religion for People_ (Calgary, AB: Bell Books, 1972)

Friesen, J. W. and V. Lyons Friesen, _And Now You Know: Fifty Native American Legends_ (Calgary, AB: Detselig Enterprises, 2009).

____. _Western Canadian Native Destiny: Complex Questions on the Cultural Maze_ (Calgary, AB: Detselig Enterprises, 2008)

____. _First Nations in the Twenty-first Century: Contemporary Educational Frontiers_ (Calgary, AB: Detselig Enterprises, 2005)

_____. *More Legends of the Elders* (Calgary, AB: Detselig Enterprises, 2004a)

_____. *More Legends of the Elders* (Calgary, AB: Detselig Enterprises, 2004b)

Fumoleau, R., *As Long as This Land Shall Last: A History of Treaty 8 and Treaty 11, 1870-1939* (Toronto, ON: McClelland and Stewart, 1973)

Furniss, E., *Victims of Benevolence: The Dark Legacy of the Williams Lake Residential School* (Vancouver, BC: Arsenal Pulp Press, 1995)

Garnier, K., *Your Elders Speak: A Tribute to Native Elders.* Volume One (White Rock, BC: Published by Karie Garnier, 1990)

Garrigou-Lagrange, R., *Reality: A Synthesis of Thomistic Thought* (London, UK: B. Herder Book Co., 1950)

Geisler, N. L., Process Theology. In S. N. Gundry and A. F. Johnson, eds, *Tensions in Contemporary Theology* (pp. 237-286) (Chicago, IL: Moody Press, 1978)

Grant, A., *Finding My Talk: How Fourteen Native Women Reclaimed Their Lives After Residential School* (Calgary, AB: Fitzhenry and Whiteside, 2004)

_____. *No End of Grief: Indian Residential Schools in Canada* (Winnipeg, MB: Pemmican Publications, 1996)

_____. The Challenge for Universities. In M. Battiste and J. Barman, eds, *First Nations Education in Canada: The Circle Unfolds* (pp. 208-223) (Vancouver, BC: UBC Press, 1995)

Grenz, S.J. and R. E. Olson, *20th-Century Theology: God & The World in a Transitional Age* (Downers Grove, IL: InterVarsity Press, 1992)

Grinnell, G. B., *The North American Indians of Today* (London, UK: Arthur Pearson, Ltd., 1900)

Gundry, S. N. and A. F. Johnson, eds, *Tensions in Contemporary Theology* (Chicago, IL: Moody Press, 1976)

Haig-Brown, C., *Resistance and Renewal: Surviving the Indian Residential School* (Vancouver, BC: Tillicum Library, 1993)

Hare, J., Learning From Indigenous Knowledge in Education. In O. P. Dickason and David Long, eds, *Visions of the Heart: Canadian Aboriginal Issues* (pp. 90-112) (Don Mills, ON: Oxford University Press, 2011)

Harrod, H. L., *Renewing the World: Plains Indian Religion and Morality* (Tucson, AZ: University of Arizona Press, 1992)

Hartshorne, C., *Man's Vision of God and the Logic of Theism* (Chicago, IL: Willet, Clark & Company, 1941)

Henderson, J. Y., Ayukpachi: Empowering Aboriginal Thought. In M. Battiste, ed, *Reclaiming Indigenous Voice and Vision* (pp. 248-278) (Vancouver, BC: UBC Press, 2000)

Henry, C. F. H., ed, *God, Revelation and the Bible*. 6 vols. (Waco, TX: Word, 1976-1983)

_____. ed, *Revelation and the Bible* (Grand Rapids, MI: Baker Book House, 1958)

Herring, J. B., *The Enduring Indians of Kansas: A Century and a Half of Acculturation* (Lawrence, KS: University of Kansas Press, 1990)

Hookimaw-Witt, J., Keenabonoh Keemoshominook Kaeshe Peemishishik Odaskiwakh [we stand on the graves of our ancestors]. Native Interpretations of Treaty #9 with Attawapiskat Elders. Unpublished Master's Thesis (Peterborough, ON: Trent University, 1998)

Hoxie, F. E., *The Crows* (New York: Chelsea House Publishers, 1989)

Hultkrantz, A., *Native Religions of North America: The Power of Visions and Fertility* (San Francisco, CA: HarperSanFrancisco, 1987)

____. *Conceptions of the Soul Among North American Indians* (Stockholm: Caslon Press, 1953)

Hungrywolf, A., *Legends Told by the Old People of Many Tribes* (Summertown, TN: Book Publishing Company, 2001)

Jenness, D., *Indians of Canada*, 7th edn (Originally published in 1932. Toronto, ON: University of Toronto Press, 1986)

Josephy, A. M., Jr., *Now That The Buffalo's Gone: A Study Of Today's American Indians* (Norman, OK: University of Oklahoma Press, 1989)

____. *The Indian Heritage of America* (New York: Alfred A. Knopf, 1969)

Kaltreider, K., *American Indian Prophesies* (Carlsbad, CA: Hay House, 1998)

Kasprycki, S. S., Northeast. In C.F. Feest, ed, *The Cultures of Native North Americans* (pp. 104-147). (Vienna, Austria: Köne-mann, 2000)

Klein, W. W., C. L. Bloomberg and R. L. Hubbard, *Introduction to Biblical Interpretation* (Dallas, TX: Word Publishing, 1993)

Knockwood, I., *Out of the Depths: The Experiences of Mi'kmaw Children at the Indian Residential School at Shubenacadie, Nova Scotia* (Lockeport, NS: Roseway Publishing, 1994)

Knudtson, P. and D. Suzuki, *Wisdom of the Elders* (Toronto, ON: Stoddart, 1992)

Kuhn, Harold B., Secular Theology. In S. N. Gundry and A. F. Johnson, eds, *Tensions in Contemporary Theology* (pp. 157-196) (Chicago, IL: Moody Press, 1978)

Küng, H., *On Being a Christian*, translated by E. Quinn (New York: Doubleday & Company, 1976)

Lame Deer, J. (Fire) and R. Erdoes, *Lame Deer: Seeker of Visions* (New York: Simon & Schuster, 1972)

Laviolette, G., *The Dakota Sioux in Canada* (Winnipeg, MB: DLM Publications, 1991)

Levine, J. L., *The Misunderstood Jew: The Church and The Scandal of the Jewish Jesus* (San Francisco, CA: HarperSanFrancisco, 2006)

Lincoln, K., *Native American Renaissance* (Berkley and Los Angeles, CA: University of California Press, 1985)

Lockwood, F. C., *The Apache Indians* (Lincoln, NE: University of Nebraska Press, 1987)

Lowie, R. H., Religion in Human Life. In W. A. Lessa & E. Z. Vogt, eds, *Reader in Comparative Religion: An Anthropological Approach*, 2nd edn (pp. 133-141) (New York: Harper and Row, 1965)

_____. *Indians of the Plains* (Garden City, NY: Natural History Press, 1963)

_____. *The Crow Indians* (New York: Holt, Rinehart, and Winston, 1956)

_____. *Primitive Religion* (New York: Grosset and Dunlap, 1952)

Lyon, L. C. and J. W. Friesen, *Culture Change and Education: A Study of Indian and Non-Indian Views in Southern Alberta* (New York: Simon and Schuster Research Study Program, 1969)

Macfarlan, A. A., ed, *North American Indian Legends* (Mineola, NY: Dover Publications, 1968)

MacLean, J., *Native Tribes of Canada* (Montreal, PQ: William Briggs, 1896. Reprinted Toronto, ON: Coles Publishing Company Limited, 1980)

Malphurs, A., *Developing a Vision for Ministry in the 21st Century* (Grand Rapids, MI: Baker Books, 2004)

McClintock, W., *The Old North Trail* (Lincoln, NB: University of Nebraska Press, 1992)

McDougall, J., *Pathfinding on Plain and Prairie: Stirring Scenes of Life in the Canadian Northwest* (Toronto, ON: William Briggs, 1895)

McGaa, E. Eagle Man, *Native Wisdom: Perceptions of the Natural Way* (Minneapolis, MN: Four Directions Publishing, 1995)

____. *Mother Earth Spirituality: Native American Paths to Healing Ourselves and Our World* (New York: HarperCollins, 1990)

McHugh, T., *The Time of the Buffalo* (Lincoln, NE: University of Nebraska Press, 1972)

McMillan, A. D., *Native Peoples and Cultures of Canada*, 2nd edn, (revised and enlarged) (Vancouver, BC: Douglas and McIntyre, 1995)

Medicine, B., My Elders Tell Me. In J. Barman, Y. Hébert, and D. McCaskill, eds, *Indian Education in Canada: Volume 2: The Challenge* (pp. 142-152) (Vancouver, BC: University of British Columbia Press, 1987)

Meili, D., *Those Who Know: Profiles of Alberta's Native Elders* (Edmonton, AB: NeWest Press, 1992)

Menninger, K., *Whatever Became of Sin?* (New York: Hawthorn Books, 1973)

Metz, J. B., New Questions on God. *Concilium*, vol. 76 (New York: Herder & Herder, 1972)

Mickey, P. A., *Essentials of Wesleyan Theology* (Grand Rapids, MI: Zondervan, 1980)

Miller, A. D., *Native Peoples and Cultures of Canada*, rev. edn (Vancouver, BC: Douglas and McIntyre, 1995)

_____. *Reflections on Native Newcomer Relations* (Toronto, ON: University of Toronto Press, 2004)

Miller, J. R., *Skyscrapers Hide The Heavens: A History Of Indian-White Relations In Canada*, 3rd edn (Toronto, ON: University of Toronto Press, 2000)

_____. *Shingwauk's Vision: A History of Native Residential Schools* (Toronto, ON: University of Toronto Press, 1997)

Milloy, J. S. *A National Crime: The Canadian Government And The Residential School System, 1879-1986* (Winnipeg, MB: University of Manitoba Press, 1999)

Mills, A. D. and R. Slobodin, eds, *Amerindian Rebirth: Reincarnation Belief Among North American Indians and Inuit* (Toronto, ON: University of Toronto Press, 1994)

Moltmann, J., *The Experiment Hope* (Philadelphia, PA: Fortress Press, 1975)

Moore, Patrick J., Lessons on the Land: The Role of Kaska Elders in a University Course. *Canadian Journal of Native Education*, vol. 27(1), (pp. 127-139) (2003)

Morgan, L. H., *Ancient Society* (Cleveland, OH: World Publishing, 1963)

Morris, A., *The Treaties of Canada with the Indians of Manitoba* (Saskatoon, SK: Fifth House Publishers, 1991)

Mullett, G. M., *Spider Woman Stories* (Tucson, AZ: University of

Arizona Press, 1979)

Nabigon, H., *The Hollow Tree: Fighting Addiction with Traditional Native Healing* (Montreal, PQ: McGill-Queen's University Press, 2006)

Neihardt, J. G., *Black Elk Speaks: Being the Life Story of a Holy Man of the Oglala Sioux* (Lincoln, NE: University of Nebraska Press, 1979)

Newcombe, Jr., W. W., *North American Indians: An Anthropological Approach* (Santa Monica, CA: Goodyear Publishing Company, 1974)

Nitsch, T. H., My heritage was so ingrained in me that I knew I would never lose it. In P. Kulchyski, D. McCaskill and D. Newhouse, eds, *In the Words of the Elders: Aboriginal Cultures in Transition* (pp. 67-94) (Toronto, ON: University of Toronto Press, 1999)

Noley, H., The Interpreters. In J. Weaver, ed, *Native American Religious Identity: Unforgotten Gods* (pp. 48-60) (Maryknoll, NY: Orbis Books, 1998)

O'Brien, S., *American Indian Tribal Governments* (Norman, OK: University of Oklahoma Press, 1989)

Packer, J. I., Contemporary Views of Revelation. In C. F. H. Henry, ed., *Revelation and the Bible* (pp. 87-104) (Grand Rapids, MI: Baker Book House, 1958)

Pannenberg, W., *The Apostles' Creed: In Light of Today's Questions*, translated by Margaret Kohl (Philadelphia, PA: Westminster, 1972)

Peers, L., *The Objiway of Western Canada, 1780-1870* (St. Paul, MN: Minnesota Historical Society Press, 1994)

Pettipas, K., *Severing The Ties That Bind: Government Repression of Indigenous Religious Ceremonies On The Prairies* (Winnipeg, MB: University of Manitoba Press, 1994)

Pfeiffer, C. F., H. V. Vos and J. Rea, eds, *Wycliffe Bible Encyclopedia*, Vol 2 (Chicago, IL: Moody Press, 1975)

Pike, N., *God and Timelessness* (New York: Schroken, 1970)

Piper, J., *The Purifying Power Of Living By Faith In—Future Grace* (Sisters, OR: Multnomah Press, 1995)

Placher, W. C., A *History Of Christian Theology: An Introduction* (Philadelphia, PA: The Westminster Press, 1983)

Porterfield, A., American Indian Spirituality as a Countercultural Movement. In C. Vecsey, ed, *Religion in Native North America* (pp. 152-166) (Moscow, ID: University of Idaho Press, 1990)

Powers, W. K., *Oglala Religion* (Lincoln, NE: University of Oklahoma Press, 1977)

Price, J., *Indians of Canada; Cultural Dynamics* (Scarborough, ON: Prentice-Hall of Canada, Ltd., 1979)

Purkiser, W. T., ed, *Exploring Our Christian Faith* (Kansas City, MO: Beacon Hill Press of Kansas City, 1960)

Rahner, K., *Foundations of Christian Faith*, translated by William Dych (New York: Seabury, 1978)

Ramm, B., The Evidence Of Prophecy And Miracle. In C. F. H. Henry, ed, *Revelation and the Bible* (pp. 251-264) (Grand Rapids, MI: Baker Book House, 1958)

Retzlaff, S., 'The Elders Have Said'—Protecting Aboriginal Cultural Values into Contemporary News Discourse. In K. Knopf, ed, *Aboriginal Canada Revisited* (pp. 330-359) (Ottawa, ON: University of Ottawa Press, 2008)

Richards, L. O. and G. Martin, *A Theology of Personal Ministry* (Grand Rapids, MI: Zondervan, 1981)

Robertson, H., *Reservations Are for Indians* (Toronto, ON: James Lewis & Samuel, 1970)

Robinson, J. A. T., *Honest to God* (Philadelphia, PA: Westminster, 1963)

Ross, J. I. and L. Gould, eds, *Native Americans and the Criminal Justice System* (Boulder, Colorado: Paradigm Publishers, 2006)

Ross, R., *Dancing With a Ghost: Exploring Indian Reality* (Markham, ON: Reed Books, 1992)

Rousseau, J. J., *The Emile of Jean Jacques Rousseau*, translated and edited by B. H. Boyd, (New York: Teachers' College, Columbia University, 1962)

Ryan, J., *Doing Things the Right Way: Dene Traditional Justice in Lac La Martre, N.W.T.* (Calgary, AB: Arctic Institute of North America, University of Calgary Press, 1995)

Scaer, D. P., Theology of Hope. In S. N. Gundry and A. F. Johnson, eds, *Tensions in Contemporary Theology* (pp. 197-236) (Chicago, IL: Moody Press 1978)

Schissel, B. and T. Witherspoon, *The Legacy of School for Aboriginal People* (Don Mills, ON: Oxford University Press, 2003)

Schmidt, W., The Nature, Attributes and Worship of the Primitive High God. In W. A. Lessa and E. Z. Vogt, eds, *Reader in Comparative Religion: An Anthropological Approach*, 2nd edn (pp. 21-33) (New York: Harper and Row, 1965)

____. *The Origin and Growth of Religion: Facts and Theories* (New York: Lincoln MacVeagh, 1931)

Schurz, C., Present Aspects of the Indian Problem. In F. P. Prucha, ed, *Americanizing the American Indians: Writings by the "Friends of the Indian," 1880-1900* (pp. 13-26) (Lincoln, NE: University of Nebraska Press, 1978)

Seton, E. T. and J. M. Seton, *The Gospel of the Redman: A Way of Life* (Santa Fe, NM: Seton Village, 1966)

Shaw, A. M., *Pima Indian Legends* (Tucson, AZ: The University of Arizona Press, 1992)

Smith, D. B., Aboriginal Ontario: An Overview of 10,000 Years of History. In E. S. Rogers and D. B. Smith, eds, *Aboriginal Ontario: Historical Perspectives On The First Nations* (pp. 418-424) (Toronto, ON: Dundurn Press, 1994)

Smith, D. L., *A Handbook of Contemporary Theology* (Grand Rapids, MI: Baker Books, 1992)

Smith, W. A., A Cherokee Way of Knowing: Can Native American Spirituality Impact Religious Education? *Religious Educa-*

tion, vol. 90 (2), (pp. 241-253) (Spring 1995)

Snow, Chief J., *These Mountains Are Our Sacred Places: The Story of The Stoney Indians* (Calgary, AB: Fitzhenry and Whiteside, 2005)

Spence, L., *North American Indians: Myths and Legends* (London, UK: Senate, 1994)

Steckley, J. I. and B. D. Cummins, *Full Circle: Canada's First Nations* (Toronto, ON: Pearson Prentice-Hall, 2008)

Stiegelbauer, S. M., What is an Elder? What Do Elders Do? First Nation Elders as Teachers in Culture-based Urban Organizations. *The Canadian Journal of Native Studies*, vol. XVI (1) (pp. 37-66) (1996)

Stob, H., *Theological Reflections* (Grand Rapids, MI: William B. Eerdmans Publishing Company, 1981)

Stolzman, W., *The Pipe and Christ: A Christian-Sioux Dialogue*, 6th edn (Chamberlain, SD: Tipi Press, 1998)

Strong, A. H., *Systematic Theology: A Compendium. Three Volumes In One.* (Chicago, IL: Judson Press. Reprinted for the 19th time in 1956)

Stumpf, S. E., *Socrates to Sartre: A History of Philosophy* (New York: McGraw-Hill, 1993)

Tanner, K., *Christ the Key* (Cambridge, UK: Cambridge University Press, 2010)

_____. *Theories Of Culture: A New Agenda For Theology* (Minneapolis, MN: Fortress Press, 1997)

Taylor, F., *Standing Alone: A Contemporary Blackfoot Indian* (Halfmoon Bay, BC: Arbutus Bay Publications, 1989)

Taylor, J. Garth, North Algonquians on the Frontiers of "New Ontario, 1890-1945." In Edward S. Rogers and Donald B. Smith, eds, *Aboriginal Ontario: Historical Perspectives on the First Nations* (pp. 307-343) (Toronto, ON: Dundurn Press, 1994)

Thiessen, H. C., *Introductory Lectures In Systematic Theology* (Grand Rapids, MI: Wm. B. Eerdmans Publishing Company, 1959. Reprinted in 1989)

Tinker, G. E., An American Indian Theological Response To Ecojustice. In J. Weaver, ed, *Defending Mother Earth: Native American Perspectives on Environmental Justice* (pp. 153-176) (Maryknoll, NY: Orbis Books, 1996)

Tooker, E., *Native North American Spirituality of the Eastern Woodlands* (New York: Paulist Press, 1979)

Treaty 7 Elders and Tribal Council, with W. Hildebrandt, D. First Rider, and S. Carter, *The True Spirit and Original Intent of Treaty 7* (Montreal, PQ: McGill-Queen's University Press, 1996)

Trigger, B. G., *The Huron: Farmer of the North* (New York: Holt, Rinehart, and Winston, 1969)

Tyler, E. B., Animism. In A. Lessa and E. Z. Vogt, eds, *Reader In Comparative Religion: An Anthropological Approach*, 2nd edn (pp. 10-21) (New York: Harper & Row, 1965)

Underhill, R. M., *Red Man's Religion* (Chicago, IL: University of Chicago Press, 1965)

____. *Red Man's America* (Chicago, IL: University of Chicago Press, 1963)

Valaskakis, G. G., *Indian Country: Essays in Contemporary Native Culture* (Waterloo, ON: Wilfred Laurier University Press, 2005)

Venne, S., Treaty Making With the Crown. In J. Bird, L. Land and M. Macadam, eds, *Nation to Nation: Aboriginal Sovereignty and the Future of Canada* (pp. 53-61) (Toronto, ON: Irwin Publishing, 2002)

Verslius, A., *The Elements of Native North American Traditions* (Boston, MA: Element Books, 1997)

Vogel, V. J., *American Indian Medicine.* (Normal, OK: University of Oklahoma Press, 1990)

Waldram, J., *The Way of The Pipe: Aboriginal Spirituality and Symbolic Healing in Canadian Prisons* (Peterborough, ON: Broadview Press, 1997)

Wallace, E. and E. A. Hoebel, *The Comanches: Lords of the South Plains* (Norman, OK: University of Oklahoma Press, 1986)

Warry, W., *Ending Denial: Understanding Aboriginal Issues* (Peterborough, ON: Broadview Press 2007)

Weaver, J., ed, *Native American Religious Identity: Unforgotten Gods* (Maryknoll, NY: Orbis Books, 1998)

Weeks, P., *Farewell, My Nation: The American Indians and the United States, 1820-1890* (Wheeling, IL: Harlan Davidson, 1990)

Wells, D. E., *The Search for Salvation* (Downers Grove, IL: InterVarsity Press, 1978)

White, J. M., *Everyday Life of the North American Indians* (New York: Dorset Books, 1979)

Whitehead, A. N., *Process and Reality* (New York: Macmillan, 1929)

Wilson, C. D., The Plains—A Regional Overview. In R. B. Morrison and C. R. Wilson, eds, *Native Peoples: The Canadian Experience* (pp. 353-357) (Toronto, ON: McClelland and Stewart, 1986)

Wissler, C., *Indians of the United States* (Garden City, NY: Doubleday & Company, 1966)

Workers of the South Dakota Writers' Project, *Legends of The Mighty Sioux* (Interior, SD: Badlands Natural History Association, 1994)

Wright, R., *Stolen Continents: The "New World" Through Indian Eyes Since 1492* (Toronto, ON: Viking/Penguin, 1992)

Wuttunee, W. I. C., *Ruffled Feathers: Indians in Canadian Society* (Calgary, AB: Bell Books, 1971)

Zeilinger, R., *Sacred Ground: Reflections On Lakota Spirituality and The Gospel* (Chamberlain, SD: Tipi Press, 1986)

INDEX

CPSIA information can be obtained
at www.ICGtesting.com
Printed in the USA
FSOW01n0825210116
15929FS

9 781320 198561